ARTHUR DOBBS

ESQUIRE

1689–1765

Governor Arthur Dobbs
1755
From the portrait by William Hoare
(by kind permission of Richard Dobbs of Castle Dobbs)

ARTHUR DOBBS

ESQUIRE

1689–1765

SURVEYOR-GENERAL OF IRELAND
PROSPECTOR AND GOVERNOR OF
NORTH CAROLINA

DESMOND CLARKE

CHAPEL HILL
THE UNIVERSITY OF
NORTH CAROLINA PRESS

Printed in Great Britain
by HAZELL WATSON AND VINEY LTD
AYLESBURY
for THE UNIVERSITY OF NORTH
CAROLINA PRESS
CHAPEL HILL

Preface

IN PRESENTING the story of the life and times of Arthur Dobbs, I have no apology to make save for sins of omission. Much, I know, has been written about colonial America, much remains to be written, but each contribution, so long as it presents something new, no matter how small or seemingly unimportant, is another piece that helps to complete the great jigsaw we call history.

By writing the life-story of a colonial Governor about whom little has been written and perhaps less known, I hope that I have rescued from the shadow of eclipse one who made a by no means small contribution to the building of a great commonwealth. With a few exceptions, historians of North Carolina have dealt harshly with Dobbs, and while I do not suggest that he was at all times above reproach, I claim that he epitomises many of the finest qualities of his age, and that his personality and ideas, his many-sided interests and activities, illuminate his age and society in many of its most dynamic aspects.

I hope this picture of a great man—whatever his faults—will brighten a dark period of Irish history, add another name to the roll of distinguished men who contributed to Britain's greatness in the eighteenth century, and provide an illustration of the type of man who helped to lay the foundation of modern America, and in particular the state of North Carolina.

In undertaking this task I have had the unstinted help, co-operation, and guidance of many good friends and critics. In the first place I must acknowledge my debt to the late Mr. Arthur Dobbs of Castle Dobbs, and his brothers Frederick and A. E. Dobbs, who were so kind and patient with me over the past few years. To Dr. Richard Hayes and his staff in the National Library of Ireland I am indebted for obtaining much of the material which provided the basis to work upon. A similar debt is due to Dr. C. C. Crittenden of the North Carolina Department of Archives and History, not only for the micro-film copy material he supplied but for reading and offering helpful criticism and suggestions in the preparation of this study. Professor T. W. Moody of Dublin University also undertook the task of reading and correcting my manuscript, and his helpful advice made my task easier.

My grateful thanks are due to Dr. E. Heathley, Deputy Keeper, Public Record Office, Belfast; Professor J. H. Plum, Cambridge University; Professor J. W. Williams; Dr. Charles Rush, Director of the University of North Carolina Library; Dr. W. Ewald, Harvard University, and many kind friends in North Carolina too numerous to mention. Among those, however, I should like to record my thanks to Mrs. Walker Taylor and the North Carolina Society of the Colonial Dames of America; Mr. E. Lawrence Lee of Chapel Hill; Mr. Clarence Griffin of Forest City; Mr. Bruce Cotten of Baltimore, and Mr. Lambert Davis of the University of North Carolina Press.

A special word of acknowledgement is due to the Right Honourable the Earl of Bangor, who permitted me to remove the valuable manuscripts from Castle Ward, which provided the hitherto unpublished material that enabled me to write this book.

Finally, I ask those whose names have not been mentioned to accept my thanks for all their help.

DESMOND CLARKE

Dublin, March 1957

Contents

To My Wife

1

Ancestry

FROM THE burning ruins of Kilcolman Castle the poet Spenser wrote despairingly to Queen Elizabeth: 'Out of the ashes of desolation and the wasteness of your wretched realm of Ireland vouchsafe, most mighty empress our dread sovereign, to receive the voices of a few most unhappy ghosts of whom is nothing but the ghosts now left buried in the bottom of oblivion.' [1] His cry was that of many other ruined, displaced, and hunted loyalists fleeing before the victorious Irish armies of Hugh O'Neill and Hugh O'Donnell. Tired and exasperated with her incompetent generals, the Queen dispatched a new and powerful army to Ireland under the able and ruthless command of two capable soldiers, Sir George Carew and Sir Henry Docwra.

In the spring of 1599, Docwra's expedition put into Carrickfergus, a stout little seaport picturesquely situated on the northern shore of Carrickfergus Bay, now better known as Belfast Lough. Among the officers on his staff was John Dobbs whose father hailed from the borders of Chester, Derbyshire, and Lancashire, and whose mother was a Buckly of Beaumaris. [2] After some days, Docwra's army sailed for Donegal, but John Dobbs remained behind with fresh troops to garrison the town, which, despite its broken and crumbling walls, was an oasis in a war-desolated land. The surrounding countryside presented a pitiful picture, for the Governor of the town had been ordered to destroy all standing crops and woods, and burn and uproot all houses and buildings likely to be used by the Irish. In this work of spoliation Governor Chichester spared neither 'house, corne nor creature of what quality, age or sex soever; he slew all fourfooted animals in their farmyards, burned the stacks of grain, and in the spring time mowed down the growing crops.' [3]

The Mayor of Carrickfergus at this time was John Dalway, who came to Ireland in 1573 with Walter Devereux, Earl of Essex, and had by a propitious marriage to Jane O'Bryne, a kinswoman of Hugh O'Neill, the Queen's enemy, obtained an estate at Braidisland and

Kilroot some few miles to the north of the town.[4] Young Dobbs was
a welcome visitor to the Mayor's house, and in a short time fell in love
with his daughter Margaret, an only child. As the war in Ireland drew
to a close, the young couple were married, and Margaret received as a
marriage portion the freehold lease of land in the neighbourhood of
Kilroot, where John Dobbs built a small castle, from which the estate
eventually derived the name of Castle Dobbs.

With the termination of hostilities in Ireland and the more or less
complete destruction of the old Irish ruling classes, the victors were
rewarded with the sequestered estates of the defeated. John Dobbs
shared in the rewards, and though he received no large land grants he
was appointed Deputy Treasurer of Ulster. His father-in-law, John
Dalway, 'in consideration of his long service to the Queen,' was amply
rewarded, and confirmed in his estates which on his death seemed likely
to pass to his daughter. When his wife died, John Dalway was 'lured
into a second marriage by a beautiful schemer, Jane Morton,' a widow,
who naturally pictured herself as the future owner of the Dalway
estate. Old John Dalway, some years before his second marriage, had,
however, drawn up a will in favour of his grandchildren, Foulk and
Hercules Dobbs. We learn from a family manuscript that Jane Dalway 'proving unfaithful to his bed, Margaret Dobbs informed her
father of the intrigues of her stepmother.' Fearing that she might be
debarred from any share in her husband's estate or that it might revert
to the Dobbs family, Jane Dalway prevailed on her aged husband to
acknowledge a certain Giles Dalway, a ne'er-do-well who lived in the
neighbourhood, to be his brother and execute a will in favour of his
two sons. The old man, despite his dotage, insisted that he had no
brother, but to placate his wife gave her protégé a small farm near
Ballyhill.[5]

In 1618 John Dalway died and a will was produced wherein he left
his entire estate to his unfaithful wife and the sons of her protégé.
John and Margaret Dobbs contested the validity of this will, and claimed
the estate by virtue of an earlier will made in favour of their son Foulk.
This is the story of a family dispute as traditionally recorded by the
Dalway family, and while the facts are more or less correct, an official
judgement inexplicably preserved among the Egmont papers shows
that Jane Dalway, besides being an adulteress, was not above forging a
will in her own favour.[6]

In a court action John and Mary Dobbs were awarded the Dalway
property, but the defendants refused to hand it over. John Dobbs, a
purposeful man and not without influence in government circles, set

out for London with his eldest son Foulk and obtained the King's letter for a grant of the land of the late John Dalway. On the return
journey the ship foundered off the bar of Chester and they were both
drowned.[7] That was in the year 1622. The surviving son, Hercules,
was eight years old, so his guardian, Marmaduke Dobbs, filed a bill in
Chancery to obtain possession of the estate. The suit dragged on for
many years until an award was agreed upon whereby 'the house and
demesne of Ballyhill and the fee farm rent of Braidisland with the land
in the liberties of Carrickfergus were allotted to John Dalway, the
elder, and to Hercules Dobbs the Cynament of Ballynure, and the
lands of Castle Dobbs, with the revision of the tenement in Carrickfergus.'

Hercules Dobbs was a delicate young man; at the age of twenty-
three he married Magdalen West of Ballydougan. A year later a son,
Richard, was born; he was three months old when his father died. For
the next seven years, in the seclusion of the castle built by his grandfather, Magdalen reared her son. Castle Dobbs was pleasantly situated
on rising ground; the fields about it were beginning to bear the fruit of
careful cultivation, and small plantations dotted the countryside so
ruthlessly destroyed by Chichester forty years earlier. A mile or two
below the castle lay the broad expanse of Carrickfergus Bay, and three
miles to the west stood the castle of Carrickfergus. From the rising
ground young Richard Dobbs could see the ships as they sailed into
Carrickfergus, and nearer still the small harbour at Kilroot and the
boats of the local fishermen.

This peaceful atmosphere did not last for long, and the flame of
Cromwell's civil war spread to Ireland. On the 23rd October, 1641,
a revolt broke out in many parts of the country, but the attempt to
seize Dublin Castle, the seat of the Government, failed. Colonel
Chichester, Governor of Carrickfergus, received secret intelligence of
the revolt and ordered fires to be kindled near the town as a warning
to the Protestant settlers of the impending danger. In the course of the
next few weeks war spread throughout Ireland, and a large number of
Protestants arrived in Carrickfergus with their families and possessions.[8]

The long struggle begun in 1641 lasted for ten years. War-ringed
Carrickfergus had its share of privations. In 1642 Scottish troops under
the command of General Munroe landed there and held the town for
the Parliamentary army. Munroe conducted a quick and decisive campaign against the Irish, ravaging and destroying anything that might
be of use to his enemy or might impede his own progress. His successful but destructive campaign resulted in hunger and pestilence, and in

Carrickfergus more than 2,500 people died. The ultimate defeat of
the Irish was followed by a violent confiscation of their lands, and the
system of plantation begun by James I was pursued on a wider scale.
The freedom English Parliamentarians gave to Englishmen did not
apply in Ireland, and the natives became slaves and helots in their own
land.

When the war ended, Richard Dobbs was a youth of seventeen.
Four years later, in 1655, he married Dorothy Williams, the daughter
of a Yorkshire squire, who gave birth to two sons: John, born in
1659, and Richard born a year later. In a more peaceful atmosphere and
with little likelihood of a fresh uprising of the defeated Irish, the now
well established settlers were in a position to develop their estates, and
this Richard Dobbs did with commendable energy, displaying a lively
interest in both the cultivation of his estate and the government of his
county. In 1664 he served as High Sheriff of County Antrim, and
seven years later was elected Mayor of Carrickfergus.

Richard Dobbs was a stern and upright man who suffered a good
deal from gout; he was blessed or cursed as the case may be with all the
prejudices of the new Ascendancy class. He looked upon Catholics,
Presbyterians, and Dissenters with a thoroughly jaundiced eye, and
considered them almost outside the pale of civilisation. When his
eldest son, John, became a Quaker, he was promptly disinherited and
driven from his home. Rutty in his *History of the Quakers in Ireland*
writes: 'John Dobbs was entitled to a considerable estate of which he
suffered himself to be deprived purely for religion sake.' The estate
of which he was deprived in 1681 was 'worth three hundred pounds
per annum.' John Dobbs went to England and studied medicine under
Charles Marshal.[9]

During a peaceful period lasting more than thirty years, Richard
Dobbs devoted himself to the improvement of his estate. The old
castle erected by his grandfather had fallen into disrepair, and he had a
new residence built close by. Writing in 1693, he remarks:

> 'My house, which is a plantation and improvement of my own time
> (though descended from my Grandfather) is opposite, northward, within
> half a mile of the Bishop's house, and has a fine view of the whole bay and
> lough of Carrickfergus, and in a few years may be remarkable for the
> orchards and gardening about it. It is called Castle Dobbs from a small
> castle here, built by my Grandfather.' [10]

With his improved estate, Richard Dobbs was the squire *par
excellence*. He was a man of wide reading and elegant taste, and his

interests extended beyond his estate. He communicated with William Molyneux, the leader of scientific thought in Dublin, who had projected a Philosophical Society, modelled on the Royal Society, which attracted the attention of many able men, including Sir William Petty. About 1683 Moses Pitt, a London bookseller who published an English Atlas, came to Ireland with the intention of publishing a similar volume of the country. Pitt placed the scheme before Molyneux, who promptly got in touch with a number of correspondents in each county, among whom was Richard Dobbs, who was requested to prepare a paper on County Antrim. The short account of Antrim compiled by Richard Dobbs with obvious care shows his love and interest in the county and in particular the town of Carrickfergus. In a letter to Molyneux dated 14th May, 1683, he wrote:

> 'You seem so well satisfied with the imperfect draft I gave you of Carrickfergus, that as you desired me, I have adventured at part of County Antrim, which I send you enclosed. . . . I have scarce time to review what I have written, and had not the least help from any other person hitherto, which you may easily guess by the many defects you will meet withal; however, where you find failures be pleased freely to let me know, and what I cannot do I will endeavour to be informed, and give you all the satisfaction I possibly can, especially in our towns and villages, situations, Rivers, Bridges, Loughs, Churches, soil or whatever else you shall desire from me. . . .' [11]

As Pitt fell into difficulties the projected atlas was never published. The description of County Antrim is preserved, however, among the Castle Dobbs papers, and was printed as an Appendix to Hill's *Historical Account of the McDonnells of Antrim* a century and a half later.

For a few years, towards the close of the seventeenth century, the parish of Kilroot and the neighbouring parishes of Templemore and Ballynure formed the first prebend of Jonathan Swift. It was not a rich living, but nonetheless a pleasant benefice offering plenty of time for the young cleric to pursue his literary work if he wished. The house occupied by Swift at Kilroot stands close by the ruins of the Bishop's house which even in Swift's day was in a ruinous state and unoccupied. Dobbs wrote that the parish was small, 'the whole tithe not worth forty pounds,' and 'the inhabitants (except my family and some half-dozen that live under me) all Presbyterians and Scotch, not one natural Irish in the parish, or a papist, and may afford 100 men.' [12]

The peace and quiet of Swift's first prebend did not appeal to the young cleric fresh from the congenial atmosphere of Sir William Temple's household. He did, however, derive some solace from a woman's society in the person of the lovely Miss Waring, whose father lived in the neighbourhood, and she has gone down to posterity as the strange Varina, the only woman who could boast of having refused Swift's offer of marriage.

Castle Dobbs was but a short distance from Swift's house, and the lonely cleric, spurned by Miss Waring, was a constant visitor there. Richard Dobbs, whom Swift invariably referred to as Squire Dobbs, permitted him the use of his library, a privilege Swift appreciated. We gather that at least one of the books borrowed from Castle Dobbs was not to Swift's liking, for in the course of a letter to the Reverend John Winder he wrote: 'The Scepsis Scientifica is not mine but old Mr. Dobbs's, and is a fustian piece of curious virtuoso stuff.' [13] Of the other books borrowed by Swift we have no record, but despite his condemnation of 'one fustian piece,' it is obvious that Richard Dobbs fulfilled the role of a cultured country squire interested in the development of his estate, and in the world of science, art, and literature.

Dobbs's second son, Richard, married Mary Stewart of Ballintoy, and built himself a house at Castletown, a pleasant inland hamlet some nine miles north-west of Carrickfergus. Early in 1688, Richard and his family returned to Castle Dobbs; this move was dictated by the fact that his father, now Mayor of Carrickfergus, had little time to look after his estate, and the growing uncertainty of political events in England and Ireland made it expedient to do so.

The thirty years of peace which had enabled the new Anglo-Irish to consolidate and strengthen their position in Ireland received a setback on the death of Charles II in 1685. His successor, James II, was a Catholic, and for a time it seemed as though the Protestants might be driven from the land they had acquired by conquest and settlement, but the policy of James, so far as Ireland was concerned, was to leave the new owners in peaceful possession of their property. He did, however, recall the Protestant Lord Deputy, Clarendon, and appointed in his place an Anglo-Irish Catholic, Richard Talbot, whom he created Earl of Tyrconnell. Protestant judges were replaced by Catholics, not universally, though, but in sufficient numbers to give Catholics a predominance on the Bench. In the army and the government of towns Protestants were replaced by Catholics, so that the greater part of the power for so many years in Protestant hands was transferred to the Catholic majority.

On the 5th November, 1688, William of Orange landed at Torbay in the south of England with some 15,000 Dutch troops and was soon joined by his English allies. After a short and futile resistance, James

II fled to France. In Ireland the Protestants banded together in support of William, and in the north of Ireland, where they were particularly strong, they formed themselves into County Associations for the 'mutual protection and defence of the Protestant religion.' The Catholics, on the other hand, declared for James, who, in March 1689, landed at Kinsale, bringing with him muskets and powder, and a large sum of money provided by his French ally, Louis XIV; so once again Ireland was to prove a warring ground for English kings. James set up an Irish Parliament at Dublin and proceeded to remove all the disabilities imposed on Catholic Irishmen; he repealed the Act of Settlement passed in the reign of Charles II, which established the Protestant minority in possession of the forfeited lands of the dispossessed Irish.

Old Richard Dobbs, who had been elected Mayor of Carrickfergus in 1687, was confirmed in his post by the Catholic Lord Deputy, Tyrconnell. His son, however, threw in his lot with the County Antrim Association, and was appointed Captain in the newly established organisation for the defence of the Protestant interest.[14] For safety, and as a necessary precaution, he sent his young wife, heavy with child, to Scotland where, at the fishing village of Girvan in Ayrshire, she was delivered of a boy 'on Tuesday morning being ye 2 of April 1689.' [15] The boy was christened Arthur.

During this period the younger Richard Dobbs took an active part in the campaign against James II. He was among those who conceived a bold plan to surprise and capture Carrickfergus, then held by the troops of James, but the plan failed. On the 13th August, 1689, the Duke of Schomberg arrived from England with a well-equipped Williamite army of more than 10,000 men, and disembarked at Bangor. Wasting little time, the Williamites took possession of Belfast, and then marched on Carrickfergus. Fearing a plot to deliver the town from within, the Governor, Colonel Thomas Maxwell, seized Mayor Dobbs and the leading Protestant citizens and held them prisoners. For an account of subsequent events the short note penned in the town records by Mayor Richard Dobbs may be quoted:

'When King William's Army under General Schomberg invested this towne (being possessed by the Irish) the 20th August, 1689, I was upon the first appearance of the army committed Prisoner in the vault next the mayn Guard, and next day was committed to the common gaole, into which I had this book, and the towne Chest (wherein all the Records, Deeds & Charters of the Towne were), brought into gaole, where they remained till the towne was delivered the 27th and the English entered;

Ireland was generally a lucrative undertaking, but unfortunately it gave rise to rack-renting on a large scale and tenants were mercilessly crushed under the thumb of landlords, agents, and petty leaseholders or middlemen. There were however good agents and good landlords, and Dobbs, while undoubtedly doing all he could to enhance the value of an estate, would appear from correspondence to have had the interest of his tenants at heart, and endeavoured to protect them from usurious rents.

Dobbs acquired a knowledge of engineering and construction during his short army career and this enabled him to engage in mineral prospecting not only in his own neighbourhood but along the Antrim coast, where, among other minerals, he discovered some workable coal seams.[3] He also undertook a prospecting survey in the neighbourhood of County Down, where his cousin Michael Ward owned a large estate on the shores of Strangford Lough. Ward, who later became an Irish judge, was a progressive landowner, and he was about the same age as Dobbs. A close and warm friendship existed between the two cousins that lasted throughout their lives.[4]

In 1719 Dobbs married the young widow of Captain Norbury. Her father, John Osburn, a silk dyer of London, was estranged from his daughter, but her uncle, Captain Osburn of Drogheda, who was her guardian, settled a large estate at Timahoe in County Kildare on Norbury contingent on his marriage to Anne with a reversion to any male issue of the marriage who took the name of Osburn. At the time of her marriage to Dobbs, Anne was in possession of the estate at Timahoe. By her first marriage she had one child who died shortly after birth, and thus her large estate became part of the Dobbs patrimony, and was later leased to Richard Dobbs, a clergyman and Fellow of Trinity College.[5]

In 1720 Dobbs was appointed High Sheriff of Antrim, and while the appointment offered little beyond some statutory fees and perquisites it was a definite step in political advancement, and brought him into contact with a number of important people. Dobbs continued to devote himself zealously to local affairs, and was elected Mayor of Carrickfergus by his fellow burgesses, thus filling the honourable position occupied by his father and grandfather under less auspicious circumstances. The old walled town had grown in size, but its importance as a port had given way to the rising town of Belfast; despite its diminishing importance, however, it was still a garrison town and returned two members to the Irish Parliament.

In 1719 the question of the establishment of a national bank for

Ireland engaged the attention of an influential body of men including Dobbs. A petition was drawn up and submitted to George I on behalf of several Lords and Gentlemen, pointing out that the extreme scarcity of coin in Ireland had 'already occasioned a general decay of trade, and reduced many families to the utmost necessities.' In order to counteract the evils arising from this scarcity which retarded the agricultural and industrial development of the country, the petitioners proposed 'to charge their estates and engage their fortunes to raise a fund of credit for circulating bills to answer the exigencies of the Kingdom.'⁶ In brief, the petitioners prayed permission to establish a bank.

The petition was favourably received, and two years later a Committee of the Irish House of Commons reported that 'the establishment of a public bank upon solid and good foundations, under proper regulations and restrictions, will greatly contribute to the restoring of credit and support the trade and manufactures of this kingdom.' There was, however, an element of opposition to the proposed bank, and when the Committee of the House of Commons issued its favourable recommendations, the opposition grew more voluble, led by the redoubtable Dean of St. Patrick's, Jonathan Swift, whose brilliance and genius was often vitiated by a narrow and unaccountable prejudice. Swift perceived the establishment of a national bank as an overt Whig conspiracy to enslave the country and make it financially dependent upon England. The tide of opposition continued to increase, and Parliament, which at the outset favoured the establishment of a bank, suddenly surrendered to the popular agitation. The main reason for the widespread opposition was due in a large measure to the fact that the commercial community, labouring under repressive penal legislation, felt that any measure of a financial nature, accepted by the Whig government, was just another attempt to strangle the economic community by controlling the monetary system of the country.

Swift's opposition to the proposed bank was mainly factious, and the scheme provided him with a platform to stir up opposition to the ruling Whigs. When the Bill for establishing a bank came before the Irish Parliament, it was promptly thrown out against the advice of its own Committee and many of its leading members. The Bill was not discussed on its merits, and the vitriolic masterpiece of Swift, *The Establishment of a Swearers' Bank*, issued a short time before, served its purpose. The initiators of the scheme were not deflected from their purpose, however, and immediately published a statement of fact, and subjoined a list of subscribers to the proposed ventures, among whom was Dobbs, listed as a subscriber of not less than £2,000, a sum which qualified him as a Deputy Governor or Director of the proposed bank. The publication of the list of subscribers, all men of wealth and influence, had not the desired effect of placating the opponents of the scheme, but actually provided Swift with material for a further onslaught. In a terse and libellous piece of vituperation entitled *A Letter to the King at Arms from a Reputed Esquire, one of the Subscribers to the Bank,* he broke down the list of subscribers and classified them in rank, his purpose being to show that generally the subscribers were men of little importance who falsely assumed the title of Esquire.

It might be pointed out that the project for a national bank for Ireland was initiated at an inopportune time. It was a period of 'Bubbles,' and the public had suffered considerably as a result of the failure of Law's South Sea Scheme and the Mississippi Scheme, which a year before was at the height of its stock-jobbing success. Great accounts of fortunes made overnight had encouraged an orgy of wild speculation, and with a plentiful supply of paper money in England a gambling mania seized the people; the failure of so many genuine and crackpot schemes had given rise to the term 'Bubbles.' The advent of a scheme for establishing an Irish bank, when so many fatuous schemes were afoot, gave thoughtful men cause for concern. Swift exploited this uncertainty to the full in a brilliant piece of invective, *An Essay on English Bubbles.* By the time the Bill for establishing a national bank reached Parliament many 'Bubbles' had burst, leaving a train of ruined and pauperised investors, a few of whom were members of the Irish Parliament. Swift adroitly classed the proposed scheme with the rest of the 'Bubbles,' and though it offered a real and genuine effort to relieve Ireland, and was not conceived in a speculative way, the terror of 'Bubbles' and the suspicion that the promoters were stock-jobbers and tools of the Whigs was sufficient to wreck the scheme.

Though ending in failure, the effort to establish a national bank was but one of the signs of a new stirring of Irish life. A spirit of nationalism and a genuine love of country were slowly developing among the more enlightened and thoughtful Anglo-Irish, who not only revolted against the appalling economic conditions of the country and the common people but deplored the impotency and diminishing power of the Irish Parliament to legislate freely in the interests of the country. Throughout the early eighteenth century, Ireland remained an undeveloped country, and almost all efforts to increase its agricultural and industrial potentialities were negatived or destroyed by successive navigation or other restrictive Acts. The enactments against

Irish trade and industry affected the Protestant business and artisan classes just as they did the enslaved Catholic majority. The economic enslavement of the country and the servility of the Irish Parliament was secured by the fact that the chief offices of Church and State were reserved for Englishmen.[7] Primates of the Irish Church such as Boulter, Hoadley, and Stone were the *de facto* rulers and saw to it that both Church and Parliament acted in English rather than Irish interests.[8] Parliament was not representative of the people, nor was it governed by the Septennial Act, but remained in existence as long as the King pleased.

The poverty of the people and the appalling economic conditions of the country unleashed the wrath of a new leader. From the deanery of St. Patrick's Cathedral Jonathan Swift emerged and fanned the flame of discontent; he found earnest disciples among the younger and more resolute Anglo-Irish. In 1720 he issued a tract, *A Proposal for the Use of Irish Manufactures*, in which he urged the people to reject and renounce 'everything wearable that comes from England,' and thus provide employment for the people of Ireland.

Though Dobbs had known Swift from his childhood days, their paths through life were widely divergent, but for all that the older man retained a warm regard for the family.[9] Swift's tract on Irish manufactures appealed to Dobbs, and though he was identified with the ruling Whigs his sympathies were with the people, and he was beginning to show a practical interest in the economic and social development of the country. Actually, while Swift was writing his tract Dobbs was engaged in distributing spinning-wheels to his own tenantry. While warmly approving of Swift's tracts on Irish trade and industry, Dobbs disapproved of what he considered his intemperate outbursts.

In 1722 a memorial was presented to the Lords of the Treasury requesting a new issue of copper coinage for Ireland because of the economic problems created by a continuous shortage of small coin. The Treasury agreed, and the privilege of supplying the coinage was granted to the Duchess of Kendal, the King's mistress, who sold the patent to an ironmonger named Wood. By the terms of the patent one pound of copper was to be coined in halfpence and farthings to the nominal value of thirty pence, but the market value of the copper did not amount to more than thirteen pence. Though the need for copper coins was very real, there were serious objections to the issue from an Irish point of view. In the first place, the patent was granted without consulting the Irish Privy Council or indeed any other authority in

Ireland, and in order to enhance the profit to the patentee more than one hundred thousand pounds' worth of small coin was to be minted when one-tenth of that amount would suffice.

Though Swift exaggerated the effect of Wood's coinage on the economic life of the country, the patent was granted when economic and social conditions were at a low ebb, and when a spirit of bitterness, discontent, and rebellion was apparent even among the Protestants; it only required a spark to set the flame alight. The explosion when it came startled the Government in England. Merchants, traders, and corporate bodies protested against the proposed coinage. In the guise of an humble Drapier, Swift issued a series of protesting tracts that were models of popular eloquence. The mass of discontent burst into a flame and spread through all classes; Walpole's foolish threat to cram the coin down the throats of the people only added to the rebellious mood. The Irish Parliament even bestirred itself and protested strongly.

Swift continued to whip the nation into fury and reasserted with passion the principles of Molyneux that the Irish Parliament had the sole right to legislate for the Irish people, and declared that government without the consent of the governed was the very definition of slavery. The English Parliament, fearful of the consequences of the outcry against Wood's coinage, hurriedly reduced by half the sum of money to be coined. The Lord-Lieutenant, the Duke of Grafton, was recalled, and the more able Lord Carteret was installed in his place. The discontent continued to spread. A reward of £300 was offered for the apprehension of the author of the Drapier Letters, and though he was well known to most people no evidence could be obtained against him. A prosecution was therefore directed against the printer, and, in spite of the efforts of the biased Judge Whitshed, the Grand Jury refused to find a bill.[10]

Throughout the country the ruling class more or less sided with Swift, and even Primate Boulter, the bitterest opponent of what he called the Irish party, strongly urged the Government in England to abandon Wood's coinage.[11] The populace joined in the opposition, and in the streets of Dublin the mob sang ballads of praise and encouragement, following Swift about the streets and lauding him as their new leader.

Town corporations issued protests against the proposed coinage, including the town of Carrickfergus of which Dobbs was a burgess, and, though he took no active part in the agitation, he appended his name to the protest. In this particular protest Wood was described as 'the greatest Alchymist who has found out the secret of turning copper into gold,' and the Corporators asserted that it was a shame 'to enrich a single Stranger who must build his fortune on the ruins of an unfortunate people.' [12] It is not difficult to understand the motives prompting Dobbs to sign his name to this protest. In every respect he differed politically from Swift and was a strong supporter of Walpole's Whig Government; he did not approve of the noisy campaign against the coinage, but he saw in the growing opposition to the Government a serious threat to the English interest in Ireland, and simply supported the demand for the withdrawal of Wood's patent so that any division between the two people could be speedily bridged.

As a result of the agitation against Wood's coinage, there was no alternative for the Government but to withdraw the patent. A deciding factor in this agitation was the fact that for the first time the native Irish and a considerable body of the Anglo-Irish had joined together, irrespective of creed, to assert their national rights, and this was something neither the Government in Britain nor the governing class in Ireland could view with unconcern. The Government's capitulation, however, could not undo the harm that had been done, and the principles which Swift enunciated had in themselves the power to destroy the narrow sectarian construction he placed upon them. He showed quite clearly the power of combination and cohesion, and preached a doctrine of liberty which far transcended that which he practised.

Though Dobbs appended his name to the protest of the Carrickfergus Corporation, he did not enter into the *mêlée* of controversy, but that he did show a practical interest in the matter of coinage and currency is evident from an unpublished tract among his manuscripts, entitled *Some Considerations on Coin in Britain and Ireland, and a Method proposed to prevent the Frauds and Abuses in the Coin from Clippers, Sweaters of both abroad and at Home.* [13]

While his more wordy compatriots added to the flood of tracts and pamphlets, Dobbs devoted his time to local politics and the improvement of his estate. At Castle Dobbs he lived the busy life of an improving landlord, taking an especial interest in the establishment of plantations and orchards, and in this regard his advice was sought by other progressive landowners, including his cousin Judge Ward. Besides giving close attention to his own estate, he acted as an agent for Ward and others, and the many letters between the two cousins give a sidelight on this activity as well as dealing with more personal matters, such as expressing a wish to see Ward 'if there are not too many visitors about him,' recording the death of a young niece, 'a hopeful girl for whom my sister grieves,' and his own domestic troubles, 'my youngest girl had also taken a fitt, but upon bleeding her she is better.' In another letter he anticipates the birth of his fourth child and clearly hopes for a marriage arrangement between his step-sister and Ward's eldest son. He writes: 'I will wait upon you at Castle Ward upon your return to the country if my wife be once laid and the child christened if all be well, and bring Betty with me if Capn. Ward will receive her after disappointing him so long.' Other letters deal with local affairs, including an exciting election in which he states that their opponents have brought 'the gouty, lame and blind against us,' but notwithstanding that 'we will have a majority.' 14

Among Dobbs's multifarious activities was a somewhat more than amateur interest in science, particularly in astronomy and meteorology. Two letters which he wrote to his brother Richard were communicated to the Royal Society and published in its *Transactions*. The first letter was an account of a Parhelion or false sun observed at Castle Dobbs in March 1721.15 Dobbs states that the Parhelion was four times as large as the sun's disc, and lay 30 degrees distant to the south-ward of the sun. His account of this phenomenon was accompanied by a fair illustration made at the time. The second letter describes an *Aurora Borealis* observed at Castle Dobbs in September 1725.16 A third letter, giving an account of observations on an eclipse of the moon, was communicated to the Royal Society by Oliver St. John, a well-known Fellow of the Society.17

Though Dobbs lived a fairly full and active life, showing a diversity of interests and tastes, he was very far from satisfied with the ordinary everyday life of an eighteenth-century landlord. He was a restless, energetic, and ambitious man with all the ambitious man's love of power, authority, influence, and wealth. Despite his restless and ambitious nature, however, he had achieved little, and his prospects, at least in Ireland, were by no means good. Dobbs realised that the path of ambitious Irishmen was strewn with many obstacles. Few important positions in State, Church, or Government were within reach of the average Protestant Irishman who lacked solid political backing and influence. Even a seat in Parliament seemed unattainable, though in this respect Dobbs could count on a strong measure of support from the rather independent electors of Carrickfergus. Normally, however, the patronage of a noble lord or the friendship of a borough patron paved the way to Parliament.

Up to his fortieth year, therefore, though acquiring some wealth and a little influence in his own county, he had attained no more responsible positions than those of High Sheriff of Antrim and Mayor of Carrickfergus. In 1728 he was again elected Mayor, and shortly afterwards Carteret, the Lord-Lieutenant, signed an order nominating him Deputy Governor of Carrickfergus. The office of Deputy Governor was not of any great importance, but it brought Dobbs into close association with the ageing Lord Conway who was Governor of the town for a considerable number of years. Conway was an influential man, and owned an estate of more than 60,000 acres in Ireland. Further, he controlled the pocket borough of Lisburn, and could influence a considerable body of freeholders in Carrickfergus. He was a member of the Irish Privy Council and the House of Lords, and, perhaps more important still, a relative of Sir Robert Walpole.[18] Dobbs accepted the old man's patronage, and in recognition of his friendship had his eldest son christened Conway Richard; one might presume, indeed, that Lord Conway acted as sponsor at the child's christening.

The death of King George I in 1727 marked a definite turning-point in Dobbs's career. The Irish Parliament that had been elected in 1714 lasted throughout the King's reign, and was dissolved only on his death. With the approval of Lord Conway and the support of a number of citizens of Carrickfergus, Dobbs offered himself for election to Parliament. The support of Conway, while by no means decisive, was helpful, for the two sitting members who represented the borough for a great many years offered themselves for re-election and from the out-set were assured of considerable support. The two members, Archibald Edmonston and Edward Lyndon, had supported the Government, and they were both friends and neighbours of Dobbs.

The election was a long-drawn-out and at times bitter affair, and though Dobbs had the backing of Conway he fought the election on his own personality and his record as a local public man. The result of the poll was a decisive victory for Dobbs, who jubilantly informed his cousin Ward that he had 'a majority of 500 in 2,000 votes cast, and more than 200 attended the poll.' His election to the Irish Parliament cost him more than £1,000 a no mean sum of money at the time.[19]

3

Member of Parliament

DOBBS TRAVELLED to Dublin towards the end of November 1727, and lodged with his brother Richard at his rooms in Trinity College; later he lodged with his friend and adviser Councillor M'Aulay, who had rooms and offices at the Sign of the Raven in Thomas Street.[1] Dublin at this time was a somewhat dirty and ill-kept city. The elegance and beauty of the Georgian capital was only beginning to show itself in a few places. Even the Parliament House was in a ruinous state, and we gather from a Parliamentary report issued in 1727 that 'the out-walls do overhang in severall places . . . the wall-plates and bottoms of all the Rafters are so decayed and rotten that if care had not been lately taken to splice all the timbers of the Roof with new stuff the house would undoubtedly have fallen.' The report ended with the statement: 'It is absolutely necessary to build a New House.' The condition of the Irish Parliament speaks volumes for the legislators of the day. A competent historian writes:

'Until their last year in Chichester House, no flame descended from heaven to encompass with any consecrated glory the understanding of the houses that met there. Rather the contrary; and they allowed the fabric of their building to fall about their ears while busy with writing the blackest pages of the statute Book.'[2]

This, then, was the Parliament House to which Dobbs, as the member for the borough of Carrickfergus, was summoned on the 27th November, 1727. Parliament opened with a pomp and ceremony that gave a glowing façade to the ruinous building, and lent an air of importance to its, at times, supine proceedings. When the members assembled, the bewigged Gentleman Usher of the Black Rod, Michael Broughton, announced that it was 'his Excellency, the Lord-Lieutenant's pleasure, that this Honourable House attend him in the House of Lords immediately,' where he was 'pleased to make a speech to both Houses of Parliament.'[3]

On this occasion the Lord-Lieutenant's speech gave little evidence of the classical scholar with the reputation of being one of the finest orators of his generation. Carteret was not one, however, to waste his oratory on a shallow Irish assembly, and despite the tributes paid to him by the members, he displayed a cynical indifference to Irish affairs. He looked upon Ireland as a nuisance which he had to endure simply because the scheming Walpole had no use for him in England.[4] In his speech he eulogised the late King as a 'gracious sovereign of glorious memory,' and, no doubt aware of the growing spirit of discontent and misery occasioned by hunger and poverty, and fully exploited by the pen of Swift, he informed the members of 'His Majesty's concern for the happiness of his people' and trusted they would support his Government 'with the greatest zeal and unanimity.'

This support was necessary, for the first business of the House was to vote sufficient money for the Establishment, not a little of which was to provide pensions for the cast-off mistresses of the King and some of his useless German friends. The great majority of the members supported the Whig Government and were its loyal tools. The more independent and critically minded members were but a handful, and though Parliament boasted many able men, its constitution was such that it lay wholly beyond the control of public opinion. An Act passed by the English Parliament precluded Catholics from membership, and by an Act of the Irish Parliament they were deprived of suffrage; nonconformists and dissenters, while not formally excluded, were debarred by the Test Clause. The national assembly was in consequence completely cut off from the great bulk of the people, and simply represented the somewhat divided interests of a small minority. The docility and servility of the Irish Parliament was ensured by the creation of pocket boroughs; this method of assuring a Government majority was common in England, too, but the creation of rotten boroughs never reached the scandalous proportions that it did in Ireland. Of the 300 members assembled on 27th November, 1727, more than two hundred were elected by boroughs and manors, and of these at least 170 were elected by individual patrons; fifty of the members, one-sixth of the House in fact, were elected by ten patrons![5]

In a Parliament of this nature even the most outrageous charges on the Irish Establishment were assured of support. These charges were out of all proportion to the wealth of the country and formed a great field of lucrative patronage, paid from the Irish revenue, at the full disposal of the English ministers, and almost wholly beyond the cognizance of the British Parliament. Swift railed against this iniquitous patronage, and pointed out that 'those who have the misfortune to be born here have the least title to any considerable employment, to which they are seldom preferred but upon political considerations.'[6] His assertion was true; no Irishman with the slightest ambition dared oppose the Government, knowing, as he did, that every advancement and preferment was attendant upon loyal support of it.

Parliament sat from the opening on 27th November until a few days before Christmas. During the session, Dobbs served on a number of Committees, including one appointed to 'report and inspect the state of the hempen and flaxen manufactures, and consider what is necessary to be done for the further improvement and regulation thereof.' He also served on an important Committee enquiring into the state of the workhouse and poor in the city of Dublin.[7]

Parliament adjourned on 23rd December and Dobbs returned home to spend Christmas with his family. The respite from parliamentary duties was short, however, and Parliament reassembled early in January, and continued in session until the month of June, when it was prorogued, having written a large number of useful Acts into the Statute Book.

The poverty, hunger, and distress of the people, due in part to the laws militating against Irish trade and industry together with a lopsided agrarian system, caused concern and began to engage the attention of many public-spirited and thoughtful Irishmen. Swift, particularly in his tracts *The Use of Irish Manufactures* and *The State of Ireland*, gave a lead to the more serious economists and philanthropists. Thomas Prior, the most practical of these men, had just published such a work —*A List of Absentees with a subjoined Essay on the State of Ireland*. Prior, in this pamphlet, listed the names of all the landlords and pensioners who lived outside the country, and set down particulars of the rents and pensions remitted to them from Ireland. This courageous *exposé* rendered Prior *persona non grata* with the Government, but earned for him the praise of Swift, who strongly deplored the evils of absenteeism. Prior, in his factual essay on the economic state of the country, made an earnest plea for the curtailment of imports, and called for the establishment of new industries, and a complete re-orientation of the Irish agricultural system.[8]

In this general movement to stem the rot in the body economic and social of the country, Dobbs was thinking on much the same lines as Swift and Prior, and devoting what little time he had to the preparation of an essay on Irish trade. In a more practical way the work of an Irish chemist, William Maple, found support in unexpected quarters, and

Dobbs, as a member of a small parliamentary committee, recommended that a grant of £200 be given to Maple to enable him to pursue his experiments in the use of Irish bark for tanning, so that it would no longer be necessary to import madder, or send green skins abroad for tanning.[9] The practical efforts of men like Maple, and the serious recommendations and suggestions of Prior, Madden, and Molesworth had the warm support and approval of Dobbs. They were earnest, patriotic men deeply interested in the economic development of the country and the well-being of the people, a sphere of endeavour in which they were later joined by Bishop Berkeley, Edward Synge, Michael Ward, and others.

Before Parliament reassembled in 1728, Dobbs published the first part of his *Essay on the Trade and Improvement of Ireland*, the second part of which was published some two years later. The complete work remains an outstanding and important contribution to Irish economic history.

The first volume of the *Essay on Irish Trade* is tiresome to read because of the great amount of space devoted to trade statistics, which are analysed with minute care and diligence. The second volume, on the other hand, is of more interest to the ordinary reader and the student of political thought. In this volume Dobbs makes many able and discerning comments on the political, social, and economic state of the country, and offers practical suggestions for increasing Irish trade, providing employment for the people and improving the standard of living of not only the very poor but also the small farming and artisan class. He writes at length on the restrictive measures imposed by the British Parliament on Irish trade, including the Navigation Acts, and the harsh measures directed against the woollen trade, which he claims were conceived by 'Jealousies and misunderstandings' and condemned the Irish people to beggary.

While Dobbs offered many suggestions for the improvement of Irish economy, he was of the opinion that all efforts to improve trade and commerce were at the best palliatives, and that the country's real salvation lay in a parliamentary union with Britain. In this regard he was looking very far ahead, clearly realising that in time the governing minority would be swept aside, and that the laws relegating Catholics to near-serfdom could not last; he saw, too, that the now relatively quiescent and subservient Parliament would throw off its shackles and demand legislative independence. An Act of Union, Dobbs contended, 'would procure us greater privileges in our foreign trade, and enlarge our commerce . . . so that we would have full employment.' Equally important, the Protestant minority in union with Britain would be assured of its privileged position and would wield the same power and security as their brothers in England. Economically a union was desirable and necessary, he wrote, for under the rule of a single parliament . Ireland would reap all the benefits of the Navigation Acts just as Scotland did.

Dobbs was a strong advocate of free trade, and in his *Essay* he condemned such artificial barriers to world trade and commerce as tariffs, duties, and penal legislature. 'Trade,' he wrote, 'makes the people of the world as one great family supplying each other's wants.' Duties and tariffs only tended to create artificial prices which 'fall upon the husbandman or artificer who raises or manufactures goods for export, and discourages industry and labour, for they either lower our market at home or raise the price of our commodity abroad, and so prevent a ready market and quick returns.' In his comments on trade and commerce generally, Dobbs was many years in advance of his time and antedated Adam Smith by more than forty years, a fact which in itself should place him high on the list of eighteenth-century economists.

In order to provide work for the workless and improve the country's unbalanced economy, Dobbs advocated the granting of premiums for the establishment of new industries, the building of granaries, and the cultivation of waste and bogland. Perhaps of more importance were his remarks and suggestions on land tenure in Ireland, one of the root causes of the country's chronic economic condition. By law no Catholic could lease land for more than twenty-one years, with the result that there was little or no encouragement for Catholics to improve their holdings, for the Catholic tenant was always conscious of the fact that if he farmed well and improved his holding its letting value, on the expiration of a short lease, was certain to be increased, often beyond the means of the tenant. 'How can a tenant improve his land,' Dobbs asked, 'when he is convinced that after all his care and toil, his improvements will be over-rated, and he be obliged to shift for himself?' High rents, bad seasons, and want of a good tenure or a permanent property, forced many farmers to leave the country. 'The present short tenures,' Dobbs remarked, 'serve only as a snare to induce the nobility and gentry to be extravagant, arbitrary, and sometimes tyrannical; and the Commonalty to be dejected, dispirited, and in a manner slaves in some places.' He suggested that there should be fixed and permanent property in farms by leases of lives renewable, or fee farms. Each freehold should have a farmhouse and be suitably enclosed and planted. He visualised the country as a 'regular plantation or garden [made so] by the industry and frugality of the people.' In suggesting such revolutionary changes in the agrarian system, Dobbs may have been an idealist; nevertheless he was a hard-headed business man, and though his ideas were many years in advance of his time, had they been accepted the course of Irish agrarian history might have been much different, and the country would have been spared many years of conflict, hardship, and hunger.

On the whole, the suggestions put forward by Dobbs were eminently practical and showed a liberal outlook far in advance of his contemporaries. Though he was a militant Protestant and strongly opposed to the Catholic Church, he favoured the granting of freehold leases to his Catholic countrymen; he was convinced that the retention of virtually all land by Protestants was not beneficial to the nation, and wished 'for the good of religion and our own public benefit that so wide a breach were not kept up between us and the Papists.' In the last pages of his book he urged the need for improved methods in agricultural practice, and pleaded for the cultivation of hops, madder, and all imported products that could be grown at home, as well as for the establishment of plantations and orchards, increased tillage, and the expansion of inland and sea fisheries. He concluded with a strong appeal for the removal of all the penal enactments against Irish industry, and a revocation of the Navigation Acts which prevented a direct trade between Ireland and the colonies. The *Essay on Irish Trade* was a thoughtful and serious contribution to the economic history of Ireland in the eighteenth century, and is clearly the work of an original thinker who had the misfortune to be born a century before his time.[10]

As a young man, Dobbs was infused with a spirit of adventure, and this no doubt led to his early choice of an army career. The death of his father changed the course of his life, but he always retained some of the spirit of the Elizabethan adventurers, an indefinable spirit that impelled merchants and prospectors to open new channels of trade and add to the power, wealth, and glory of Britain. Now, at the age of forty, with little hope of success in Ireland, and stirred no doubt by the blended motives of patriotism, religion, and profit, his thoughts turned to the rich American colonies then evoking the envy of France and Spain, who vied with Britain for their possession. To the patriotic Dobbs it seemed probable that these rich colonies would fall into the grasping hands of France and Spain unless Britain bestirred herself from the drugging content, lethargy, and complacency of Walpole's prosperous and peaceful administration. This was no idle conjecture, so about 1729 Dobbs prepared a long memorandum calling for a vigorous colonisation policy, and suggesting how the colonies might be secured and strengthened in the face of French encroachment and exploitation.

As Dobbs had little or no influence in governing circles and was unknown outside of Ireland, he placed his memorandum or scheme before Primate Boulter, and requested him to provide the necessary introduction to Walpole, the Prime Minister. Boulter readily agreed, and in a letter dated 4th January, 1730, he wrote:

'The gentleman that waits upon you with this, is Mr. Dobbs, one of the Members of our House of Commons, where he on all occasions endeavours to promote his Majesty's service. He is a person of good sense, and has for some time applied his thoughts to the improvement of the trade of Great Britain and Ireland, and to making our colonies in America of more advantage than they have hitherto been, and has written his thoughts on these subjects, which he is desirous to offer to your consideration. As he has not the honour to be known to you, he has applied to me to open a way for his waiting on you. I need say nothing of what his thoughts are on those subjects, since he will be better able to explain them, and you are more capable of judging them than I can be. I presume no farther than to recommend him for an audience at leisure, and to do afterwards in the affair as you think most proper.' [11]

Though armed with Boulter's letter of introduction, Dobbs did not proceed immediately to England, for Parliament was sitting at Dublin, and the journey to London in winter was by no means pleasant. In order to pave the way for a future interview, however, he wrote to Walpole and enclosed a copy of his scheme, which he hoped would not be looked upon as a criticism of the administration of the colonies, but rather as the thoughts and ideas of an ordinary, patriotic citizen who realised that

'in the administration of a government of so extended a dominion as Britain and the dependencies it is impossible for such ministers so employed to lay schemes and concert proper measures for enlarging and looking after the outskirts of our colonies, trade, and commerce.' [12]

Dobbs envisaged the publication of his scheme, for he firmly believed that he had a mission to perform, and that it was his duty to arouse in a growingly lethargic nation, sated and drowsy with power, a fresh zeal and interest in the neglected colonies. There were others in England at this time who thought on much the same lines as he did, and the more enterprising merchants and business men were concerned that Walpole's peaceful policy of appeasement served to strengthen French and Spanish influence throughout the world, and actually threatened the growth and expansion of British trade. Dobbs leaned strongly towards the views of these imperialists, but he felt at this stage that it would serve him ill to appear critical or opposed to the colonial policy of the Government; this is clear from the concluding paragraph of his letter to Walpole. He wrote:

'Since this project if divulged and prosecuted by its consequence would arouse misunderstandings and jealousys between his Majesty and the powers of France and Spain, I hope you'll pardon my ambition in laying it thus privily before a Prime Minister whose capacity and genius will at once comprehend and improve it, and whose integrity and love of your country and application in discharge of the great trust reposed in you by his late and present Majesty, will incline you if it be found feasible and convenient, to push it with great zeal.' [13]

We do not know what Walpole thought of the ambitious scheme, but we do know that from this time onward Dobbs could count Walpole among his patrons, and the new friendship opened a door hitherto closed to the ambitious Irishman.

4

Friendship with Walpole

DOBBS'S SCHEME for the enlargement and development of the American colonies was succinctly summarised in a letter to Walpole in which he asked him to accept and patronise the scheme which he had 'calculated to his utmost of my capacity, to increase in an eminent manner the fame and glory of His Majesty, and the wealth and naval power of Britain by increasing our trade and colonies in America.' In the course of his lengthy memorandum in which he traced the growth of colonial empires from the earliest times, he stressed the need for strengthening the American colonies by providing more settlers and settlements, and pleaded for a just treatment of the Indian natives. He set down plans for the education of the colonists and Indians alike, and as a staunch Protestant appealed for a new missionary outlook so as to ensure the establishment of the Protestant religion. In the field of economics he suggested practical plans for increasing the wealth of Britain and the colonies, and, as in his *Essay on Irish Trade*, he pleaded for a repeal of the Navigation Acts so as to permit the free flow of trade between Britain, Ireland, and the colonies.

Dobbs deplored the *laissez-faire* policy of the Board of Trade, and claimed that if the Government failed to take a more practical and realistic interest in the colonies they would fall easy prey to other nations. He forecast with accuracy the effect of French expansionist policy in Canada, the encroachment down the Ohio and the probable linking of Louisiana in the south with the northern French possessions. He suggested that French expansionist policy could be forestalled if Britain took possession of the string of lakes stretching almost from Quebec to the Ohio and established forts and settlements thereon.

Though much of Dobbs's colonial scheme is clothed with wordy rhetoric, a fiery crusading Protestantism, and some impractical suggestions, it is not without merit. Indeed, his observations on colonial trade, development, and education are important, and his suggestions and plans for containing the French and eventually wresting their colonial possessions from them are interesting in the light of later events. Dobbs was not ignorant of military matters, and his suggested attack at the heart of the French colonial empire—Quebec—by a land advance from the south and a naval expedition from the east was the plan eventually laid before Pitt by Pownall and others some twenty-five years later and successfully carried out.

Armed with Primate Boulter's letter of introduction to Walpole, Dobbs crossed to London in April 1730, and at once made himself known to some of the influential city merchants, among whom was Joshua Gee, a prosperous Quaker with considerable business interests in London and America. Gee introduced him to other merchants, notably Murray Crymble, James Huey, Henry McCulloh, and James Campbell who were interested in the American colonies. There was much in common between Dobbs and Joshua Gee, for about the same time as Dobbs published his *Essay on Irish Trade*, Gee published a somewhat similar essay—*The Trade and Navigation of Great Britain Considered*. The two essays were complementary in many respects, and the ideas set down by both men regarding the eradication of poverty, the development of agriculture and industry, and the provision of full employment for the man-power of each country, were identical. Further, Gee's comments on the economic relations between Britain and Ireland were very similar to those enunciated by Dobbs. Gee's essay created quite a stir when published, and was praised and used by Adam Smith some years later.[1]

An interesting sidelight on the meeting of Dobbs and Gee is contained in a letter from Gee to Judge Ward, who apparently effected the introduction. Gee writes:

> 'I happened to be out of town when thy kinsman Arthur Dobbs first called at my house, and left word he had a letter for me. . . . As soon as I had an opportunity of returning to town I enquired at his lodgings . . . He was so kind as to give me his company yesterday, and take a short dinner with me, when we had a sound discussion upon Trade and the Linnen manufactures of Ireland. I was surprised to find a man not born to trade knowing so much as he did.'

Gee assured Ward that he would do what he could to help Dobbs, with whom he was impressed.[2]

A few days later Dobbs called on Walpole to discuss his scheme for the colonies with him. Though Walpole may have signified his approval of the scheme, it is obvious he could do little about it without arousing French antagonism, for the scheme, generally speaking, was the antithesis of the *quieta non movere* policy of his Government. In other respects the interview was not a failure, for Dobbs had made himself known to Walpole, and apparently impressed him.

Dobbs returned to Ireland filled with a new enthusiasm for colonial enterprises, an enthusiasm no doubt engendered by his discussions with the London merchants. Despite his new interests, he did not neglect his obligations at home. During the years 1731 and 1732 he played an active part in the Irish Parliament; he served on a number of committees, formulated schemes for the development of agriculture, and introduced some Parliamentary Bills, the most important and far-reaching of which was a Bill to encourage tillage, improve waste land, and establish plantations. The paucity of tillage and the increase in pasture contributed in no small way to the appalling economic conditions prevailing in Ireland, resulting in almost endemic famine. This condition has been described by many who witnessed it. Swift wrote about the old and sick dying by the hundreds, and rotting from cold and famine, filth and vermin.[3] Bishop Nicholson, on his transfer to the See of Derry, tells us that the unfortunate people fell upon one of his horses left to die upon the roadside and devoured it.[4] Boulter, in a letter to Newcastle, wrote: 'The dearness of corn was such that thousands of families quitted their habitations to seek bread elsewhere, and many hundreds perished.'[5] The Bill introduced by Dobbs to encourage tillage was a practical measure to repair this state of affairs, but unfortunately its usefulness was largely negatived by a Bill rendering pasture land tithe-free, and this measure, quite naturally, tended to increase the area of pasture land. Notwithstanding this, the tillage Bill served a useful purpose, and Lord Mountmorris, writing some years later on the need for increased tillage, remarked: 'The principal Act upon this subject was introduced and carried through the Irish Parliament by Arthur Dobbs . . . a gentleman well known and esteemed at the period for his tracts and able calculations upon political arithmetic.'[6]

With hunger and poverty widely prevalent, it became increasingly clear to a number of the more thoughtful Irishmen that something of a more practical nature than Acts of Parliament and the charity of kindly people would have to be done to provide work for the workless and food for the hungry. With this end in view, fourteen men met in the rooms of the Philosophical Society in Trinity College and formed a Society for the Improvement of Husbandry, Manufactures, and other Useful Arts.[7] The prime mover in this new venture was Thomas Prior, the selfless patriot whose *List of Absentees* had roused the enmity of Primate Boulter, and with him were associated Dobbs and his kinsman, Judge Ward, as well as his fellow-member for Carrickfergus, Colonel Upton; two other members of the Irish Parliament, Le Hunte and Warburton, were also present. Among the others who helped to found the Society were Thomas Molyneux, Dr. Whitecomb, John Madden, Dr. Stephens, a well-known physician and physicist, and the chemist Maple whose experiments in tanning had been recognised by Parliament.

Though the initial efforts of the Dublin Society to create a new social, cultural, and economic standard for the country may have been small, it grew in strength and stature, and in the course of the next two hundred years played an important part in the life of the nation.[8] The historian Lecky remarks that it filled an eminent role in the history of Irish agriculture and industry, and attracted to itself a great number of able and public-spirited members. It was from this Society, which Dobbs warmly supported and on whose committees he served for many years, that most of the modern institutions of the country came into being. For more than a century and a half the Society was in fact the counterpart of a modern Department of Agriculture, and was responsible for the establishment of a National Library, Botanical Gardens, a College of Art, a College of Science, a Veterinary College, and other institutions; it predated kindred agricultural societies by many years. The Society created a spirit of self-reliance and independence in the more nationally minded and public-spirited Anglo-Irish, and developed a system of voluntary and unselfish public service which has marked its manifold activities for more than two centuries.[9]

About this time Dobbs became interested in the Northwest Passage to 'the great southern and western oceans,' the existence of which had engaged the attention of explorers for many years. The question of a Northwest Passage so far as Dobbs was concerned arose indirectly from his efforts to increase the trade and commerce of Britain, and may have been suggested to him by Gee or some of the other London merchants with whom he was now associated. Since the prospect of such a discovery opened up a whole new vista of adventure and enterprise, Dobbs proceeded to make a methodical study of the subject, eventually reaching the conclusion that a Northwest Passage existed; this conclusion he set down 'by way of a letter which was first writ in the year 1731.'[10]

In the meantime the political scene had changed in Dublin. Carteret, the Lord-Lieutenant, had been recalled, and the Duke of Dorset, a courtier 'with an ambition for years to represent the King in Ireland,' was appointed in his place. Dorset was the perfect English courtier and nothing more. 'He had the good fortune,' Shelburne wrote, 'to come into the world with the Whigs, and partook of their good fortune to his death.' Walpole entertained no high opinion of his Irish Viceroy, and remarked that in spite of great dignity in appearance he was in private the 'greatest lover of low humour and buffoonery.'[11] In spite of Walpole's low opinion of Dorset, his initial address to the Irish Parliament was a more statesmanlike effort than that of Carteret, and he was not averse to living in Dublin. The city had grown in size and importance; new houses were being built, new streets laid out, and there was about it an air of wealth and refinement; among the new buildings adorning the city was the magnificent Parliament House, now in the first stage of completion under the able guidance of Sir Edward Lovet Pearce and a group of skilled craftsmen.

Dobbs had met Dorset in a purely official way as a Member of Parliament. He had waited upon him with his Bill to encourage tillage, and two minor Bills he introduced into Parliament, but by one of those curious and fortuitous twists of fate or circumstances which so often affect the lives of men, he came to know the Lord-Lieutenant somewhat more intimately and to his own good fortune. Dorset found the Irish capital a very pleasant place, and it was not until the prorogation of Parliament in 1732 that he decided to return to England. On 23rd April, Dorset and his party sailed from Dublin. Their ship encountered very heavy seas in the Irish Channel, and two days later it was driven ashore at Ranbury, a rocky inlet in Carrickfergus Bay. Dobbs, and the members of his household, hastened to the help of the stranded party, which included the Duchess of Dorset, Lord Forbes, the friend and protégé of Godolphin, and Sir Holden Lambert, a man who exerted some influence in Government circles. The party was welcomed to Castle Dobbs, where they enjoyed rest and hospitality for three days before again embarking for England.[12]

A short time before this event, Dobbs had written a long memorandum setting out his views on the possible existence of a Northwest Passage. In this memorandum he urged the need for a voyage of discovery so as to open up the western ocean to British trade, and thus forestall any French discovery of a Passage to the Pacific, and also to counter French expansion in Northern Canada, particularly in the Hudson Bay area. Dobbs forwarded his memorandum to Walpole, and in the course of an accompanying letter wrote:

'You may be surprised that I should at this time endeavour to revive an attempt to discover the Northwest Passage to the Great Southern and

Western oceans of America, which has been in a manner explored since the year 1631, a century ago when Captain James and Captain Fox both attempted it in the same year . . . Since that time it has been revived but once by Gillam in 1667.'

He then remarked that having read and studied all the journals and papers dealing with the subject, he had a 'very strong reason to believe there is a Passage.' [13]

Dorset's stay at Castle Dobbs was availed of by Dobbs to discuss his plans and ideas, and he laid his project before the Viceroy, who was apparently sympathetic and promised his support and patronage which were by no means negligible. Dobbs crossed to England with the Viceregal party, and his reception by Walpole and other important personages was infinitely more propitious and promising than his reception a year earlier. He was introduced to Colonel Bladen of the Board of Trade, who evinced an interest in his Northwest Passage proposals, and laid them before Wager, the First Lord of the Admiralty. Wager, while approving of the proposals and offering the support of the Admiralty, felt that any new voyage of discovery should be carried out by the Hudson's Bay Company in the first instance, and accordingly provided Dobbs with a letter of introduction to Sir Bibye Lake, Governor of the Company. Lake appeared at the outset to be enthusiastic; he promised Dobbs he would use his influence and request the Company to undertake a voyage of discovery as soon as conditions and circumstances permitted.[14]

While in London, Dobbs had a number of meetings with Walpole, who appears to have taken a friendly interest in him. This friendly interest may of course have been just as shallow as much of Walpole's friendship, for the great intriguer gathered about him and cultivated the friendship of any man who could be useful to him. There is evidence in one or two letters from Dobbs to Walpole of an arrangement of this nature, which in fact was of mutual benefit to both men, and Dobbs was not slow to use the advantage of his friendship with Walpole to press his claims for an appointment under the Crown.[15]

In the course of a letter to his friend and adviser Councillor M'Aulay, for whom he also sought an appointment, Dobbs wrote:

'Sir Robert has been so good as to give directions, that I should be recommended to the Chancellor to be the sole agent and receiver in Ireland with a salary annexed and to have power to appoint who I will under me. Mr. Fortescue his secretary as Chancellor of the Exchequer is appointed lawyer here, and things (are) to be directed by him here. I told him

I thought it proper that some young lawyer should be retained here, and that I should choose a proper person for it.' [16]

Despite Walpole's promise and recommendation, the post of Receiver-General was bestowed upon Luke Gardiner at the behest of Primate Boulter.[17] Dobbs was disappointed and quite rightly felt that Boulter's interference at this juncture was unfair and unwarranted. The office of Receiver-General was one of the plums of the administration, and was reputed to be worth close on £8,000 per annum.

Dobbs was not to be left in the wilderness, however, and, pending a suitable appointment, Walpole, on the death of Lord Conway, asked him to take over the management of the Conway estate in Ireland, and act as legal adviser and Court agent of the heir, who was a minor. The agency was not quite what Dobbs sought or expected from Walpole, none the less it was an undertaking with possibilities, and in a letter to Walpole he spoke of the 'favour and Hon^r you have done me in putting Lord Conway's affairs here under my care.' [18]

The Conway estate comprised more than 60,000 acres, and provided one of the largest rent rolls in Ireland. As agent for the estate, Dobbs was paid a fixed salary of £300, and also received fees reckoned to yield in the neighbourhood of £200 per annum. He was not particularly happy or satisfied with the agency of the Conway estate, and remarked to Walpole that until 'things are put into a regular method it Ingrosses all my time.' [19] From the outset the management of the estate was attended with difficulties, and appears to have given little monetary return for the labour and trouble involved. Writing to the young Lord Conway, Dobbs complained:

'I have been living in a more expensive manner, and in an extensive place and larger neighbourhood, paying the highest rent for my house and fields to promote the keeping up the rents and keeping a more plentiful table at my own expense among your friends and tenants, which I thought myself obliged to do in honour to your Lordship in the station I was placed in, so that I speak within bounds when I say that two hundred pounds per annum did not make up the difference of my expense by living at Lisburn and living upon my own demesne which I was obliged to let at a very low rent, and for all this trouble and expence I have only had £300 salary as agent and from £87 to £165 annually receivers' fees.' [20]

From this letter it would appear that Dobbs had set up house at Lisburn, the manorial town, and brought his family there. His troubles in regard to the Conway estate were further complicated by the action of his principal clerk, a man named Wogan, who formerly acted as an

agent or land steward for the late earl, and was continued in employment on the strong recommendation of Lady Conway. Wogan, who
was on friendly terms with Lady Conway, objected to his inferior
position under Dobbs, and for some reason or other it would appear
that Lady Conway did not take kindly to Dobbs; it would seem,
indeed, that she would have much preferred if her more subservient
protégé was charged with the agency of her late husband's estate.
Between Lady Conway and the clerk Wogan, Dobbs found matters
a little difficult, and in a letter to Walpole he complained that Wogan
was employed by Lady Conway 'to lye upon the watch and find me
tripping.'

A growing enmity between Dobbs and Wogan persisted for some
years and finally reached a climax when Dobbs refused a demand from
Wogan for fees amounting to £250, which he claimed was due to him
for drawing leases. Wogan thereupon threatened that he would expose
Dobbs, and charged him with a dereliction of duty, and also with
appropriating funds that should have been remitted to Lady Conway.
The charges were palpably false, and Dobbs had no choice but to
submit Wogan's letter to Walpole, who readily agreed that he should
be discharged from his position.[21] This brought matters to a head.
Wogan drew up a list of charges which he immediately transmitted to
the young Lord Conway; among the charges levelled against Dobbs
was that he had neglected Conway's affairs by lowering his rents,
taking fees for drawing leases to which he was not entitled, and charging heavy costs against the estate for repeated visits to London,
ostensibly to see Walpole or Conway and discuss estate matters, but
also to attend to his own interests there; finally he was charged with
misappropriating sums of money remitted by Lady Conway for the
payment of her accounts.

Dobbs reacted vigorously to the charges of his clerk, pointing out
their falsity in a long valedictory to Conway and claiming that he
carried out his duties 'with diligence, uprightness, and integrity.' He
insisted that the trust was discharged to the entire satisfaction of Sir
Robert Walpole. In accepting responsibility for the agency and trust
at the request of Walpole, Dobbs informed Lord Conway that he had
at the same time to provide security amounting to £18,000, and that
the collecting of rents of close on £10,000 per annum occupied so
much time and energy that 'I had greatly neglected my own private
fortune.' In the course of his communication to Conway he set down
in detail particulars of the Conway rents, and the fees and salary he had
received, as well as the disbursements attendant upon the agency.

Having cleared himself of all charges of misappropriation and mis-conduct in the discharge of his duties, he turned the spotlight upon Wogan, who, though only an underling, had all the appearance of a well-to-do man, boasting a fine house, fields, and also a vineyard, adding 'it may seem a little malicious to hint that Wogan offered the Master in Chancery a small bottle of Usquebaigh to make a favourable report for him.' [22]

With the discharge of Wogan there was no further trouble, and Dobbs remained the trusted agent of the estate for some years more until the burden of other duties necessitated his relinquishing it.

From the time of his appointment to the agency of the Conway estate Dobbs communicated regularly with Walpole on matters of a purely administrative nature. In the course of one of his letters, however, he submitted proposals for putting an end to the lucrative smuggling trade carried on from the Isle of Man to 'the great prejudice of the Revenue Receivers,' and also suggested clauses in a Bill to increase the revenue which were embodied in Walpole's celebrated excise scheme in 1733. In submitting these proposals, Dobbs reminded Walpole of 'the Hon^r you did me when I left London of allowing me to communicate to you my thoughts in writing,' and goes on to assure him that 'all the spare time I have, you Sir are justly entitled to.' [23] The friendship with Walpole soon brought its reward, and when, in 1733, Sir Edward Lovet Pearce, the Engineer and Surveyor-General of Ireland, and 'the contriver' of the new Parliament House died, Dobbs was appointed to the vacant post. [24]

The completion of the Parliament House was the most important task falling to the new Surveyor-General, and though the greater part of the building was complete we note 'that all the Portico from the archtrave up, roofing and ceiling same, part of the carving of the Voluta columns, and the whole pavement under the colonade, the levelling of same with the steps of the pavement in the area in front of the Portico, the Balustrade, and iron Palisadoes are yet to be finished.' [25] This work was carried out under Dobbs's supervision, and thus his name is associated with the craftsmen and artists responsible for this noble building, still regarded as one of the finest pieces of Georgian architecture in Dublin. Many other public buildings in Dublin and throughout the country were erected or rebuilt in part under Dobbs's supervision, but few of these works remain either as reminders of his term of office or of his skill as an architect.

The office of His Majesty's Engineer and Surveyor-General was of considerable importance and was first established in the sixteenth century; it was by no means a sinecure, and, though lucrative, had from the outset lent itself to considerable fraud and speculation, and large sums of money set aside for the building of barracks and such-like establishments found its way into the pockets of a host of office-holders and tradesmen. At the time of Dobbs's appointment the office of Surveyor-General carried a salary of £300 per annum, but a considerably larger sum accrued in fees and undisclosed payments, to which from time to time were added *ex gratia* payments by Parliament; Pearce was voted no less than £2,000 in recognition of his work in the construction of the Parliament House.

5

The Northwest Passage

FOR THE next two years Dobbs hammered on the doors of the Admiralty and the Hudson's Bay Company in an effort to arouse interest in a Northwest Passage to the Pacific. The existence of such a Passage had engaged the attention of explorers since the days of Jacques Cartier, and though many lives and ships had been lost in the unchartered Hudson Bay, Dobbs was convinced that a properly organised expedition would have little difficulty in finding the Passage. Bladen and other officials of the Admiralty gave Dobbs grudging support; they were not unenthusiastic but claimed that the Admiralty would not like to interfere in the affairs of the Hudson's Bay Company. Though Dobbs had a number of interviews with Sir Bibye Lake, and received a promise that efforts would be made at an opportune time to discover the Passage, the Company appeared unwilling to dissipate its large profits on what seemed a doubtful venture. Dobbs pointed out that it was incumbent on the Company to undertake such voyages of discovery, claiming that the Charter was granted in 1670 by reason of the fact that the original proprietors had 'at their owne great cost and charge undertaken an expedicion for Hudsons Bay in the northwest part of America for the discovery of a New Passage into the South Sea.'

This extraordinary Company owed its origin to two adventurous French traders, Medart Chouart Sieur des Groseilliers and his brother-in-law Pierre Esprit Radisson, who having quarrelled with their French masters promptly offered their services to Britain. The services of the two men were accepted and Charles II granted a charter to Prince Rupert 'and severall others, and Incorporated them by the name of the Governours and Company of Adventurers of England Trading into Hudson's Bay.' Though primarily a trading venture, the masters of the Company's first ships, the *Eaglet* and *Nonsuch*, which sailed northward in 1688, were instructed 'to have in your thoughts the discovery of the Passage into the South Sea, and attempt it as occasions shall offer.'[1] The Company over the years had lost much of this pristine spirit of discovery.

When Dobbs first submitted his proposals to Walpole, Bladen, and Sir Charles Wager he was not fully conversant with the Charter of the Company and the monopoly it conferred. Writing to Ward in 1734 he said:

'I have been pushing my scheme for the Northwest Passage, and finding by the Hudson's Bay Company that they have the sole benefit to be made by a discovery I laid my observations upon the Journals before Sir Bibye Lake, their Governor. They made an attempt about eleven years ago which cost them £6,000, which has frightened them, but yet he is willing a new attempt should be made in the manner which I desire would be no expense to them, and is to consult the rest of the Company upon it.' [2]

Dobbs suggested to Lake the formation of a new company to undertake the discovery of the Passage, and invited Lake and his directors to join with him and his friends in the venture. Lake gave Dobbs an assurance that 'they would come into it'; at the same time he informed him that instructions would be sent to the governor at Churchill River, 'their most northerly settlement which is about one hundred leagues from where the Passage is, if any, and send out in the season as often as he can a sloop to coast along and make the attempt by degrees.' [3]

Early in the year 1735, Dobbs was in London. The main purpose of his visit was to confer with young Lord Conway and Walpole on matters pertaining to the Conway estate. While in London he renewed his acquaintance with the influential merchants John Hanbury, Murray Crymble, James Huey, and Henry McCulloh, who some years earlier had shown an interest in his colonial projects, and were now prepared to back his Northwest Passage scheme. Dobbs must have been a man of strong personality and more than ordinary persuasiveness, for the merchants whom he interested in his projects were shrewd business-men with little or none of his idealism. He was warmly welcomed in their circle, and however impossible or improbable his schemes and projects may have appeared to the Government, the merchants were wide awake to the possibilities inherent in them, and accepted him as a man of acumen. The interest evinced by the merchants in the North-west Passage project was responsible to some extent for the eventual break between Dobbs and the Hudson's Bay Company. Up to April 1735 the relations between Dobbs and Lake were cordial. In a letter to Ward, Dobbs wrote:

'I have got the Hudson's Bay Company to undertake once more the Northwest Passage, but as they are apprehensive of a war they are to be fully employed this year and next in finding a stone fort at their settlement on Churchill river, but when that is finished they will instruct their governor there to renew their attempt by sloop from that settlement.' [4]

Whether the Company had any intention of undertaking a voyage it is difficult to say, but it would seem that Lake and his associates, having considered the proposals put forward by Dobbs, realised that the new Company would be somewhat different from the tightly knit Company which they controlled. Undoubtedly in 1735 there was a certain amount of apprehension and fear of war, but this state of nervousness had existed for ten years, and was described by Hervey as a period of 'broken peace and undeclared war.' [5] At all events, Dobbs was growing impatient, and, probably urged by the city merchants, he reached the conclusion that the Hudson's Bay Company had no real interest in the discovery of a Northwest Passage, the existence of which would seriously affect their chartered rights. While this doubt was growing in his mind, he introduced himself to John Middleton, one of the Company's captains, who wrote: 'Mr. Dobbs made strong application to me, then a stranger to him, to quit the Company's service, in which I continued many years with much reputation, in order to undertake a Discovery of a Northwest Passage into the Western American ocean.' [6] Middleton declined to leave the Company, but agreed to provide Dobbs 'with all the Journals and memoirs I was possessed of, which were most likely to direct him to the place where such a Passage might most probably be found.'

Increasing international tension, eventuating in a declaration of war between Britain and Spain in 1739, tended to push the Passage scheme into the background, and gave the Hudson's Bay Company an excuse for doing nothing. With the scheme hanging fire and the Company uninterested, Dobbs was impelled to proceed on more vigorous lines. Assured of the support of the merchants who were opposed to the trade monopoly of the Hudson's Bay Company, and backed by a number of politicians who believed, as he did, that the Company's lack of enterprise and obvious ineptitude not only retarded British trade but encouraged French encroachment and consolidation in North America, Dobbs was in a strong position to lay his plans before the Government and claim attention.

With solid support behind him and a firm belief in himself, he proceeded to attack the Hudson's Bay Company, in public, with the avowed intention of destroying it. When he initiated his attack, the Company had undergone a considerable change from its earlier days, and with some justification he claimed that it failed to carry out the objects contained in its charter, and in consequence it forfeited the rights conferred upon it. George Bryce, a painstaking historian, writes:

'When peace had been restored by the Treaty of Utrecht, the shores of the Bay, which had been in the hands of the French since the Treaty of Ryswick were given over to Britain. . . . The Company, freed from the fears of overland incursions by the French from Canada, and the fleets that had worked so much mischief by sea, seems to have changed character in the personnel of the stockholders, and to have lost a great deal of its pristine spirit. The charge is made that the stockholders had become very few, that the stock was controlled by a majority who, year after year, elected themselves, and that considering the great privileges conferred by the charter, the Company was failing to develop the country, and was sleeping in inglorious ease on the shore of Hudson Bay.' [7]

These were precisely the charges made by Dobbs in a new memorandum submitted to Walpole. He denounced the Company with vigour and charged that it deliberately violated its Charter by refusing to undertake a voyage to discover a Northwest Passage, or attempt exploratory journeys into the interior of Canada. While Dobbs was whipping up public opinion, the Company was experiencing a period of great prosperity, and was naturally ill-disposed to jeopardise its profits on an expedition that, in the light of previous experience, seemed futile. The investment of the original 'Lordes and Proprietors' had been a mere £10,500, but their ninety-eight successors, with no galaxy of great names, held stock valued at £103,950, so that the 'comfortable operation conducted by a secretive management' saw no reason to embark on foolish schemes, even if such schemes eventually enhanced the greatness of Britain, and opened up a new trading route.[8]

Dobbs continued to pursue his attack and enlist more and more support; the city merchants backed him strongly, and a growing number of influential politicians came to his aid. He conducted his campaign against the Company with vigour and energy, and not unnaturally those envious of the Company's financial success were easily won to his side. Commenting on this campaign, Bryce remarks:

'At this period a man of great personal energy appears on the scene of English commercial life, who became a bitter opponent of the Company, and possessed such influence with the government that the Company was compelled to make a strenuous defence. This man was Arthur Dobbs, an Irishman of undoubted ability and courage. He conducted his campaign against the Company along a most ingenious and dangerous line of attack.' [9]

This ingenious line was simple, and one that appealed to the people of a great and growing empire, especially the commercial interests that contributed in no small way to the Empire's greatness and affluence. Dobbs fired the English imagination by recalling the prowess of the Elizabethan voyagers and the courage of the Elizabethan soldiers; he appealed to the blended interests of religion, patriotism, and profit permeating every aspect of English life. Pictures of untold wealth and great financial rewards from across the sea were sufficient to stir and excite the most lethargic Englishman. But the vast wealth—the rich fur trade, the as yet unopened mines—were falling into the hands of the French because of the inertia and ineptitude of the Hudson's Bay Company, and the Company's sole rights in the northern hemisphere prevented discovery and settlement there. Dobbs made a good case for a voyage of discovery, and the people were willing to believe that the restrictions on Canadian trade and the ever-recurring trouble with the French arose solely from the exclusive rights of the Company, rights which also precluded a search for the Northwest Passage, and left the entire Canadian hinterland unsettled and in the hands of French traders.

The rising tide of public opinion, formented by Dobbs, at length compelled the Company to act, and give some proof of its earnest to help British trade. Two ships, the sloop *Churchill* under Captain Napper, and the *Musquash* under Captain Crow, were sent to the western coast of Hudson Bay, and 'ordered to sail to the Northward' with the pious injunction 'God send the good sloops a successful Discovery.' No records of this expedition have survived, and the ships returned home after a few months having accomplished nothing, nor indeed added anything to what was already known of the western coast of Hudson Bay.

The voyage was a pitiable effort and satisfied nobody, least of all Dobbs, who now pressed the Admiralty more vigorously to undertake an independent voyage of discovery. His persuasiveness and the influence which his powerful friends, who included Sir Charles Wager, First Lord of the Admiralty, exerted on the Government at last bore fruit. Towards the end of the year 1740, the Admiralty provided two ships. A short time before this, Captain Middleton had written to Dobbs that the failure of the *Musquash* and *Churchill* expedition was due to the fact 'that the people on board were not duly qualified for such an undertaking,' and he added significantly, 'If you should be in London this winter or next spring, I shall be extremely glad of the honour to wait upon you and tender my service in anything that may be in my power.' Dobbs accepted this offer, and on Middleton's return from Hudson Bay he offered him the command of the expedition. Middleton readily agreed, provided that the ships were fitted out in a proper manner to undertake the voyage.

Almost eight years had passed by since Dobbs first presented his memorandum on the Northwest Passage to Walpole, and now it seemed that his perseverance and tenacity were about to be rewarded, though much work still remained to be done. In a letter to Ward, dated April 1741, he wrote:

> 'As to myself, I shall lye by until I know what my expedition turns to. I have got all fixed for my Captain. He is to be fitted out with sixty men and fourteen guns, six swivel guns in the *Furnace Bomb*. She is a kalk and has a new deck made for the conveniency of the men and to store her provisions, and on Monday the tender was bought, a strong new built collier. I have got the mate made master of her. She is to have thirty men in her and twenty guns in case we meet any Spanish ships at the entrance of the Straits where they generally go. This tender is called the *Discovery Pink*.' [10]

For the next few weeks Dobbs worked hard to ensure the success of his venture. Crews were recruited for the two ships, provisions were purchased and stored for a long voyage, and though the Admiralty had provided the ships, the expense of fitting was borne by Dobbs and a number of city merchants. Early in May both ships were ready to sail, and the instructions, drawn up by Dobbs and displaying an uncanny knowledge of the Hudson Bay area, were handed to Middleton. Up to the last moment there were difficulties to be faced, not the least of which came from the Hudson's Bay Company. In a letter to Ward, Dobbs complained that 'the Hudson's Bay Company do all they can to prevent us taking effect. They took an Eskimaux Indian away from my Captain who would have been a good interpreter.' [11] This action, of which details are lacking, tended to embitter Dobbs still more against the Company, and strengthened his resolve to destroy it at all costs. In the same letter to Ward he wrote: 'I have a copy of their Charter from the Plantation Office to lay before Council to see if we can open the Trade since they have none but King Charles' grant for an exclusive trade.'

The two ships, the *Furnace* under the command of Middleton, and the *Discovery* under William Moore, an experienced seaman who had been in the service of the Hudson's Bay Company, were expected to sail about 10th May, but vexatious delays prevented departure until the middle of the month. In August the ships reached Prince of Wales Fort in Hudson Bay, where it would appear that Middleton was cordially received by Robert Pilgrim, who was temporarily in charge pending the arrival of James Isham from York Fort. As the season was getting late and ice was forming in the Bay, Middleton decided to proceed no farther and accordingly made arrangements to spend the winter anchored in the Churchill River.

With the Northwest Passage expedition safely off his hands, Dobbs returned to Ireland in June 1741, and was shortly afterwards elected Mayor of Carrickfergus for the third time, a unique distinction in the annals of the town. Other events at home also engaged his attention, particularly the emergence of a strong and vocal opposition party in the Irish Parliament, which necessitated meticulous attendance by the Government supporters in order to stave off defeat and protect the English interest in important matters of policy. A period of relative prosperity resulted in a surplus revenue which many members of the Irish Parliament claimed should be set aside to redeem the national debt. This suggestion did not meet with the approval of the Administration, and the growing opposition was bluntly informed that all surplus revenue belonged to the Privy purse and could only be disposed of as the King wished and not as Parliament decreed. The opposition revolted and the Government was defeated on this issue by the vote of Colonel Tottenham who, in a hasty ride from Wexford, appeared on the floor of the House in a mud-bespattered riding suit.

In spite of the many calls on his time and a not unnatural anxiety regarding the outcome of his expedition, Dobbs found time to write and present new memoranda to the Government in England on divers aspects of colonial trade and development. Among the memoranda was a long communication entitled *Reasons for the Great Price and Scarcity of Beaver and other Furs*, which was in effect a skilfully prepared attack on the Hudson's Bay Company, which was held responsible for the scarcity by reason of the fact that it lacked enterprise, and permitted the French trappers to trade at will throughout the northern parts of Canada.[12] A serious result of the scarcity of furs was that considerable unemployment existed among hat-makers and furriers in England and Ireland, which Dobbs exploited by drawing up and presenting to Parliament a petition setting out their unhappy plight. He also prepared a lengthy communication entitled *Some Reasons to show the Expediency of settling and securing the Coast of New Britain otherwise called Labrador . . . and to Show the Benefits that should accrue from it to the Trade and Navigation of Britain*, which he addressed to Lord Halifax.[13]

In this communication he directed attention to the neglected state of Labrador, which at the time contained no European settlement of any consequence. Dobbs asserted that the settlement of Labrador would effectively seal off the northern parts of Canada from French encroachment and provide safe harbours for the British fleet in American waters. As in the case of his memorandum on the scarcity of furs, this communication was intended to undermine the position of the Hudson's Bay Company; Labrador was considered to be an outlying part of the Company's territory and any settlements established there would result in a competitive trade and threaten its monopoly.

Walpole's fall from power in 1742 while not affecting Dobbs in so far as his schemes were concerned may have had a deleterious effect on his ambitions. Walpole had proved a good friend and an influential patron. Undoubtedly he found Dobbs useful, just as he had most of those whom he gathered about him. An interesting sidelight in this respect is to be found in a letter from Dobbs to Walpole shortly before his fall from power. In 1741 Walpole requested Dobbs to make private enquiries into the financial affairs of Colonel Henry Cunningham and his brother William. This Dobbs did, and in a letter submitting the result of his enquiries he concluded:

> 'Thus far I have endeavoured to the utmost of my capacity to fulfil y^r commands which I hope will be satisfactory, and wish it were as much in my power as in my inclinations to contribute to y^r ease and satisfaction. I shall obey all your future commands with the utmost readiness and pleasure, having the most grateful sense of all y^r favours.' [14]

Dobbs had little faith in the succeeding Government; he did not think very highly of Newcastle, Pultney, Pelham, or even Carteret the new Secretary of State with whom he was on fairly intimate terms and to whom he dedicated his *Essay on Irish Trade*. Beyond ambitious dreams of office, the fall of Walpole and change of government made little material difference to Dobbs. He was no longer an unknown Irishman vainly knocking on the doors of His Majesty's ministers, but a man of importance with influential friends, some of whom, such as Colonel Selwyn and Lord Holderness, had the ear of the King. A growing number of Members of Parliament supported his schemes, and he had the backing of wealthy merchants who endorsed his colonial plans, and accepted him as a partner in the purchase of large tracts of land in North Carolina and on the Ohio River.

While Dobbs embarked on new ventures with the prospecting merchants, the ships of his expedition in Hudson Bay patiently awaited the passing of the long winter. The trading station at Churchill River was a bleak, inhospitable place which has been described by James Knight, one of the Company's most indefatigable servants, as the most miserable place he ever saw in his life. While there was little or no fraternisation or friendship between the Company's employees and the expedition's crew, Captain Middleton appears to have been treated in a somewhat different manner, and he enjoyed the comfort of quarters in the fort.[15]

It was almost the end of June 1742 before the ice broke sufficiently to permit the expedition to sail again. Middleton's journal for the northward journey is a meticulous record containing detailed observations on the weather and tides, with descriptive notes on the coastline and particulars of soundings of bays and rivers. He mapped his course with great accuracy, and every point and inlet charted and named by him stands out on our maps to-day as a memorial to his painstaking care. The largest inlet which showed promise to be the long-sought Passage proved to be a bay and was appropriately christened Wager after Sir Charles Wager who supported Dobbs and pressed his case at the Admiralty. Farther north the ships passed a ragged headland which Middleton named Cape Dobbs 'after my worthy friend.'[16] The presence of ice caused a vexatious delay and Middleton was compelled to weigh anchor in Wager Bay. However, this delay gave an opportunity for a thorough investigation of the opening, and confirmed his opinion that it was not the entrance to the Passage—'the strait of Anian and the great door to the Pacific.' On 3rd August Middleton resumed his northward journey to Welcome Bay. Here a majestic headland appeared to mark the extreme northern limit of the coastline which he optimistically named Cape Hope. But Cape Hope was another mirage in this snow- and ice-clad region, for upon rounding it Middleton found his way blocked by still more land, and no signs of the elusive Passage; the ice-strewn sea, half locked in arms of desolate land, was named Repulse Bay. There seemed no way out but the way he came, and Middleton was convinced, in fact he proved beyond reasonable doubt, that no Passage existed on the western coast of Hudson Bay as far north as Southampton Island and the entrance to the Frozen Straits.

On reaching Repulse Bay and encountering the ice-packed Frozen Straits, Middleton consulted with his officers, and it was agreed to call off the search there and then. The expedition set sail for home fairly certain that there was no prospect of finding a Northwest Passage in the area of Hudson Bay. Thus one more voyage of discovery ended in failure, but in spite of failure Captain Middleton added a bright page to English exploration, and charted a hitherto uncharted region. To Dobbs must go some of the credit for such success as this expedition achieved, for it was his initiative, his drive and energy that made it possible, and his efforts are imperishably enshrined in the northern cape that bears his name.

Word reached Dobbs at Lisburn early in September informing him of the return of Middleton's ships, but he had no precise information regarding the expedition until about mid-September, when he received a letter from Middleton together with an abstract report which had been dispatched from the Orkneys. In the course of this letter, Middleton informed Dobbs of his failure to discover a Passage, and said that a full report and journal of the voyage had been dispatched from Churchill by one of the ships of the Hudson's Bay Company, but Dobbs had not yet received this. He was very disappointed at the turn of events, but hastened to congratulate Middleton on his 'safe arrival with the ships after so dangerous a voyage; and at the same time express my concern at your not having found the Passage, as we had reason to have expected it.' [17]

Dobbs was unable to cross to London owing to other engagements, but he requested Middleton to forward to him without delay his full journal, together with maps and charts of the voyage, so that he might study them at his leisure. About the middle of December Middleton wrote and promised he would transmit his charts, journals, and other observations 'by the first convenient opportunity.' He concluded his letter, however, with the firm statement that

'there is no hope of a Passage to encourage any further search between Churchill and as far as we have gone; if there be any further way to the northward, it must be impassable for the ice, and the narrowness of any such outlet in 67° or 68° of latitude, it cannot be clear of ice one week in a year, and many years, as I apprehend, not clear at all. In any attempt I shall give you all the assistance I can, and furnish you with any information that you may think needful to promote your design; but I hope never to venture myself that way again.'

In acknowledging Middleton's letter, Dobbs more or less accepted his findings and admitted that he had carried out his mission to the best of his ability, and that no useful purpose would be served by searching for a passage farther north, 'as navigation would be difficult and dangerous.' He added: 'I am fully convinced that there can be no passage northwest by sea as we have reason to suspect.' Though

apparently setting aside the possibility of a Northwest Passage, Dobbs
was deeply committed to his plan to break the monopoly of the
Hudson's Bay Company, and accordingly requested Middleton to
prepare a summary account of the climate, coastline, rivers, and trade
in Hudson Bay, and transmit it to him so 'that I may prepare matters
to attack the Company's charter, and open the trade, which I think
would be of great advantage to Britain by making settlements higher
up upon the rivers in better climates, and by that means securing the
country and trade from the French.' He asked Middleton to join with
him in a scheme to establish a rival company, assuring him that Lords
Carteret, Winchelsea, and others 'would come in.'

Middleton's reply to Dobbs early in the year 1743 was as cold as the
wintry blasts of the season. He asserted it would be impracticable to
make settlements in the more northerly parts of the bay, and he
doubted if people could be found in sufficient numbers to undergo the
'fatigue of travelling those frozen climates,' nor did he know what
'encouragement would be sufficient to make them attempt it.' As for
the summary account of the climate and conditions prevailing which
Dobbs requested, Middleton in a somewhat brusque manner referred
him to his Journal 'as well as the accounts of those that attempted the
discovery before me.'

In the meantime the long-awaited journals and charts of the Hudson
Bay area as re-plotted and discovered in part by Middleton reached
Dobbs, who, after careful perusal,

> 'found many things mentioned in the Journal which I thought very
> material to prove a Passage which he had altogether concealed in his letters
> to me, and found from his journal, that he had not made anything like
> a search or discovery of the coast from Cape Dobbs to Brook Cobham,
> having not been within five or six leagues of the headlands, and passed
> a great part in the night, and had never gone ashore to look for any inlets,
> or try the heights and direction of the tides.' [18]

Middleton's Journal revived Dobbs's interest in the Passage, and he
concluded from his reading of the Journal that Middleton 'had been in
the Passage or Streight without his knowing it to be so.' Belief in the
existence of a Passage was further strengthened by the reports Dobbs
received from Lieutenant Rankin, and Moore, the Master of the
Discovery, both of whom had sailed some miles up Wager Bay and were
of the opinion that it was the opening of the Passage. As their reports
were not included in the Journal, Dobbs concluded that Middleton

had deliberately suppressed them because they cast some doubts on his own conclusions.

At this juncture Dobbs communicated with Lord Carteret, and informed him of his 'intention of proposing to have settlements made in Hudson Bay, and lay open the trade, and by that means we should recover our fur trade which the Company has lost to the French, and in time secure the whole country.' He suggested that if Carteret found his scheme practicable, he would go over to London immediately and initiate it in a proper manner. He arranged that his attorney Samuel Smith should show the letter to Middleton before it was delivered to Carteret. Middleton, in the course of a letter to Dobbs, expressed approval of his scheme, and, though he doubted if it would be possible to break the Company's charter, added: 'I would be heartily glad if you could dissolve the Company, for they have used me, and all my men who were with me, very ill: and those who voluntarily entered at Churchill they refused to pay their wages.' [19]

Dobbs was puzzled by the tenor of Middleton's reply and suggested that he only supported the scheme because 'it would be impolitick in him to oppose it, least he should be suspected of being in friendship with the Company.' Further, the reports of Moore and Rankin convinced him that Middleton had suppressed vital information regarding the Passage. With a seed of doubt growing in his mind, he hastened to London to consult with his supporters. Middleton, hearing of Dobbs's arrival, called to see him at his lodgings, and found him 'with a good deal of company, who all withdrew when I came into the Room.' He expostulated with him and hotly denied that he had suppressed vital information; in turn he charged Dobbs with having secret dealings with his officers. Dobbs admitted interviewing the officers, and informed Middleton that he only sought the full facts in order to satisfy the Lords of the Admiralty. A few days later Dobbs called on Middleton and, having checked his logbook, asked a few questions hurriedly and left him.

During the next few weeks Dobbs proceeded to build a case against Middleton, and charged him with deliberately failing to search for the Passage at the behest of the Hudson's Bay Company. By a high order of logic-chopping, he succeeded in turning the case for the time being against Captain Middleton. Seldom indeed had greater skill been used to win a case. No doubt Dobbs genuinely believed that Middleton had deliberately suppressed all material parts of his discovery. There had been enough in Middleton's conduct to arouse suspicion in a less perverse man than Dobbs. From a proposal to attack the Company's trade

Middleton had veered to protecting it; from a lifelong advocacy of a Northwest Passage he had fallen to denying its practicability even if it existed; and he had spent the winter in which he was supposed to be preparing to demonstrate the incapacity and lethargy of the Company in the undisguised conviction that the Company's factor James Isham was better company and better informed than his own officers.[20] The methods adopted by Dobbs and the charges he formulated against the hapless Middleton were unjust, and in the light of later events entirely false. Middleton was charged with suppressing vital information, and also advancing falsehoods in his Journal and dissuading others from prosecuting the discovery of the Passage by insisting that it did not exist. 'It seems evident,' Dobbs complained, 'that both the Hudson's Bay Company and he are convinced that there is a Passage, and are equally afraid of being detected in having neglected and prevented the discovery of it.'[21] In seeking to discredit Middleton, Dobbs also pointed an accusing finger at the Company, which he charged with offering a bribe of £5,000 to Middleton either to return to their service or search for the Passage in the Davis Straits or Baffin Bay.

Early in May 1743 Dobbs lodged a series of charges with the Lords of the Admiralty, and these were immediately transmitted to Middleton with a letter stating:

'Mr. Arthur Dobbs having laid before my Lords Commissioners of the Admiralty objections to your conduct in your late Voyage in the *Furnace* sloop, together with the *Discovery*, in order to find out a Northwest Passage; and having proposed several Queries relating to your proceedings in that voyage, to which the late Lieutenant, Master, Surgeon and Clerk of the *Furnace* sloop have given answers, I am commanded by my Lord Commissioners of the Admiralty to send you copies of the objections, queries and answers, and am to acquaint you that the Publick have been at a great expence in fitting and sending out the said Sloop and Pink, in order to make the aforementioned Discovery, which would be of great Publick utility, their Lordships think it is a matter of a very serious nature, and that they ought to be thoroughly satisfied, that the person entrusted with the execution of such a Design, has strictly performed his duty therein; and therefore they expect, that you give a very particular and clear answer to the several points of misconduct, which you are charged with by the aforesaid papers.'[22]

Middleton had little difficulty in convincing the Commissioners that he had carried out the task assigned to him conscientiously and to the best of his ability. And it was clear that there was no dereliction of duty or evasion on his part. The Admiralty expressed its satisfaction by giving him a naval command, and the Royal Society acknowledged his efforts by bestowing a gold medal on him; later explorations substantially confirmed his reports. To clear his name before the public, he published the following year his *Vindication of the Conduct of Captain Middleton . . . In Answer to Certain Objections and Aspersions of Arthur Dobbs, Esq.* Middleton's *Vindication* gives a full account of the entire proceedings of the unfortunate dispute between himself and Dobbs, and would indicate that he was an ill-used man.

Middleton's *Vindication* did not mark the end of the dispute, but actually provoked something more than just a reply from Dobbs in the form of an important contribution to the literature of North American travel and exploration. In 1744 Dobbs published a large volume with the lengthy title *An Account of the Countries Adjoining Hudson Bay in the Northwest part of America . . . with an Abstract of Captain Middleton's Journal . . . the whole intended to Show the Great Probability of a Northwest Passage, so long desired, and which (if discovered) would be of the highest advantage to these Kingdoms.* This book, while containing many inaccuracies in the light of subsequent discoveries, is remarkable in many ways, and strangely enough has little bearing on the author's controversy with Middleton. It is clearly the work of a painstaking man who devoted much time to patient study, and as a result of wide reading had acquired an intimate knowledge not only of the history of exploration but of the nature and geography of Canada and its almost unknown interior. Of very considerable interest is the author's account of the travels of Joseph La France, a 'French Canadese Indian' who worked his way from Lake Superior to York Factory on Hudson Bay by way of Lake Winnipeg about the year 1740.

Joseph La France was born at Michilimakinac about the beginning of the century. His father was a French trader, and his mother an Indian of the Saulteur tribe. When La France was five years old, his mother died, and his father took him to Quebec to learn French; at the age of sixteen, when his father died, La France made his way to Montreal with a cargo of furs which he traded. He later made a trip to the Mississippi, travelling as far as the mouth of the Missouri. A few years later he made a second journey to Montreal, where he endeavoured, unsuccessfully, to purchase a licence from the Governor to trade; this was refused, and, as he was in danger of being arrested, he slipped out of the fort at night and began trading in furs again. He was later seized by the French but managed to escape and made his way to one of the forts of the Hudson's Bay Company. He set out on this long journey in 1739, travelling along the north shore of Lake Superior, and then continuing westward to the Pic River. In April

1740 he reached Grand Portage, and then followed the familiar route of the Indian and French traders to Du Plius; he reached Winnipeg in September and eventually came to York factory on the shore of Hudson Bay on 4th June, 1742, having spent three and a half years travelling in a roundabout fashion from Sault Ste Marie. This long journey is set down in detail, and gives a glowing picture of the great wealth of the Canadian interior.

As the Hudson's Bay Company was forbidden to harbour Frenchmen, La France on his appearance at York fort was sent to England where, according to Dobbs, he was maintained at the expense of the Admiralty 'on the prospect of his being of service in the discovery of a Northwest Passage.' While in England he was continually at Dobbs's command, who wrote the story as the half-breed told it to him. Regarding this amazing journey, Burpee writes: 'Considering that the narrative of La France's journey was communicated verbally to Arthur Dobbs, it furnishes a remarkably full and accurate account of the country between Lake Superior and Lake Winnipeg, as well as the tribes that inhabited that country.' [23] Despite the amazing description of the country, its lakes, river, and people, many parts of the journey appear to be inaccurate, and many places difficult to identify, but this is not to be wondered at, for, as Burpee remarks:

> 'It must be remembered that Dobbs is reporting a conversation with an uneducated half-breed, and that he himself knew literally nothing of the country described by La France, and that he had every opportunity of confusing the narrative. That he did confuse it, to an almost ludicrous extent, will be clear by a reference to his map which is a literal interpretation of the narrative, and it is therefore clear that he got an entirely erroneous idea of the topography of the Winnipeg country from La France's description.'

We can overlook these inaccuracies and acknowledge the fact that the name of La France fills an important place among the great discoverers of Canada, and to Dobbs belongs the credit for committing his journey to paper and making him known to the world.

Though the journey of La France occupies a large part of *An Account of the Countries adjoining to Hudson Bay*, the work gives a very clear summary of the history of discovery in the area, and sets down in detail an account of the trade and wealth of the country with plans for its development and exploitation.

> 'Dobbs rounded out the story with his own sharp enthusiasm,' Mackay notes, 'and the book was widely read among all who had interests in colonial expansion and overseas trade. He thumped hard on the drum of the Empire,

contrasting all the glories of English seamanship and exploration with the Company's smug content with dividends while the Northwest Passage awaited discovery.' [24]

It is true that Dobbs thumped hard on the drum of the Empire in an effort to arouse enthusiasm in the phlegmatic and contented Englishman of the day who had grown smugly content and satiated with a surfeit of colonies which he was in dire danger of losing.

'Dreaming at his desk in Dublin,' Morton writes, 'Dobbs was achieving for the English on paper what La Vérendrye had already gone far towards making a reality for the French—the occupation of the great central plain of America. To the dreamer there was no obstacle on the way but the monopoly of the Hudson's Bay Company. Patriotic Englishmen who hated to think that the French were getting the better of the English, others again, who regarded all monopolies as vicious obstacles to progress, manufacturers and merchants eager for new markets for their goods, rallied to his support and precipitated a crisis for the Company.' [25]

Though the Northwest Passage expedition had ended in failure and proved a disappointment to many, the campaign against the Company was only beginning to gather strength, and the way was being slowly prepared for yet another attempt to find the Passage.

6

The Second Voyage of Discovery

FOR MANY years Walpole in England and Fleury in France endeavoured to maintain peace between the two countries. It was an uneasy peace built up by a series of defensive alliances which on the Continent broke down through contending rivalries. In 1744 France declared war on England. Dobbs was in London at the time conferring with the city merchants and devising plans for another voyage to discover the Northwest Passage. The time was anything but propitious for such a venture, as a state of near-panic prevailed in England. In a letter to Ward, Dobbs wrote: 'I believe you will be glad to know at this critical time what news we have here. We are still certain that there has been a great sea fight in the Mediterranean, and from the silence of the French court we believe it to be greatly to our advantage, but very bloody.' Despite this rumoured victory, fear of invasion was uppermost in all minds. 'The French still go on with Imbarking their troops,' Dobbs wrote, 'and by the storm on Saturday we were told there were eight forced ashore, but cant hear yet what has happened to their fleet in the Channell.' In spite of the panic, however, a wave of patriotism swept the country, and Dobbs wrote jubilantly: 'All Protestants now find it necessary to unite against the common enemy, and the Protestant spirit begins to show itself in defence of our Royal Family our only safety; mock patriotism is no longer popular.' With the threat of invasion hanging over the country, Dobbs informed Ward, 'My affairs stand as they did but nothing can be thought of until we are safe at home.'[1]

Though the thoughts and energies of the Government and people were directed to the successful prosecution of the war, the question of the Northwest Passage was not permitted to recede into the background, but was kept before the public by a spate of pamphlets. The first of these was issued by Dobbs under the title *Criticism*, and made public the charges against Middleton that had been presented to the Admiralty. Middleton's *Vindication* was actually a reply to this pamphlet, and quick on its publication came half a dozen other pamphlets written alternately by Dobbs and Middleton; each one was more bitter and libellous than its predecessor. While numerous pamphlets, broadsides, and anonymous letters kept the question of the Passage before the public, the bitterness of the controversy tended to obscure the real issues, and on the whole did not add to the credit of either Dobbs or Middleton, but debased a serious and important controversy to the level of the vituperative pamphleteer of the day.

Behind the façade of noisy controversy, and in spite of the gloom occasioned by the news that the French General, Marshal Saxe, had entered Flanders and taken Ypres, that Bohemia had been invaded by Frederick, and that the inept and fumbling action of elderly and incompetent admirals had brought disgrace to the British fleet in the Mediterranean, Dobbs continued to press the Government to undertake another voyage of discovery. A committee of leading merchants and influential politicians was formed to finance another voyage, and obtain a charter for a rival company to trade in Hudson Bay. Under the adverse circumstances of war it was difficult, however, to make the Government move. In March 1744 Dobbs wrote to Ward:

'The French war is likely to disconcert all my scheme with the Admiralty for this season, as I foresaw this I petitioned the King in Council for two ships or sloops to go the voyage, or in case that could not be granted at this time to grant a reward as he thought proper to encourage Private undertaking to find the Passage, this the Council have referred directly to the Admiralty to save time without referring it to a Committee of the Council.'[2]

Lord Winchelsea promised to expedite the petition, and assured Dobbs that the discovery of a Passage would be beneficial to British trade, but it would be difficult to supply ships to undertake a voyage. He suggested, therefore, that Dobbs and his committee should apply to Parliament 'for a vote to give £10,000 to any who shall find the Passage.' Dobbs fell in with this suggestion, and informed Ward that he intended applying immediately for this amount. In the meantime the Committee drew up plans for fitting out two ships, and raising a sum of £10,000 to cover the expense of the undertaking. In the course of a long letter to Ward giving details of the scheme, Dobbs asked him to let him know of any persons in Ireland who wish to be 'Adventurers with me.' He assured Ward that he had the utmost faith in the project, and that he was employing Captain Moore 'master of the *Discovery* upon the late voyage' to command the new expedition as he is 'convinced of there being a Passage, and has made several voyages into the Bay already, and is very sober and careful, and will be an Adventurer himself.' Other members of the previous expedition also agreed to take part in the new venture, which, Dobbs remarked, 'cant be called a lottery except from the dangers of the sea, there being almost a certainty of all the Packets being prizes. I hope to hear from you soon,' he concluded, 'and by that time we shall be fixed in the voyage.' [3]

From this letter to Ward we gather that the plans for a voyage of discovery were well advanced, and that a number of merchants had come in with him as Adventurers, and subscribed liberally to his fund. His plan found warm support in governing circles, and he counted among his friends and supporters such influential men as Carteret, Winchelsea, Pelham, and Chesterfield who had just been appointed Lord-Lieutenant of Ireland; with these men behind him, and the assurance of strong support in Parliament, it seemed there would be very little difficulty in obtaining a promise of a parliamentary grant as a reward for the discovery of the Northwest Passage. His enthusiasm and certainty received a slight shock, however. Pelham, a careful and cautious politician like Walpole, with a strong sense of economy and a love of peace as first Lord of the Treasury felt that the time was not propitious to embark upon a new voyage of discovery, and in consequence asked Dobbs not to pursue the matter for the present. On 19th April Dobbs wrote to Ward:

'All thoughts of my discovery are dropt until next year. I had a meeting with some merchants on Monday who were to be concerned as Adventurers, and we found there was no depending upon getting a proper ship ready. . . . On Tuesday I waited upon Mr Pelham, who advis'd me, since ships could not be provided not to apply to the Commons or ask the King's approbation for a Premium now, but to come over in the beginning of the next session and have everything then properly fix'd, and the discovery effectually prosecuted, for it being now late in the session, and the House very thin we would not desire to have any objection arise against it in the House upon such an account which might damp it, especially since it could not be prosecuted this session, and he was pleas'd to say that he advis'd this both upon my acct. and for the good of the Publick, as he thought the scheme beneficial to the Publick. I told him I would be advised by him and acquiesce until next session, so that I shall now prepare to go over in a fortnight.' [4]

Dobbs returned to Ireland, not to rest but to clear up his own affairs at home, many of which had become involved, entangled, and neglected owing to his long absence in England. His new Northwest Passage project and the task of framing a case against the Hudson's Bay

Company, as well as involvement in the colonial enterprises of his merchant friends, necessitated his resignation from the office of Surveyor-General. Though so many activities engaged his attention, he managed to carry out his duties as Engineer and Surveyor-General in a satisfactory manner, though it cannot be said that he earned the same repute as his predecessor Sir Edward Lovet Pearce; nonetheless good public work was done during the period he held office. On the completion of the Irish Parliament House, a Select Committee was pleased to report that 'Mr. Dobbs, His Majesty's Engineer and Surveyor General had acquitted himself of the trust reposed in him with great care and frugality,' and recommended that a sum of £500 be granted him for his 'care and pains.' This recommendation was not accepted in full, but Parliament granted him £250.[5]

Dobbs remained in Ireland for a few months and played an active part in the parliamentary proceedings. He was diligent in his attendance and served on three important committees set up by the Irish Parliament to examine the possibility of establishing a tanning industry and the manufacture of paper and glass. These industries, for which the raw material was readily available in Ireland, had been suggested by the Dublin Society with the approval of Viceroy Chesterfield, who in a short term of office did all he could to encourage Irish industrial development. Chesterfield was an admirer of Prior and his associates, and was instrumental in obtaining a grant from the privy purse of £500, to assist the Dublin Society.[6]

When Parliament was prorogued in 1744, Dobbs drafted his petition to the Government requesting financial aid and support to undertake another voyage in search of the Northwest Passage, and praying for a repeal of the Charter of the Hudson's Bay Company. In his petition he claimed that the Company's charter was a barrier to the growth and development of British trade and commerce, and that the Company's lack of enterprise and initiative encouraged the growth of French power and influence in Canada. He attributed the failure of the last voyage to a dereliction of duty on the part of Captain Middleton. In the closing passages of his petition he beat hard on the drum of the Empire, recalling the genius, achievements, and sacrifices of Frobisher, Hudson, Baffin, Davis, and a host of other explorers whose names conjured the spirit of British enterprise and ability.

Early in the following year Dobbs returned to London and, having consulted with his merchant associates, he presented his petition to the Lords of the Admiralty, who immediately referred it to a Committee of the House of Commons. The Committee wasted no time in getting down to work, and as soon as procedure was arranged Dobbs was called to give evidence in support of the petition. He was closely examined by Admiral Edward Vernon, a bitter opponent of Walpole, who insisted in calling Captain Middleton to prove that any further attempt to discover the Passage would be futile.[7] The Committee having examined all the evidence put forward by Dobbs and a number of those who took part in the previous expedition were impressed. A month elapsed before Dobbs could convey the news of his success to Ward.

'The Commons in a Committee of the whole House,' he wrote warmly, 'came yesterday unanimously into two resolutions in my favour, the first that the finding a Passage betwixt Hudson's Straits and the Western Ocean of America would be of great advantage to this Kingdom, and the second that a Publick reward should be given to such as should perfect the discovery of it.'

In view of this recommendation, and the promise of a Bill in Parliament, Dobbs continued:

'We shall now immediately open our subscriptions and prepare the ships. We propose that the merchants shall petition the Admiralty for the loan of the *Furnace* which we had before and was fitted for that voyage and even to pay the men, etc., which if we can get will lessen the expense and the Crown may have her again. I hope in a month now to be ready to go away once everything is put forward and in a proper way.'[8]

In spite of the heavy commitments of war, and rumours of an impending invasion of Scotland by the Young Pretender, a Bill offering a reward of £20,000 for the discovery of a Northwest Passage was passed without difficulty. It was made clear to Dobbs, however, by both the Lords of the Admiralty and Pelham that the Government had no ships to give him, and that he and his Committee would have to purchase their own ships and find their own crews. Undeterred by this task, Dobbs immediately opened a subscription list to raise a sum of £10,000. The prospectus, backed by many influential people, asked for the names of one hundred subscribers willing to subscribe one hundred pounds each. The appeal for subscriptions was not entirely successful, due in all probability to the fact that England was at war, and also because of the failure of Middleton's voyage. The appearance of the Young Pretender in Scotland, and his victorious drive into England had a chilling effect upon people and turned their thoughts in other directions. However, seventy-two subscribers advanced a sum of

£7,200, and the deficit was willingly made up by Dobbs and some of his personal friends. The list of subscribers contained the names of people from many walks of life; among the noblemen who subscribed were the Earl of Chesterfield and Lord Southwell, ecclesiastics included Dr. Holt, Archbishop of Tuam, and the philosopher George Berkeley, Bishop of Cloyne, who at the time was actively engaged in discovering his famous panacea—Tar-water. Among the lesser notabilities were Charles Stanhope, Member of Parliament for Harwich, and one-time under-Secretary for the Southern Department, and Solomon Dayrolles, Chesterfield's godson, and Master of the King's Revels; there were also a number of city merchants and personal friends such as the Earl of Granard, Sir John Rawden, and Judge Ward, who entered a subscription for his son who was then actively engaged in the suppression of the 1745 rebellion in Scotland; the Reverend Richard Dobbs applied for two shares, thus showing his faith in his brother's enterprise.

A committee to administer the undertaking was elected and comprised the following: Lord Southwell, James Douglas, Rowland Frye, John Thomlinson, Robert Mackay, Henry Douglas, William Bowden, Samuel Smith, and Dobbs himself. Early in 1746 the Committee purchased two ships, the *Dobbs Galley*, a sloop of 180 tons, and the *California*, a slightly smaller ship of 140 tons. The two vessels were speedily commissioned and placed under the command of Captain William Moore and Captain Francis Smith. Both captains had experience of sailing in northern waters, Moore accompanying Middleton as Master of the *Discovery*, while Smith had served with the Hudson's Bay Company since he was a boy. Both men were bitter critics of Middleton and the Hudson's Bay Company, and were keenly enthusiastic. Dobbs trusted them implicitly, certain that if there was a Passage they were the men to find it. The manning of the ships presented little difficulty, even though a war was in progress, for the rewards offered were sufficient to tempt even the most timorous of seamen. Premiums were settled on each man in the event of success; the Captains were to receive £500, while every officer was promised £200, and the men proportionately; at the same time it was agreed that all prizes taken at sea were to be divided entirely between the officers and the men.

Throughout the earlier part of the year 1746 the work of fitting out and equipping the ships proceeded apace.

'Each ship was perfectly well repaired and strengthened,' Henry Ellis,

A.D. — 5

who acted as agent, wrote, 'and in all respects fitted as well as could be desired. . . . They also had a sufficient quantity of Provisions, military and naval stores.' He added: 'The diligence used in equipping the vessels was such that the care of the Committee outstripped the coming in of subscriptions, so that they fell somewhat short of the necessary supply; which so far from either discouraging or abating their endeavours, that on the contrary, the Gentlemen comprising the Committee, came to a full resolution of not letting the season pass, and therefore made up out of their own pockets the deficiency of the subscription, towards defraying the expense for the outset of this voyage.' [9]

Ellis was a young man of means with an adventurous disposition who spent the greater part of his life travelling throughout Europe. He was a subscriber, and with Dobbs's approbation sailed on the expedition as the agent of the Committee. He shared Dobbs's interest in colonial development. He was a scientist of no mean merit, and though officially agent to the expedition he also acted as hydrographer, surveyor, and mineralogist, and in later years contributed numerous publications to the Royal Society of which he was a member; some of these papers were on the subject of the Northwest Passage, in which he paid warm tribute to Dobbs. Ellis was later appointed Governor of Georgia.

By mid-May the ships were completely fitted and ready to sail. Dobbs in a letter to Ward wrote:

'I propose going to Gravesend tomorrow where I expect our ships will be, to take leave of them, their convoy is waiting for them at the Nore under orders to sail on the 15th with the fresh fair wind for the Orkneys without waiting for the Trade. I propose setting out on Friday having taken a place in the stage, but my man has fallen ill, and I must either wait till Monday or leave him. I have heard nothing new here. Yesterday I was told 4 of the Brest Squadron are sail'd to the Western Isle of Scotland to try to bring off the young Pretender, and twas said five or six of them were seen off the Lizard; if that be true they cant all have sailed with their transports for America, in case they are sail'd and Martin is at sea with 13 stout ships we apprehend here that Antwerp will soon fall into the hands of the French as our army is obliged to give way to the French superior force until the Hanoverians and Hessians join us.' [10]

This letter, besides giving Ward news of the impending departure of the expedition, marks the final curtain in Charles Stuart's brief appearance upon the Scottish scene. A month before this his hungry army had been destroyed by the ruthless Cumberland, and the Prince was hiding in the Western Isles with a price of £30,000 on his head. In spite of a victory against poorly armed Scots, British prestige was low, and the armies of Marshal Saxe had swept on to capture Brussels, Antwerp, and Liège; except for the exploits of Anson and Hawke at sea the mounting ruin of war lay heavy upon the country.

Dobbs reached Gravesend on 20th May, and waved farewell to the ships that carried with them all his hopes and dreams. From the outset the expedition was beset with ill-fortune; the *California*, encountering heavy seas, received some minor damage and had to refit at Yarmouth. A day or two later the chief mate was accidentally left ashore at Tynemouth, and the ships had to sail without him. On 4th June the expedition, in company with two ships of the Hudson's Bay Company, sailed for the Orkneys in convoy with the frigate *Loo* of forty guns. The voyage to the Orkneys passed without incident. A fortnight later the ships parted company, leaving the *Dobbs Galley* and the *California* to make their own passage to Hudson Bay. Three days later an incident occurred that almost wrecked the prospects of the voyage; a serious fire broke out in the great cabin of the *Dobbs Galley*, due, apparently, to the negligence of a cabin-boy. The fire spread towards the powder room directly under the cabin, which contained some thirty or forty barrels of powder, besides 'candles, spirits, matches and all manner of combustibles.' Ellis, in his account of the voyage, gives a vivid picture of the ensuing panic where 'you might hear on this occasion all varieties of sea-eloquence; cries, prayers, curses and scoldings mingled together.' Prompt measures were taken, however, to save the ship, but of the panic that prevailed we note that

> 'some were for hoisting out the boats; accordingly the lashings were cut for that purpose, but none had the patience sufficient to join and hoist them out; others were for setting more sail to come up with the *California* . . . that if any should be alive after the Ship's being blown up, they might have a chance of saving themselves aboard her.'

Fortunately the fire was extinguished and the damage speedily repaired by the ship's carpenter.[11]

On 8th July Resolution Island, at the entrance to Hudson Straits, was reached, but thereafter progress was slower owing to ice-floes. By 19th August the expedition had crossed Hudson Bay to the west coast in the neighbourhood of Marble Island, where Dobbs maintained the Passage lay. Owing to the lateness of the season, no survey could be made, and the ships proceeded in a southerly direction exploring the coast from Rankin Inlet to Hayes River, the wide area which, Dobbs claimed, had not been properly surveyed by Middleton. At the mouth of the Hayes River the ships sought winter anchorage, and according to Ellis received little help or co-operation from the governor of the Hudson's Bay station. When the *Dobbs Galley* went aground and the crew were in obvious distress, the governor 'sent his boats and people to cut down the beacon, which was the only proper mark we had to guide us into a place of safety when we might get the ship afloat.' [12] The *Dobbs Galley* was refloated and anchored close to the *California* in the mouth of the river, but the governor of the factory intervened and issued a letter 'desiring us not to come any nearer the factory without sending a proper authority from the Government or the Hudson's Bay Company for so doing, or he would use his utmost strength and endeavour to prevent us from doing so.' Ellis writes bitterly of the callous attitude of the Company's officials from whom 'we expected shelter and assistance as subjects of Great Britain, and people who had no intention to molest the Hudson's Bay Company's trade.' [13] Isham defended his attitude on the grounds that as Britain was at war the expedition might have been an enemy, but that when the Captains produced their papers he sent a boat to assist them.[14]

Following the departure of the expedition, Dobbs proceeded to set on foot his projected rival company, but it soon became evident that no new company could hope to trade in either Labrador or Newfoundland while the well-established Hudson's Bay Company enjoyed chartered rights over this vast area. The success of any new venture depended upon the enjoyment of equal rights in North American waters, and to be assured of this equality it would be necessary to induce Parliament either to abrogate the charter of the Hudson's Bay Company, or at least repeal some of its clauses. This was a new task Dobbs undertook to perform, but with other important commitments on hand, particularly his purchase of large tracts of land in North Carolina which called for immediate settlement, he was content to let matters lie until the return of the expedition.

While a long winter of silence enveloped the expedition, Dobbs never lost faith in its successful outcome. Early in the year 1747 he wrote to Mathew Rowan, the Surveyor-General of North Carolina, who had undertaken to survey and plot his land in the province, voicing his optimism. 'I hope,' he said, 'to go to London in the autumn upon the return of our ships gone to find out the Northwest Passage, which have been out a year, and expect to hear of their return with success by next August or September.' [15] About the same time, in the course of a letter to the Reverend Charles Westein, Chaplain and Secretary to the Prince of Wales, concerning the distance between

Asia and America, Dobbs wrote: 'I am sensible it will give the learned and ingenious professor great pleasure to think that we may yet hope for a Passage by Hudson's Bay to the Western American ocean without being obstructed by ice after passing Hudson's Straights.' This letter was a criticism of a paper communicated by Leonard Euler, Professor of Mathematics at the Imperial Society of St. Petersburg, to the Royal Society on recent Russian discoveries in the Bering Straits which more or less ruled out the possibility of a Northwest Passage. Dismissing Euler's defence of Bering, Dobbs ended his letter with the words: 'However, a few months now, if our ships return safe, will give us a certainty on one side or the other, although I am sanguine enough they have by now sailed through and discovered this much wished for Passage.' This letter to Westein was later communicated to and published by the Royal Society.[16]

Some months before the return of the ships from Hudson's Bay, Dobbs suffered a serious loss by the death of his wife to whom he was deeply attached. Her death shocked him, and for a time he appeared to lose interest in the activities hitherto engaging his attention. In the course of a letter to Rowan in North Carolina he said:

'My situation has changed since I last wrote to you by the death of my wife ... I have time if my health continues to take a trip to North Carolina, and take over some families with me, and some servants to settle them there. This will depend principally upon the encouragement you will give me of the goodness of the land, and the benefit it may be to me settling there.' [17]

Dobbs did not go to North Carolina, and a few months later was fully engrossed in all his former activities, and initiating plans for the development and settling of his North Carolina property. The Hudson's Bay Company was still his *bête noire*, and he eagerly awaited news of the discovery of the Northwest Passage before resuming his attack upon it.

During the long winter months the *Dobbs Galley* and the *California* lay anchored in the Hayes River. The crew spent their time building a longboat which would enable them to explore the coves and inlets of the western shores of the bay. During these months the men suffered a great deal from scurvy, which Ellis claimed was brought about by drinking brandy and by a lack of fresh meat which they were unable to obtain because James Isham would not permit the members of the expedition to trade with the Indians and Eskimaux. Scurvy was undoubtedly rampant and scarce a month passed without members of the crew sickening and dying of it. The blame for this state of affairs, however, could hardly be placed on Isham, who would appear to have gone out of his way to help, and actually provided warm clothing out of his meagre store as well as gunpowder and shot so that the members of the expedition could obtain game. We gather from Isham's Journals that the utmost discord existed between the two Captains, Moore and Smith, who were continually at loggerheads, and did not actually speak to each other for some months.[18]

The longboat was finally launched on 10th May, 1747, and the summer months were spent in making a minute search of the openings and river mouths as far north as Cape Dobbs. The search revealed no passage and the most it achieved was to vindicate Middleton and prove conclusively that no Northwest Passage existed in the Hudson Bay area. Ellis, in his account of the voyage, suggests that Dobbs was mis-led by Lieutenant Rankin into believing that Wager Bay marked the entrance to the Northwest Passage, and in loyalty to his patron wrote:

'It ought to be observed that it was from Mr. Dobbs zeal for the Pub-lick, and a laudable concern for the glories of Britain that Mr. Dobbs took so much pains in this affair. It must likewise be considered that he could not be expected to be farther in the right than he was properly informed, and it must be allowed, that he argued very justly and judiciously, though from facts that were wrong stated, so that his errors, if they be errors prop-erly so called, were not only involuntary, but inevitable; since reasoning as he did from what was laid down to him by others, he could be answer-able only for the rectitude of his own conclusions, and not for the certainty of the premises which lay entirely out of his reach to discover.' [19]

This is a just and kindly verdict. To his dying day, however, in spite of failure, Dobbs firmly believed that a Northwest Passage existed, but a century and a half had to pass before this dream was realised and by then its utility was of little importance.

7

Colonial Proprietor

DOBBS FIRST showed an interest in colonial affairs in 1729 when he drew up his scheme on the American colonies and presented it to Walpole. Though his scheme awoke no interest in Government circles, the London merchants, Gee, Hanbury, Huey, Crymble, and McCulloh were impressed by it, and when, in 1735, Dobbs approached them with a view to settling Protestant families from Ireland in North Carolina they readily agreed to facilitate him; indeed, the suggestion was most acceptable, as the merchant landowners had found great difficulty in getting settlers for the more backward and thinly populated parts of the colonies. The plan to bring to America a large number of Irishmen, particularly the distressed Protestants, or more correctly Presbyterians with a strong admixture of Scottish blood, fitted in with Dobbs's own ideas of planting, extending, and strengthening Britain's overseas possessions.

With regard to this plan, Osgood states that before the end of the year 1735, Dobbs, with other gentlemen of prominence in Ireland, and McCulloh, the London merchant and a relative of Governor Johnston of North Carolina, had begun to make enquiries about facilities for settling poor Protestants in the province, and with this end in view had, through their attorney, purchased a tract of 60,000 acres on the Black River.¹ This is true only in part, for Dobbs had no financial interest in the purchase, nor were any prominent Irishmen associated with him. At this time his interests were purely altruistic, but his ideas were considered to be sufficiently practical to be exploited by such shrewd and capable men as McCulloh, Crymble, Hanbury, Huey, and Smith, who had been associated with him in his Northwest Passage ventures. Early in the following year, McCulloh petitioned the Board of Trade for two tracts of 132,000 acres; a later petition was made in conjunction with Crymble and Huey, for tracts near the heads of the Peedee, Cape Fear, Neuse Rivers of a million and a quarter acres for early settlement. The prospect of settling this

vast area of land in accordance with the patents was, however, far
beyond the ability of the merchants concerned, and in the course of
the next few years they disposed of considerable tracts of land to other
speculators, including Dobbs.[2]

In 1745, Dobbs, with Colonel John Selwyn, purchased from
McCulloh and his associates 400,000 acres of land lying in what
roughly comprises the present counties of Mecklenburg and Cambanus
in North Carolina. Colonel Selwyn, whom Dobbs met through his
association with young Lord Conway, was the father of the celebrated
wit George Selwyn. He had had a distinguished army career, having
served at Malplaquet, and was aide-de-camp to Marlborough. On the
accession of George I, Selwyn was appointed Controller of Customs,
and later Groom of the Bedchamber to George II; he was also
Treasurer to Queen Caroline and the King's son—the Duke of Cambridge. Shortly before his death he served in a similar capacity to the
Prince of Wales, later George III. Selwyn was a Member of Parliament for Gloucester from 1734 until his death in 1751. He was a kind
and amiable man, blessed with a great deal of worldly wisdom; Walpole
remarked that he was a shrewd, silent man, humane and reckoned
honest. As the close friend and adviser to the King, and closely associated with the ruling Whigs (he was actually a relative of Walpole's),
his influence was fairly considerable.[3] Dobbs had known Selwyn for a
number of years, but a closer and more intimate friendship developed
by reason of his association with the young Lord Conway who, as a
schoolboy at Eton, was passionately attached to Selwyn's eldest son,
and both boys often spent their holidays together at Selwyn's house.
Dobbs was a welcome visitor to Cleveland House, the London home
of the Selwyns and the resort of the leading political figures of the day
—Walpole, Pelham, Newcastle, Chesterfield, and other important
Whigs, as well as the merchants Hanbury and Smith. A younger member of the Cleveland House circle was Robert D'Arcy, Earl of Holderness, who was a senior contemporary of Conway and the Selwyn boys,
John and George.

The land obtained by Dobbs and Selwyn contained about 400,000
acres, 'lying in the extreme part of North Carolina with a quit rent of
4s. Proclamation money for every hundred acres, payable to the Crown
after the expiration of ten years.' This grant, like all similar grants
from the Crown, contained the provision that the grantee should settle
one white person on every two hundred acres of the grant, and that
all unsettled land at the end of ten years should revert to the Crown.

Having acquired the status of a colonial proprietor, Dobbs lost little time in making suitable provision for the immediate settlement of his property. Fortunately Mathew Rowan the Surveyor-General of the colony hailed from County Antrim, and Dobbs, being acquainted with his family in Ireland, entrusted him with the agency of the grant. Early in the year 1747 Rowan carried out and completed a survey of the land, and we gather from a letter written by Dobbs that his affairs in North Carolina had been placed on a very satisfactory basis.[4] In the course of this letter, Dobbs wrote:

'I am glad to find that Mr. McCulloh and you have at last settled, and that the patents are passed for my lands which you expect to receive from him at New Bern, the present seat of Government. . . . I am pleased also to hear that my lands are fixed upon Peedee in the King's division, and may expect them clear of quit-rent for ten years from the passing of the patents.'

Owing to the scramble for colonial grants and the fact that titles were not properly registered, land in the colony had been granted over and over again to different grantees, and much confusion existed regarding boundaries and the fixing of quit-rents; many blank patents were also issued which only added to the confusion. Dobbs was much too shrewd a business man and too well acquainted with land tenure to leave such matters to chance, and informed Rowan that on the question of his grant being free of quit-rent for ten years he intended applying 'to ye Council in England to have it out of doubt.'[5] At the same time he requested Rowan to supply him with a full and accurate description of his lands which he hoped were as good 'as they are on Peedee.' He added: 'In your former letter you mentioned these lands to be good, and I expect that Mr. McCulloh will have them properly surveyed in baronies of 12,500 acres each, I having paid him £250 for that purpose over and above the purchase.' Dobbs, in his letters to Rowan, displayed an intimate knowledge of the colony, its people and requirements, and also of the lands bordering North Carolina which Virginian planters had recently settled. In order fully to acquaint himself with conditions, however, he requested Rowan to supply him with full details of the number of acres, terms of lease, rents which might justifiably be expected, and the produce of different parts of the Province, 'so that I may know how to conduct myself in any bargain I shall make.'[6]

From the moment Dobbs acquired his North Carolina property he proceeded with his accustomed vigour and enthusiasm to plant settlers there. He sought out likely families in his native county of Antrim, and approached small farmers on his Kildare estate, offering

them every inducement to take up some of his land. In his impulsive
and impatient way, he spoke about chartering a ship and providing free
passage for settlers. He did not take kindly at all to the advice of Rowan
and others living in the colony when they pointed out the difficulties
and dangers facing prospective settlers. North Carolina, unlike the
New England provinces, was relatively backward, and ranked as the
least commercial of the thirteen colonies; further, it had a background
of turbulent history.

The first settlers in Carolina were restless traders and adventure-
some people who found the laws of the more civilised and exacting
Virginia burdensome, and sought the untrammelled freedom of a
vast new country, flanked by the sea on one side and the Appalachian
mountains on the other. The Virginians called the colony the sanctuary of runaways, but whether lawless or not, these hardy, virile
people poured across the border from the north and staked their claims
where they fancied. Some years later these colonists learned that King
Charles II had set up a province of the area called Carolina, and had
presented it to eight proprietors, among whom were Lord Granville,
Sir William Berkeley, and George Monck, Duke of Albemarle. A
few settlers were sent over from England, and a representative of the
proprietors, William Drummond, was empowered to set up a form of
government, which met in 1663, constituting the first Assembly of
Carolina.

In 1669, a simple constitution was framed for Carolina, and for
half a century the scattered population was content to keep to its own
simple primal government, despite the efforts of the proprietors to
induce them to accept the grand model of government prepared by
the Earl of Shaftesbury and the liberal philosopher John Locke. From
the earliest days, therefore, a spirit of hardy independence, divorced
from the trappings of the English constitution and disdainful of the
prerogatives of kings, was evidenced in the province. By the end of
the seventeenth century, while under the governorship of Philip
Ludwell, an able and upright man, Carolina was divided into two provinces—North and South Carolina. Though a large number of settlers had come from England and Ireland and there was a continuous
flow of migrants from Virginia, the province remained relatively poor
and backward, and suffered from a surfeit of unscrupulous governors.
The establishment of a Huguenot settlement at Bath, and Swiss and
German Palatines, led by Baron de Graffenried, at New Bern on the
Neuse River mark an epoch in Carolinian history. Graffenried was supported in his work of settlement by a Scot, John Lawson, who de-

scribed the area in which they settled as a 'delicious country, being placed in that girdle of the world which affords wine, oil, fruit, grain and silk, with other rich commodities, besides a sweet air, moderate climate and fertile soil.' He concludes his description with the remark that the country is suitable 'to spin out the thread of life to its utmost extent.' [7]

As the industrious German and Swiss settlers moved farther west into Indian land their difficulties increased, and the rich hunting-ground of the Indian became the graveyard of many settlers. In 1711, the Indians fell upon the white settlements at New Bern and Bath, killing many hundred men, women, and children, including Lawson. Despite a punitive expedition from South Carolina, the settlers continued to suffer, and their numbers were further decimated by an outbreak of yellow fever.

In 1714, the proprietors sent out Governor Charles Eden, who until his death eight years later was the ablest governor the colony had yet had. He established his seat of government at Edenton, a village of fifty small cottages. On the death of Governor Eden, King George I, jealous of his prerogatives, arrogated to himself many of the privileges of the proprietors and appointed George Burrington as Governor. Burrington was a vulgar ruffian, a rake who had served a term of imprisonment for an infamous assault on an old woman. After some years of wretched government he was replaced by Richard Everard. By 1729 conditions in the colony had grown so bad that the proprietors, with the exception of Carteret, were quite willing to sell their interest to the Crown for less than £50,000. Thus North Carolina reverted to the Crown with the 'peaceful assent of all parties.' [8]

When the colony became a royal province, George II sent out the infamous Burrington as Governor for the second time. Burrington's rule brought down all the wrath of the colonists upon his head, and in the course of a letter to Newcastle he complained that they were 'indolent and crafty, impatient of government, and neither to be cajoled nor outwitted by any Ruler.' The colonists refused to enact legislation or support Burrington, whom they charged with using scandalous, opprobrious and malicious words, as well as being a drunkard, and guilty of the most outrageous conduct and tyranny. [9]

In 1734, when Dobbs, McCulloh, Crymble, and Huey were first showing an interest in the colony, the King appointed Gabriel Johnston as Governor. Johnston, unlike other royal governors, did not come from the army or Court party, but was a scholarly gentleman, and a professor of Oriental languages at St. Andrews University. His rule lasted for twenty years, and though it was on the whole wise and prudent, it was by no means serene or peaceful. Years of ill-government had taken their toll, and towards the end of his rule Johnston complained that the colonists were 'wild and Barbarous' and paid 'the servants of the Crown scantily and tardily.' [10]

It was at this stage in the history of the province that Dobbs entered the scene. As a landed proprietor he was untiring in his efforts to establish settlements, and in this he was aided by the unfavourable economic state of Ireland which accelerated the flow of workless Presbyterians to the new world. The collapse of the Jacobite rising in Scotland in 1745 also accounted for a large influx of Scottish emigrants. The effect upon the colony of this accretion of industrious Scottish and Irish Presbyterians was important, and contributed greatly to the growth and prosperity of North Carolina. It has been said, perhaps with some exaggeration, that the newcomers who 'quite made over the once lawless and shiftless colony were the old Scotch stock from Ulster.' [11] Nevertheless, these Presbyterian settlers were a sturdy and independent people, fugitives from economic and religious oppression.

Though North Carolina was steadily growing in importance, and developing a trade in tar, pitch, and resin from its vast forests, as well as growing rice and maize in the alluvial about Cape Fear, the internal government and public accounts bordered on chaos. Efforts to raise taxes to support the Government and administration, and provide for some kind of army or militia to meet the ever present threat of French encroachment from the Mississippi and Indian incursions, were solidly resisted by the colonists; even the quit-rents due to the King were not paid. In 1746, Johnston complained that his salary was eight years in arrears, and the salaries of other officials were in the same state.[12]

The administration of North Carolina grew more and more chaotic, and it is difficult to know whether the blame for the state of the colony could be laid against the Governor, the Board of Trade in London, or the colonists themselves; indeed, we might apportion the blame to all three in varying degrees. So far as the administration was concerned, Johnston neglected to send either letter or report to the Board of Trade for a period of five years from 1742 to 1747. At a later date, when he was taxed with neglect, he claimed that he had written and sent reports regularly to the Board of Trade, but that his letters and packets had miscarried. Undoubtedly he was guilty of some neglect, which might be excused because of the conditions under which he laboured, and the woeful lack of interest displayed by Britain in her colonies. In many matters of administration the Board of Trade failed to sustain the hapless Governor. In the internal affairs of the colony Johnston had to contend with a bitter rivalry for representation between the older settlers in the north and the new settlers in the south. In his efforts to provide equal representation in the Assembly, he reduced the number of members elected by the northern counties, and was immediately faced by a stern opposition which, oddly enough, had the support of McCulloh and his London associates Crymble, Huey, and Dobbs. Johnston, in a letter to the Board of Trade, wrote:

'It is with great difficulty we make shift to meet twice in a year. All the rest of our time is spent at our own little plantations which are some fifty, some a hundred and some two hundred miles distant from one another; and this will always be our case until our salaries are regularly paid . . . which makes it impossible for us to remain long in any of the towns of this Province where, small and despicable as they are, living is dearer than in London.' [13]

At this period the Governor's salary was almost £13,000 in arrears.

With no reports coming from Johnston and a series of complaints arriving from McCulloh, the proprietors in London were naturally anxious about their property. It was clear to them that if the unsettled conditions continued in the colony, all their efforts to send out settlers and make settlements would fail, and in time their properties would revert to the Crown. Dobbs was particularly anxious, for he had his heart and soul fixed on this new colonial venture, which offered an opportunity to put into practical effect some of the plans and schemes he had submitted to succeeding governments for almost thirty years. Early in 1749, in concert with McCulloh and Francis Corbin, who for a short time had been Attorney-General for North Carolina, Dobbs preferred charges of neglect and maladministration against Johnston, and to add weight to these charges he alleged that the Governor was in sympathy with the Jacobites. The charges were submitted to the Duke of Bedford, with whom Dobbs was on friendly terms, and he immediately referred them to the Board of Trade for an enquiry and report thereon.[14]

The Board of Trade, in a report to the Duke of Bedford, summed up the case against Johnston with the brief comment that there was clear evidence of considerable disorder and confusion in the colony. Johnston immediately wrote a series of letters to the Board of Trade in defence of his governorship. In subsequent proceedings before the Board, Dobbs and McCulloh appeared as spokesmen for the colonists, while James Abercrombie, the agent for the colony, defended the Governor on instructions from the North Carolina Council. The controversy between the parties dragged on for some years, and a settlement was only effected when the governorship passed into Dobbs's hands, by which time he had settled some five hundred people on his land.

At this stage in Dobbs's career we must retrace our steps to the autumn and winter of the year 1747. In October, the two Northwest Passage ships, the *Dobbs Galley* and the *California*, returned to England. Dobbs, who had been in Ireland, hurried to London to meet the agent, Ellis, and interview the captains, Moore and Smith. From the journals and records of the voyage it was clear that no passage to the Pacific existed in the Hudson Bay area, but the members of the expedition did not rule out the possibilities of a Northwest Passage elsewhere.

From his lodgings at St. James's Coffee House, Dobbs called a meeting of his Committee, and it was then decided to petition Parliament for a Charter to form a new trading company.[15] The Petition was drawn up by Dobbs, and a strong case was made for the repeal of the Charter of the Hudson's Bay Company, on the familiar grounds that the Company failed to increase trade between Britain and Canada, retarded the development of the rich interior of the country, and permitted French traders to gain a monopoly of the fur trade; further, the Company failed to undertake voyages of discovery, and placed insuperable difficulties in the way of the more enterprising Company of Adventurers. By the end of the year Dobbs had completed the Petition and prepared a case for submission to the Government.[16] He remained in London over the Christmas, and on 26th December wrote to Ward:

'I have delayed writing to you on my coming here until I had seen some of our Ministers and consulted them upon what I had to propose to them upon my Northwest Passage scheme. Some of them I have not yet seen as they have taken the opportunity of the recess to go to the country. Those whom I have seen think well of my project and wish it success; the Duke of Dorset has promised me all the assistance he can give and dispatch as Lord President; Lord Chesterfield as Secretary will give my petition to the King whenever I am prepared; my friend Patten will give it all necessary dispatch in his office. The Duke of Newcastle I have been with at his levee and have desired an audience of him when I am prepared at his leisure, and Mr. Stone approves of it, and wishes me success, and I expect will prepare him for it. I have not seen Mr. Pelham as he is gone to the country. Lord

Anson and Lord vere Beauclerk are strongly for it and want it to be pursued and will prepare the Duke of Bedford for it, by whom I expect to make Lord Governor Privy Seal Lord Duplin in the Board of Trade assist me, his only objection is the spirit of the times against all charters. But as we dont wish for an exclusive trade but only for a term of years during the infancy of our settlement and discovery, it is easily obviated. My Lord Chancellor I have not yet been with. Our Committee has empowered me to retain the Attorney and Solicitor General for his opinion before I petition the King, his opinion I have already had as to the exclusive trade absolutely in our favour. The only point now is as to the King's right in giving the lands already granted upon acc^t of the Company's not settling and occupying the lands in so long a time; whether he cant grant them to others who will settle and improve them. Most people think that the Company will be glad to drop their Charter and come in as sharers in the new Charter upon our terms we stipulate with the Government, as they must unavoidably lose their present exclusive trade.' [17]

In March 1748, Dobbs succeeded in getting Parliament to set up a committee to enquire into the state and condition of the countries and trade of Hudson Bay and 'the rights the company pretend to have by Charter to the property, land and exclusive trade of these countries.' [18] The object of this move was to expose the Company in public, and bring its private affairs into the open, and thus show that beyond making large profits for a handful of shareholders it had no interest in further discovery, nor in the development of the territory over which it ruled. About the same time as the Select Committee was appointed, Dobbs submitted a petition to the King in Council, stating that the aims and objects of the petitioners were to discover a passage 'to the western and southern ocean of America' and to 'extend the Trade and increase the wealth and power of Great Britain by finding out new countries and nations to trade with.' The Northwest Passage Committee, the petition claimed, had already expended a considerable sum of money organising one expedition, which, though failing to find a passage, had made many new discoveries. The Committee believed that there was a reasonable prospect 'of finding a Passage to the southern ocean,' and with this end in view had procured 'men of resolution, capacity, and integrity to pursue it effectually.' To carry out those designs the petitioners desired a Charter to establish a trading company, and pointed out that the reward of £20,000 offered by Parliament was 'not adequate to the expences the Adventurers must be at to perfect the Discovery, they having already expended more than half that sum in their last expedition.' If a Charter were granted, the petitioners stated they were prepared to pursue the discovery of a passage, settle and improve the land in all the countries of the northern continent, civilise the natives, convert them to Christianity, and make them happy and industrious subjects of His Majesty the King, and prevent French encroachment on His Majesty's territory.[19] The seemingly portentous aims of the petitioners were by no means impossible, and showed considerable acumen and foresight, for French encroachment and influence were threatening to destroy not only the British fur trade but British possessions in North America. Regarding these aims, George Bryce remarks:

> 'Arthur Dobbs, judging by his book, which shows how far ahead he was of his opponents in foresight, saw that this must come, and so the new Company promised to penetrate the interior, cut off the supply of furs from the French, and save the trade to Britain. A quarter of a century afterwards, the Hudson's Bay Company, slow to open their eyes, perceived it too, and . . . rose from their slumbers, and entered the conflict.' [20]

The Parliamentary Committee began its hearings early in March. The charges against the Hudson's Bay Company as delivered to the Committee may be summarised briefly:

1. The Company had not discovered, nor sufficiently attempted to discover, the Northwest Passage into the Southern Seas.
2. They had not extended their settlements to the limits given them by Charter.
3. They had designedly confined their trade within very narrow limits:
   (*a*) Had abused the Indians.
   (*b*) Had neglected their forts.
   (*c*) Ill-treated their own servants.
   (*d*) Encouraged the French.

In support of these charges, besides the written and carefully prepared case of the petitioners, some twenty witnesses were produced, in the main ex-employees of the Company, and some merchants who supported the case for the opening up and enlargement of the trade of the Hudson Bay area. On the whole, the evidence against the Company was inconclusive and for the most part readily rebutted. The investigation was conducted with judicial detachment, and a year later Lord Strange presented the report of the Committee to Parliament, a report which in its final summation stated: 'On consideration of all the evidence laid before us, by many affidavits on both sides, we think these charges are either not sufficiently supported in point of fact or in a great

measure accounted for from the Nature of Circumstances.' With regard to the granting of a Charter to a rival Company, the Committee
suggested that if Dobbs and his associates wished to have the Charter
of the Hudson's Bay Company repealed, and make a case for the
granting of a new Charter, he should pursue his trade and explorations
into Hudson Bay, and 'carry his freedom of trade to law and get some
judgement of a Court of Justice to warrant it.' [21] This suggestion was
more or less in accord with the advice of the Attorney and Solicitor-
General to the Privy Council, but Dobbs considered it unsatisfactory.

In a final effort to stay the report of the Parliamentary Committee, he
hurried to Scotland to interview the Duke of Argyle 'and staid with him
two days.' [22] In the course of a letter to Ward he wrote:

> 'My principal view was to consult with his Grace upon the Attorney's
> and Solicitor's report which advised the Crown not to grant us an immedi-
> ate Charter, setting forth our objections to the validity of the H. B. Charter
> from their grants being without limits and the exclusive trade a monopoly,
> but think upon account of their long undisturbed possession the Crown
> should not interfere until a judgement in a court of justice is obtained
> against it, as an exclusive grant to us would be an objection against us as
> well as them.' [23]

The Duke of Argyle 'was extremely friendly and civil' but was not
able to help; when, however, Dobbs pointed out that he had obtained
further evidence which could invalidate many of the sworn statements
of the Company's officials, the Duke thought

> 'the Committee of the Council might if they please allow them to be read
> and then refer it to the Attorney General for a further report, but [he]
> thinks it will be the shortest and best way to bring it into Parliament, which
> if we do so he has promised me his friendship and interest in it, as he is in
> principle with us, and thinks it is promoting a publick spirit.' [24]

Though both the Parliamentary Committee and the Privy Council
were, on the whole, sympathetic and even favourable to Dobbs and
his associates, it was fairly clear that he had failed in his efforts to break
the Company's monopoly or obtain a Charter for a rival Company.
The Committee, however, expressed its appreciation of his public
spirit, and commended him for his progressive views and patriotic
outlook.[25]

8

The Ohio Company

THE IRISH Parliament was in session when Dobbs received the final report from the Parliamentary Committee, and though he was aware of the nature of the findings he had hoped in the end for some direction in his favour. The more or less complete vindication of the Hudson's Bay Company was a bitter blow to him. For close on sixteen years he had carried on an unremitting campaign against the Company, which he conceived, rightly or wrongly, to be an obstruction to British trade and commerce, and responsible, by its neglect, for the growth and expansion of French power and influence in Canada. Though supported by the London merchants and a number of able politicians, Dobbs, in the main, waged a lone fight, and the money and energy he had poured into the effort, while earning him a meed of praise, was to all intents and purposes irretrievably lost.

Immediately the report of the Committee was issued, Dobbs crossed to London to make one last effort to launch a company and test the validity of the Hudson's Bay Company's Charter, but the merchants who already had their fingers burnt had lost interest. Despondent and disappointed, he returned to Ireland, and retired to the pleasant quietness of Castle Dobbs to rest and plan for the future. On 22nd October, 1750, he wrote a letter to his friend Charles Stanhope, a subscriber and loyal member of the Northwest Passage Committee, which was later transmitted to the Royal Society as a communication *Concerning Bees and their Methods of Gathering Wax and Honey*. In the course of this letter he said:

'Since my view of doing good by making discoveries of the great world has been disappointed, upon my retirement into this little corner of it, amongst other rural amusements I have been consulting the inhabitants of the Little World, particularly the most useful and industrious society of Bees, and have had time to revive the curious, ingenious, and entertaining account given by M. Reaumier of that inimitable insect.[1]

In this communication we get a picture, not so familiar perhaps, of Dobbs as the scholarly and thoughtful squire keenly interested in his estate and enamoured of the mysteries of Nature.

During this period of disappointment and apparent failure he turned to scientific investigation, and constructing a number of glass observation beehives he methodically studied the life-cycle and habits of the honey bee. His observations, he informed Stanhope, were made by using a microscope and looking into 'glass hives.' In the course of his observations he crossed swords with the first recognised biologist to make a serious study of the physiology of the honey bee. Reaumier's communications to the French Academy on bees and their behaviour attracted considerable attention, and Dobbs, though in error himself, showed that Reaumier was wrong in his assertions that bees gathered farina or crude wax from different species of flowers on their legs, and that the refined wax was discharged as fæces. While not making the same error as Reaumier, he was nevertheless incorrect in his own observations. On the whole, however, he was more accurate than the French biologist, and showed that not only was he a capable and painstaking observer, but was well acquainted with the works of the foremost naturalists, including Swammerdam, whom he closely followed in his investigations.

Though no longer a young man, Dobbs had lost none of the restless energy that was such a marked characteristic of his entire life, and he soon grew tired of the quiet, unhurried life of a country squire which at no time offered sufficient scope for his mental or physical abilities. Ireland was always much too small, much too circumscribed and parochial to contain him for any length of time. Besides, his work in the field of colonial development had earned him a reputation among the merchants and colonial prospectors in London, and they invariably sought his assistance on matters pertaining to the development of the colonies and British trade. Events nearer home also played a small part in drawing him away as it were from his country retreat. In the Irish Parliament the English interest was feeling the full impact of a strong and bitter opposition party, and the attendance of Government supporters was vitally necessary to stave off defeat, and keep the 'Patriot' Party in order. Added to this was the fact that his eldest son, Conway, had married, and had more or less taken over the management of the family estate. Thus, at the age of sixty-one and a grandfather, Dobbs once more embarked on the active life he had known for more than thirty years, and his fertile brain conjured new schemes and put forth new ideas to stir the Government to action.

In Dublin the Duke of Dorset took office as Viceroy for the second time. He was an old and valued friend of Dobbs, and his influence and patronage over the years was, on the whole, ample repayment for the hospitality Dobbs had shown him in 1732. Dorset's reappointment was by no means a happy choice, more particularly as his son Lord George Sackville accompanied him to Ireland as Chief Secretary, and forthwith allied himself with the unpopular leader of the English interest, Primate Stone. Despite Parliamentary clashes over the disposal of the surplus funds in the Irish Exchequer, Ireland had known a certain amount of good government, particularly during the short viceroyalty of Chesterfield. His successor, the Earl of Harrington, was received with considerable disapproval, however, not only by the Patriot Party, but by many liberal-minded Anglo-Irish. The opposition to the Whig Government and the English interest in Ireland reached back, at least in embryo, to the days of Swift, but much had happened in the last ten or twenty years to instil a more independent outlook in the ruling Ascendancy. Thoughtful men objected to the colonial status of the Irish Parliament, and the rule of English primates in the person of Boulter and his successor, Stone. Some years earlier Boulter complained that 'some foolish and other ill-meaning people have taken the opportunity of propagating a notion of the independency of this kingdom on that of England.' [2] This spirit of independence was a natural growth, and the sovereignty exerted by England, with its deleterious effects on Irish economy, injured not only the Anglo-Irishman's pride, but hurt him in his pocket. A new generation of Anglo-Irish, secure in their Ascendancy, were devoting their talent and energy to developing the natural resources of the country, and endeavouring to instil a spirit of self-reliance in the people.

The question of the disposal of the surplus revenue accruing in the Irish Exchequer first engaged the attention of the Patriot Party in 1731. Then, as already noted, the Irish Parliament directed that the surplus be utilised in repaying the national debt. The Government, which Dobbs supported, opposed this measure, contending that all surplus revenue belonged not to Parliament, but to the King, who could dispose of it as he wished. By 1750 the question of surplus revenue as well as the independence of the Irish Parliament had assumed national importance, and gained considerable support both in Parliament and throughout the country.

A period of unusual prosperity in Ireland followed the peace of Aix-la-Chapelle, and resulted in a surplus revenue of £200,000. Parliament resolved to apply this surplus for the repayment of the

national debt. Heads of a Bill for this purpose were accordingly introduced, and sent to England for approval. The Government took the
view, as on former occasions, that the surplus belonged to the Crown,
and could only be disposed of as the Crown directed. On this occasion
the Government faced a sullen and bitter opposition, and its action
produced another Swift in the person of a crippled apothecary named
Charles Lucas, whose courage and vituperation earned him the condemnation of the Government, so that he had to flee the country.[3]

In Parliament the mood of the opposition was anything but favourable to the Government or the establishment, and when in 1751 the
Duke of Dorset, in his speech at the opening of Parliament, signified
the Royal approval for the appropriation of part of the surplus revenue
for the repayment of the national debt, the members, incensed with
what they considered to be a breach of privilege, passed an appropriation
Bill pointedly omitting to take any notice of the King's assent. When
the Bill was returned from England, it was found that a preamble had
been inserted signifying that the King had assented to the appropriation of the surplus for the repayment of the national debt. Parliamen
on this occasion accepted the altered Bill, but in a rebellious mood and
fully prepared to fight for its rights at a later date.

The appointment of Dorset as Viceroy at this stage was impolitic,
and his support of the unpopular and licentious Primate Stone was no
helpful. The opposition, gathering strength each day, was not entirely
patriotic, or even wholly national ; it earned the name of being the
Patriot Party, but it drew to its ranks all the elements of discontent and
rebellion in the House.[4] This formidable opposition in Parliament was
organised and led by Boyle, the Speaker of the Commons, who was
bitterly opposed to the rule of Primate Stone, and he was supported by
the foremost lawyer and orator—Prime Serjeant Anthony Malone.
Boyle had been a Member of the Irish Parliament for forty years and
had been Speaker since 1733; he was a man of considerable ability,
wealth, and influence. A jealousy had developed between the Speaker
and the Primate, who, like his predecessors, was the *de facto* ruler of
Ireland. This jealousy was increased by the appointment of Dorset's
son—Lord Sackville—as Chief Secretary, who entered into a close
alliance with the Primate, and when the Irish Parliament, led by
Boyle and Malone, rejected the King's assent to the appropriation
Bill, Stone and Sackville, incensed by the insubordination of the Irish
Parliament, actually prepared a warrant for the Speaker's arrest which
Dorset signed; fortunately, no attempt was made to execute the
warrant.

Throughout the stormy sessions of Parliament, Dobbs was assiduous in his attendance and warmly supported the Government against the opposition, though quite clearly he was not very happy about it; he had, in fact, long reached the conclusion that the Irish Parliament was an unnecessary luxury, and did not contribute to the well-being of the country at large. He viewed the growing opposition with discomfort, and felt that if some of the evils of the day were to be redressed, an independent Irish Parliament could only do so by destroying the Protestant Ascendancy, whose survival, he felt, was dependent upon the Crown and Parliament in England. In a letter to his friend and patron, Conway, now Lord Hertford, he touched briefly on the controversy between Boyle and the Government. 'Things continue unsettled here,' he wrote, 'between the Duke of Dorset and the Speaker, though the Speaker's friends say it is betwixt Lord George and the Primate, and him putting his Grace of Dorset out of the question.' [5]

The opposition to the Government in Parliament continued to grow and gather more strength each year until by 1753 it was sufficiently strong to defeat the Government. Again it was the perennial question of the disposal of the Irish surplus revenue. As on a former occasion, the King had graciously consented to the appropriation of part of the surplus for the repayment of the national debt, but in the Bill drawn up by the Irish Parliament there was no mention of the King; the Bill was returned from England with the changed preamble as in previous years. The Parliament decisively rejected the Bill in its altered form. The Government, stung by defeat, reacted strongly to this show of independence. Office-holders—and there were many of them—who voted against the Government were dismissed from their posts, and without the consent of Parliament the surplus was allocated towards the repayment of the national debt. A number of influential opposition members were brought over to the Government side by the usual method of conferring titles and offering preferment and promotion. Despite this action, however, the nucleus of a Patriot Party had been established, and the seed sown some years earlier flowered in all its grandeur for a brief period in the last quarter of the century.

The victory of the opposition gave rise to a flood of pamphlets, argumentative, scurrilous, and libellous, and among these was a broadsheet setting down in red and black print the names of the Members of the Irish Parliament who voted for and against the altered Bill. Those who voted in favour of the Royal consent appeared under the heading *Hic niger est hunc tu Romane Caveto*, while the opposition was listed under the words *Vindices libertatis*; Dobbs, noted as Governor of North Carolina, appeared under the former head.[6]

Though the Irish Parliament had been prevented from asserting its free and independent right in this matter, it did in subsequent years manage to circumvent the overriding power of the English Privy Council by adopting an expedient which has been described as cutting off its nose to spite its face. Unable to obtain control of Exchequer surpluses, Parliament decided to keep expenditure at the highest possible level, and thus bring about a position where there would be no surplus. From 1753 onwards the Irish Parliament granted large sums of money for public works, such as the building of canals and bridges, and the encouragement of industry generally, all perfectly laudable enterprises, but in reality much of this expenditure was frittered away in the private aggrandisement of members and their friends.[7] A system of bounties for the establishment of new industries was certainly worth while, and had been warmly advocated by Dobbs almost a quarter of a century earlier, but he was careful to point out that bounties and premiums were not payments for idleness and inefficiency, nor in perpetuity, but simply to encourage industry in its formative years. He wrote:

'Premiums are only to be given to encourage manufactures or other improvements in their infancy, to usher them into the world, and to give an encouragement to begin a commerce abroad; and if after their improvement, they cannot push their own way by being wrought so cheap as to sell at par with others of the same kind, it is no value to force it.'[8]

This was a practical suggestion which the Irish Parliament might have carried out, but though many useful public works were assisted, the excessive expenditure in this field led to great private speculation and political jobbery, and weakened the spirit of self-reliance and enterprise.[9]

Though occupied with colonial ventures and endeavouring to obtain a governorship in America, Dobbs found time during this controversial period to enquire into the vexed question whether a parliamentary union with Britain might not be better for Ireland. Early in 1753 he prepared a long memorandum on this matter which had come very much to the forefront following the bitter controversy between the Government and the opposition. Dobbs approached the question of a parliamentary union from two angles which were in accord with the principles he had advocated throughout his life. In the first place, he saw no solid reason for an independent Irish Parliament, whether

as at present constituted or as envisaged by Molyneux, Swift, and
Lucas. In the second place, he was strongly of the opinion that a legislative union with Britain provided the only real solution to Ireland's
social and economic problems. A single Parliament in England legis-
lating for Ireland as it did for Scotland would assure for all time the
dominant position of the Protestant minority in Ireland. With this
secure domination, it would be possible to ease or relax the penal laws
against Catholics, which under an independent Irish Parliament were
considered necessary to safeguard and protect the Protestant minority.
With regard to the economic state of Ireland, it was clear to Dobbs,
and indeed to many others interested in the country's welfare, that a
union would at least secure for Ireland the benefits of free trade and
give to the country the same commercial liberty as that enjoyed by
England.

Dobbs actually wrote two pamphlets on the question of a legislative
union between Britain and Ireland.[10] They are more or less identical,
and cover the same grounds and arguments, but one appears to have
been written some years earlier, possibly in 1731, while the later paper
was written in 1753, when the defeated Government seriously thought
of bringing forward a Bill to abolish the Irish Parliament. Neither
pamphlet was ever published, as Dobbs considered that it would be
impolitic and dangerous to do so in view of the volatile nature of Irish
public opinion. He did, however, communicate his views to the
Government in England, and in a letter to Ward, in April 1753, he
wrote:

> 'Mr. Pelham has seen my manuscript upon a Union, and is so struck with
> it that he has desired a copy of it to consider it at his leisure, and has since
> spoken to Lord Hillsborough upon it, who has spoke also to me to have
> a copy of it, and Lord Hertford who had been formerly prejudiced against
> it, tells me he is almost fully convinced and I have got it in full light. But
> it is thought proper not to publish anything till it is fully considered, and
> people are properly prepared to avoid disputes and altercations, so that
> probably it may be taken up by a new Parliament, or at furthest on a new
> Reign. It seems to be agreed that something should be settled in Ireland.'[11]

The manuscript submitted to the Government by Dobbs was
entitled *A short Essay to show the Expediency if not Political necessity of
an Incorporating Union betwixt Britain and Ireland*. In the course of
his essay Dobbs remarked that it resulted from 'a thorough consideration of what might be said for and against a union,' and he was of the
opinion that 'a union upon equitable terms would be of the greatest

benefit to both Britain and Ireland, and add vastly to the power, wealth, and far-reaching influence of the British Empire.'

With regard to the controversial issue of the disposal of Irish surplus revenue, Dobbs advanced a practical suggestion which might have been acceptable to the Irish Parliament, but apparently did not commend itself to the British ministry. The suggestion or proposal was embodied in a memorandum entitled *A Proposal to extend and Increase the Trade, and settle the Countries upon the Labrador Coast*, which he submitted to Newcastle.[12] He suggested that the Government should buy out the Hudson's Bay Company with the Irish surplus revenue, and transfer the colony to the Irish establishment as a purely Irish possession. He envisaged the colony as being garrisoned by Irish troops who, having served some years there, would be given free grants of land and helped to settle thereon, a scheme somewhat similar to that adopted by Lord Halifax in Nova Scotia. In seeking approval for his proposition, Dobbs enlisted the support of his friend Colonel Selwyn, and also asked Lord Hertford to place the proposal before Lord Holderness, Secretary for State. In the course of a letter to Holderness, Dobbs wrote:

'The proposal as to encourage Ireland to be at the expense which may be done to the satisfaction of the British monarchy and without injuring any man's property by giving the proprietors of the Hudson's Bay Company the full value of what they make by the net balance of their trade, and opening that trade to all his Majesty's subjects of Britain and Ireland, upon condition of Ireland paying the purchase and being at the sole expense of settling, improving and defending these countries, which can in no way hurt, but greatly increase the trade as well as the sale of manufactures of Britain and Ireland, which trade is now locked up by the Company from Britain, and likely to continue so while in their hands, and as the Revenue of Ireland is now in so happy a situation as to pay our debt to be able to make the purchase, and be at the whole expense without any new tax or encroaching upon the Revenue granted for the support of the Establishment, and all exceedings and emergencies of Government, I humbly beg leave to lay the enclosed proposition and scheme before your Lordship for your consideration.' [13]

Holderness does not appear to have displayed any more interest in the scheme than his fellow ministers. Acutely disappointed, but more alive than the Government to the growing French threat to the British colonies in America, Dobbs wrote again to Newcastle:

'I hope you will pardon the freedom I have taken at several times in communicating my thoughts to your Lordship upon subjects beyond my sphere of action, and which your Lordship is entirely master of without any information I can give. I am therefore at a loss to know whether my correspondence or communicating any further thoughts which occur to me to promote the settlement and extend British trade throughout our North American Continent is in any way agreeable to your Lordship since the several papers I communicated by my late friend Colonel Selwyn upon the colony of Nova Scotia and also upon the improvement of our fur trade to your Lordship, and the proposal I sent last winter about the settlement of New Britain or the Labrador coast I have never known whether your Lordship received them or whether they were acceptable to your Lordship.'

He reminded Newcastle that a gentleman 'who has great experience and knowledge of our North American colonies has paid me in an epistle he has lately published a very high compliment which far exceeds any merit I can claim by my unfortunate attempts to serve my country.' Reverting to his Labrador scheme, he concluded:

'If the plan appears to be of public utility I would not give it to a clerk to transcribe since it ought not to be made publick until it be ready for execution, I therefore only communicated to Lord Holderness, also a few friends, Mr. Stone of Liverpool and Mr. Smith in London and consulted some merchants. If you disapprove of the Scheme, and the Ministers think proper not to countenance it, it is the last thing I shall probably ever trouble your Lordship and the Government with, but shall sit quietly down contented with my private lot after endeavouring for twenty years to guide my country without success.' [14]

The plans, proposals, and suggestions regarding the colonies, their trade, settlement and defence, which Dobbs submitted to successive ministries were not the vague and impracticable plans of a crank or busybody. On the contrary, they constituted a serious effort to awaken interest in colonial development, and bring home to the Government and the people the danger of neglecting the colonies, particularly in view of the growing expansionist policy of the French. Though his plans and proposals failed to find favour with the Government, they continued to arouse interest among the London merchants who were keenly aware of the gradual deterioration of British power and influence in America. And while the Labrador and Nova Scotia schemes lay unread in some Government office, John Hanbury invited Dobbs to join with him and other merchants in a new project—the Ohio Company of Virginia.

The Ohio Company was organised in 1748 by a group of influential

men, most of them Virginians, for the purpose of securing a share of
the Indian trade of the Alleghenies, and for the exploitation and settlement of the Ohio Valley. It was not entirely a speculative venture, but
a well-conceived scheme of imperialistic expansion, intended to bring
to a climax the struggle between Britain and France for possession of
North America.[15]

By the year 1748 the American frontier was moving westward with
increasing momentum, and the rich land and prosperous fur trade in
the region west of the mountains, especially the Ohio Valley, began to
attract the attention and interest of the merchant, settler, and trapper.
The lack of a definite colonisation policy, and the apparent indifference
of the British Government to the growing need for strengthening and
consolidating newly acquired territory, played into the hands of the
French, who were quick to realise that command of the Ohio was the
key to the rich hinterland of America, a fact long apparent to men like
Dobbs, Hanbury, and Dinwiddie. With the westward advance of
English settlement and encroachment from the north by the French,
it was clear by the end of 1748 that the Ohio Valley was the most vital
of any disputed territory in America. If the French gained the Ohio,
as Dobbs pointed out some years earlier, British expansion would be
seriously impeded, and French possessions in America would stretch
from Canada to Louisiana. To prevent this linking of French possessions, it was essential that the Ohio Valley should be settled and
strengthened, though the act of doing so would inevitably precipitate
war.

In Virginia, Thomas Lee, Thomas Cresap, Lawrence Washington, and others planned the formation of the Ohio Company, and
requested Sir William Gooch, the Governor, for a grant of land lying
on the western side of the Alleghenies.[16] Gooch was slow to accede to
the request, fearing that he might give offence to the French, but he
sent the petition to the Board of Trade. In the meantime the Virginians got in touch with Hanbury, and requested him to petition the
Board of Trade.[17] Hanbury, with whom Dobbs had been associated
for some years, thereupon presented a petition requesting a grant of
500,000 acres of land

'betwixt Romanettos and Buffalo Creek on the South Side of the River
Aligane otherwise the Ohio, and betwixt the two Creeks and the Yellow
Creek on the North side of the River, or such other part of the West of the
said Mountains as shall be adjuged most proper for that purpose, and that
200,000 acres of the said 500,000 acres be granted immediately.'

The purpose of the grant, the petition stated, was to enable the petitioners to make settlements, advance and strengthen the frontier, carry on trade with the Indians, and 'at the same time promote the consumption of our British Manufactures, enlarge our Commerce, increase our shipping and navigation, and extend your Majesty's empire in America.'[18]

The petition presented by Hanbury to the King on behalf of the Ohio Company contained the names of thirteen Virginians, and referred to the unnamed members of the Company as their Associates. Some time earlier, however, Hanbury had invited Dobbs, Robert Dinwiddie, who was later appointed Lieutenant-Governor of Virginia, and Samuel Smith, Dobbs's personal agent in London, to participate in the venture. Bailey notes that Dobbs was a distinct outsider as far as the Virginian aristocracy was concerned, but was, politically, a definite asset.[19] This, of course, is true, and Dobbs played an important part in the formation of the Ohio Company. In the first instance, he helped Hanbury to prepare the petition to the King, and exerted his influence in ruling circles to obtain the grant. The Ohio Company was not a speculative venture, but a sound imperial scheme.

> 'The leaders of the British Government,' Bailey writes, 'were not trusting England's future in the Ohio country and in the west to fate or an unequipped miscellaneous group of business adventurers. They were placing that future squarely on the shoulders of some of the most influential men in London and the colonies. With such a personnel as the backbone of this venture, the outlook appeared promising indeed.'[20]

While negotiations were taking place in London between Hanbury, Dobbs, and the Government, the formation of the Company was proceeding apace, and twenty shares of stock were issued with a subscribed capital of £4,000. In 1749, the King granted the Company 200,000 acres of land, with a promise of a further grant of 300,000 acres on either the northern or southern bank of the Ohio if the Company succeeded in settling the first grant; the land was given free of quit-rent for ten years, and the projectors agreed to settle 100 families thereon, and build two forts, one at or near the head of the Ohio River—this fort marked the beginnings of the town of Pittsburg.

Christopher Gist, an explorer of note, was employed by the Company to survey the land, and from his report the shareholders learnt that the territory comprised some of the best and richest land in America, which by careful exploitation was capable of giving a return beyond their wildest dreams.[21] Unfortunately, the chief difficulty facing the Company was the fact that French traders and settlers, both active and well armed, had encroached upon the territory. Despite the difficulties of enforcing their claim and settling the Ohio territory, because of the growing French threat, the Company went ahead with the project. Dobbs was enthusiastic, and displayed once more the pioneering zeal with which he essayed so many tasks in the past. In the spring of 1750 he wrote to Ward:

'I have an acct. that our Ohio Company of which I am a member goes on briskly, we have sent away £2,000 in goods to trade with the Indians, and the King has given us goods to give in presents to them. The French Government has sent threatening letters to our several Governors not to come near their limits which they extend far enough, but as we have over 10,000 Germans gone this year to Philadelphia alone, this besides what are gone to other colonies, and 3 or 4,000 more from Britain and Ireland, I shall laugh at their threats if our Commissaries protract the time and give up nothing . . ., and insist upon all unoccupy'd lands when purchas'd from the natives to which the French have no right but by the consent of the natives, and if we gain them our Germans will preserve our new boundaries.' [22]

In 1754, with the threat of war and the imminent danger of invasion by the French, the Ohio Company petitioned the Board of Trade for a further grant of 300,000 acres. This second petition was drawn up by Dobbs and signed by himself, Hanbury, Smith, and James Wardrop, all of whom constituted the Committee in England.[23] The need for enlarging the grant and settling the boundaries had become very real since the French erected a series of blockhouses on the Ohio and Allegheny River, which seriously threatened British settlement and trade in the Ohio Valley. Dinwiddie, a shareholder in the Ohio Company and Governor of Virginia, sought to discourage French encroachment; he dispatched young George Washington with a strong diplomatic protest to the French military commander, but this had no effect. A month later Washington was sent with a company of militia, but on encountering a French force he rashly opened fire, killing the French commander and forcing the French to retire. Washington's success was short-lived, for he was trapped in the fittingly named Fort Necessity by a superior French force and constrained to surrender.

Though fate was unkind to many of the pioneering companies of projectors in America, their contribution to American colonisation was very great in spite of the feeble support and encouragement of the Government of the day. Indeed, had the Government paid more heed to men like Dobbs and assisted their efforts in a more generous

manner, the story of British colonisation in America might have been
very different. Banta, in his *History of the Ohio,* commenting on the
neglect and lack of interest, not only in the development of the American colonies but in the welfare of the unfortunate settlers, remarks
that this neglect resulted, twenty-five years later, in the loss of these
colonies, not to the French, but to its own neglected people. The same
author reminds us that the Ohio Company was in the main responsible
for the ultimate fate of the Ohio Valley, but adds that little credit
accrued to the investors who 'presently lost their figurative shirts.' [24]
The Ohio Company was undoubtedly a direct challenge to France,
and led to the final struggle between Britain and France for supremacy
in America. Nobody realised this more clearly than Dobbs, and in one
of his later letters he said:

> 'I thank God for sparing me so long among so many contemporaries,
> with health and money sufficient as to finish what I engaged in, and live to
> see my long projected plan of driving the French out of the continent and
> I hope out of America . . . and what is a great addition to my pleasure is
> that I have been instrumental in so soon entering into this American war
> by my soliciting with Mr. Hanbury the grant to the Ohio Company,
> which was the means of bringing on the war before the French were pre-
> pared to begin their attack against our colonies.' [25]

Though the final fate of the Ohio Company occurred many years
later, its remaining history may be briefly summarised. From time to
time the Company's grants, privileges, and exemptions were extended
by the Crown, until in 1773 it was finally merged with the Grand
Ohio Company, but, as Banta notes, the merger was a gesture as
futile as may be imagined, for within two years of its consummation
the Crown of Britain ceased to have authority for granting Ohio River
land, and the Company died with the birth of the United States of
America. While the Ohio Company was a failure in so far as it failed
to recompense its shareholders, it marks an important milestone in
American history.

> 'Anyone who thinks of the Ohio Company as merely a land speculation
> scheme,' Bailey asserts, 'is doing scant justice to such great men as Colonel
> Thomas Lee, Lieutenant-Governor Robert Dinwiddie, Lawrence Wash-
> ington, Arthur Dobbs, and George Washington. These men, in the early
> years of the Company's history, were patriotic Virginians and Englishmen.
> Its political objectives were worthy and ultimately successful. History is
> often lenient in its judgement of success because it looks not to the immedi-
> ate but to the ultimate.' [26]

9

Governor Designate

FOR MANY years a steady stream of north of Ireland families sailed for America, and Dobbs found little difficulty in persuading many of them to settle on his land in North Carolina. In his efforts to make new settlements, he willingly defrayed the cost of transport, and on at least one occasion he chartered a ship to takes his settlers across the Atlantic. His enthusiasm in this direction was at times dampened by the not too glowing accounts he received of actual conditions in the province. Early in 1750, William Faris,[1] a settler in the Cape Fear region, wrote to him:

'I heard you thought of seeing this country this year yourself, but I fear the settlement is yet too much in its infancy to give you much satisfaction, and the accommodation in many parts so bad, that I doubt you would soon tire of it. The Fall is the best time to attempt it, October particularly, and your arriving just to that time is precarious in so long a voyage, and in the two preceding months agues are rife. I am certain if you were here a little time you would be better able to form a judgement than you can by any description, and should you send out a number of people, and they met with disappointments, and became unhappy, I know it would give you great uneasiness; so that whether you come or send I would by no means have you send many at first, a few well-chosen industrious farmers, either Irish or German . . . be settled with the necessary provisions. . . . The necessary tools of Hoes, Axes, etc., are easily got here if you dont send them, with a few for a carpenter & blacksmith which are useful hands in a new settlement, with nails, hinges, etc., and a few Cooper's tools. Course striped duffel blankets & course bed ticks will be necessary with low priced clothes or house furniture, viz., Potts, Panns, etc. Course shoes, and cheap pumps or brogues with stockings, hatts, etc., will be wanted, and if you send many people, plenty of oatmeal or grits may be useful over here after they arrive.'[2]

Faris did not speak of all the difficulties encountered by settlers, but he warned Dobbs of the danger of sending too many at a time, particularly if they were insufficiently supplied with food and equipment to tide them over the first season. Rowan and others, however, viewed his enthusiasm with considerable misgivings. Indeed, about the time that Faris wrote, Dobbs had been informed that a white woman was murdered by Indians on one of his settlements. In spite of warnings, and the need for exercising care and caution, Dobbs, with the ebullient enthusiasm of a child with a new toy, continued to provide his quota of settlers. In a letter to Rowan in April 1751, he wrote:

'This I hope will be delivered to you by Robert Milhouse who with Mr. Samuel Wyly and their families, and several other of my tenants, neighbours and friends go to settle in North Carolina, and have freighted a ship from Dublin to land them in Cape Fear River at Brunswyck, it is to them and their ancestors[?] I have disposed of one of the 12,800 acre tracts, or two half tracts in the great survey, number two and five at £500, or a shilling per acre forever free of quit-rent to Lady day '55. I want you to befriend them and assist them in their settlement and advise them for the best. They want to have it in their option to settle on my land on the Black river, and take that as so much of the 12,800 acres. I have agreed with them on paying a fair rent fixed at the time they enter into it for they will fear planters if they settle at Peedee, so that if they agree upon that I give you power to give them possession of it. Their reason for deserving it arose from your letter to me acquainting me that a woman had been killed on my land by an Indian, so that until they arrive there they cant tell how far it may be safe for them to settle on the Peedee till most of the Planters fix in their neighbourhood.'[3]

Dobbs was not unaware of the difficulties and hazards encountered by white settlers, and at all times showed a thoughtful interest in the welfare and care of those whom he sent to North Carolina. This interest is perhaps best exemplified by the fact that despite his age he was quite willing to face these difficulties, and start a new life himself in the colony. He wrote to Rowan:

'I still have some hopes of visiting you in Carolina, and hope, if I keep my health, of fixing my affairs here with my son, so as to carry over my second son with me, by which time my friend Milhouse will have a lodge built where I can stay when I go over, till I am better provided with a house.'[4]

While Rowan was willing to help Dobbs and do what he could for his settlers, he was doubtful from long experience in the province if his efforts to make settlements were correct. In a letter to Samuel Smith, he wrote:

'Mr. Dobbs was pleased to write to me in April last, and mention his sending out some families for his land on Peedee. I have advice from Cape Fear that the ship was arrived there. I wish the method may answer his expense if he is at the charge of their freight, but I would not recommend it to any friend to attempt transporting and settling on land in this country. People who come from Europe have extraordinary expectations formed of any new enterprise going commonly far beyond whatever can succeed. If they engage on conditions to settle lands and they come here and see the affairs of the country that they can take up land on easier terms than perhaps they contract for, they grow out of humour with all that has been done for them, and seek all means to be disengaged and seldom do anything for themselves or benefactors. I hinted this much to Mr. Dobbs when in England, and told him that tale of the people who were sent over by Mr. McCulloh and others to make settlements all miscarryed.' [5]

Despite Rowan's advice, Dobbs continued to pursue his active policy of settlement. This policy was dictated by the twofold idea of settling his own grants and at the same time strengthening the colonies to counteract French expansionist policy in the new world. Since the end of the Austrian War of Succession and the subsequent treaty of Aix-la-Chapelle in 1748, French influence had increased not only in Europe but in America and elsewhere. Dobbs and statesmen like Pitt were fully alive to the dangers inherent in the complacent and selfish policy of the Pelham-Newcastle administration. It was clear that a lack of serious interest in the American colonies, and the policy of permitting them to fend for themselves under, for the most part, the care of incompetent, disinterested, and inept governors, served Britain and the colonies ill. Dobbs insisted, both in practice and in letter, on the need for a vigorous policy of settlement in America in order to counteract French designs. His failure over many years to make any serious impression on the Government in so far as his ideas on the colonies were concerned, at length compelled him to seek a role wherein he could play a more active part in British colonial development. With this end in view, he wrote, early in 1751, to his friend Selwyn:

'The favour you have always been pleased to show me and approbation of my endeavours to serve the publick, encourages me to apply to you for your countenance and recommendation in an application I am making not only to serve myself but also have it in my power to serve the government and British interests whilst I have health and strength to live an active life, which is for a government on the continent of America, where I could hope to be of service not only in promoting such improvements as might be use-full to the British commerce, but also to extend our commerce into the continent by taking proper methods to instruct and civilise the natives, and so lay a foundation for their becoming Christians, and promoting a lasting friendship with them, by giving them an equitable trade, and good usage would make them a Bulwark to our colonies against the French and prevent their encroachment, and gain the trade upon the lakes and so break all the French scheme of uniting Louisiana to Canada, and so far strengthen our colonies against another war, as by our Indian allies we might secure the whole northern continent from the French, and only by confronting them in their own way would give no handle to break with them until a proper opportunity happens to make them pay for their perfidy and encroachment.

'With this view I have applied to Lord Hertford who has been so good as to recommend me warmly to Lord Holderness who has received it with great friendship, but my Lord thinks it very proper that I should procure a recommendation to his grace of Newcastle that I may have his approbation and if possible his recommendation to Lord Holderness which from your goodness to me, and my Lord Primate's being so good as to interest himself in my favour I have hopes will be attended with success.' [6]

Selwyn's influence at this juncture was not inconsiderable, for he had just been appointed Secretary to the Prince of Wales. Dobbs's patron, Lord Hertford, was at this time Lord of the Bedchamber, and his friend Lord Holderness held the office of Secretary of State. Unfortunately, Selwyn died a few days later, and Dobbs lost a very good friend at Court, but this sudden loss did not prevent him pressing his claim. A week or two later he wrote to Newcastle. 'The goodness you have always shown to me,' he said, 'encourages me to apply for a governor upon the continent of America, and my endeavours would entitle me to your favour.' [7] In this letter he emphasised the need for cultivating friendship with the Indians whom the French were using for depredatory raids on isolated English settlements. He also pointed out the immediate necessity for strengthening the colonies which he felt were likely to fall easy victims to French aggression.

So far, letters and appeals seem to have been in vain, and when the Pelham administration was reorganised in 1752, Dobbs wrote again to Newcastle:

'Your constant goodness and friendship to me upon all my applications to you, emboldens me to put in again for your favour, and at the same time express the pleasure of your Lordship's appointment at the Head of the Council. Lord Hertford has been so kind to recommend me to Lord Holderness for a government in North America upon a vacancy, and as your Lordship has always approved of my endeavours, and shown

a steady friendship for me that you will upon this occasion grant me your
favour in whatever manner may be most agreeable to you.' [8]

As in his former letter, he set down his thoughts and ideas on the
American colonies. He deplored the complacency of the Government
following the peace of Aix-la-Chapelle. Britain had learnt nothing
from the wars of the Austrian Succession, while France, though
beaten on the Continent, had lost none of her North American possessions and little indeed of her influence. The danger that Britain
would revert to her pre-war state of unpreparedness was very real,
and prompted Dobbs to remark: 'Our misfortune has been that when
we make peace we never think of strengthening ourselves and preparing for a new war.' [9] These words were to be repeated by many
other far-seeing Englishmen, including Pitt who, like Dobbs, felt
that the treaty of Aix-la-Chapelle, instead of strengthening Britain's
position in America, tended to weaken it. The position, however, was
not entirely irreparable, and Dobbs was still of the opinion, despite the
Treaty's confirmation of French possessions, that the Government
should take active steps to contain the French, and prevent any
encroachment or expansion. He went further and suggested a plan for
the eventual expulsion of the French from the American continent.
In closing his letter to Newcastle, he wrote:

'Whilst I have strength I could wish to have it in my power to assist in
so laudable an undertaking, and if your Lordship thinks me worthy in
being an instrument to procure so great an advantage to my king and
country it would lay me under a perpetual obligation to your Lordship,
as you have it in your power to set the wheels agoing to bring such a scheme
about.'

Dobbs spent the next few months canvassing his influential friends.
In the meantime Governor Johnston died, and Dobbs, with the aid of
his patron Lord Hertford, pressed his claims for the vacant governorship. This time his efforts were successful, and towards the end of the
year 1752, he wrote from Hertford's London house to his son Conway:

'My being governor of North Carolina is so far agreed to that Lord Halifax expects to lay it before the king before the holidays for his approbation,
and has recommended to me Mr. Pownal, the clerk of the Board of Trade,
to take out my commission, which if done before the holidays I shall go to
Bath, and be in town again when they do business.' [10]

As he was unable to take out his commission, he went to Bath,
where he spent the Christmas and New Year enjoying the mild cli-

mate and taking the waters. While at Bath he had his portrait painted by the then fashionable artist William Hoare. The portrait depicts a man of character, energy, and ability, and though Dobbs was almost sixty-three years old at the time, the impression is that of a much younger man. The artist skilfully suggests the many activities of the sitter, who, compass in hand, studies a map of the Arctic regions. There is considerable life and vigour about the portrait, which gives the impression of a tall, active man, austere and spartan in an age noted for the flabbiness of dissipation.[11]

Dobbs returned to London about the middle of January, and, full of that optimism which governmental dilatoriness could not subdue, he wrote to Conway: 'I am uncertain yet whether my instructions will be made out whilst I stay so as to go over from Ireland to Carolina, or whether I will return here before I go.'[12] In February, Pownal wrote to him that the Board of Trade had postponed consideration of his affairs for a few weeks, and though his appointment was confirmed from 25th January, 1753, almost a year and a half elapsed before he sailed for North Carolina.

In the meantime, despite the fact that his patience was sorely tried, he continued to promote various colonisation schemes, and made an effort to get a group of French Protestants, experienced in the culture of silkworms and the winding of silk, to settle in North Carolina. When this scheme failed, he decided to approach the Moravians, who had successfully established a prosperous colony in the province. He drew up plans for bringing a group of them from Europe to settle on his lands. The Moravians, he suggested, would 'not only go into the silk industry, but also send missionaries among the Indians, and begin my scheme to civilise and make friendship with them.'[13] While devising these plans, he asked Conway to make enquiries among his tenants whether any of them would care to accompany him to North Carolina. He wrote: 'I will engage a ship from Liverpool well appointed to carry them over, and I will take over tradesmen of several kinds.'

Though now very actively engaged in making preparations for his departure for North Carolina, Dobbs still showed a deep interest in Irish affairs, and particularly in the development of his Irish estate. In a letter to Conway, he informed him that he was sending him 'a barrel of split peas and a catalogue of garden seeds,' and he wanted to know what 'is being done by the labourers as I believe you have put a stop to the building for this winter.' At this time a large number of men were employed in the rebuilding and enlarging of Castle Dobbs, and so that they might not be idle, he instructed Conway that 'they had better finish any of the March ditches when the weather is proper for it, and at other times work in the garden, or set up the old ditches in the kiln garden, and make up any deficiencies in the apple trees that are wanting in the garden or elsewhere so as to plant out young trees that have been grafted.'

The traveller Pococke who visited Castle Dobbs in 1752 noted the improvements being carried out there. The old castle, he wrote, was in a low situation behind a hill, but 'Mr. Dobbs is now building on a very fine spot on rising ground.' [14] Dobbs's attachment to his old servants is evident from his letters to Conway, and in one he tells him to 'ask Nelly Hay if she and Arch. McDowell will venture to go with me to Carolina for I shall want both a cook and a mill-wright there.' Both agreed to go with their master and actually sailed for North Carolina some time before he did, together with other North of Ireland settlers, including the Reverend Alec Stewart; unfortunately, McDowell died on the voyage out.[15]

While Dobbs awaited the final drafting of his instructions by the Board of Trade, he returned to Ireland to take part in the bitter and hotly contested Parliamentary debates in the year 1753, when the Government suffered defeat on the question of the disposal of the Irish surplus revenue. In the same year, another contentious matter arose, when Boyle and Malone moved that Arthur Neville, who assisted Dobbs and later succeeded him as Surveyor-General, should be removed from office for failing to comply with a previous resolution of the House that 'he at his own expense should rebuild and put in order certain barracks for which he had been previously paid.' [16] Neville was openly charged by the opposition with the embezzlement of public funds, but he was a Member of the House, and had the support of the governing faction, including Primate Stone and the Secretary of State for Ireland, Lord George Sackville. The opposition in Parliament dragged Neville's peculations into the House, and saw therein an opportunity to defeat the Government, behind which Neville sheltered. The motion for Neville's expulsion occasioned a heated debate, and ended with the defeat of the Government by a majority of eight votes. Dobbs voted with the defeated minority. A fortnight later, the debate on the disposal of the Irish surplus revenue took place, and again the Government was defeated, this time by a majority of five votes.

The effect of these victories by the Patriot Party gave new hope to the growing body of intelligent people who rightly objected to the subservient role of the Irish Parliament, and the vested power of the

'English interest' in Ireland. Even the masses, who had no direct representation, were stirred by the defeat of the Government, and when the result of the division on the disposal of the surplus was made known, a multitude escorted the Patriot members home in triumph; bearing lighted torches and burning sheaves of furze on pitchforks, they marched before the Speaker's carriage through streets ablaze with bonfires, while the bells of the city rang out joyful peals.[17]

Dobbs, by his support of the Government, found himself in the opposite camp to many of his friends, among whom were young Bernard Ward, Colonel Upton, his fellow-member for Carrickfergus, Robert Echlin, a near kinsman, and many others; even in his own constituency, his action in identifying himself with the Government, and especially with Dorset, Sackville, and Primate Stone, found little support. For more than twenty-five years he represented the town of Carrickfergus in the Irish Parliament, but now, on the eve of his departure for North Carolina, the Corporation at a special meeting presented an address of thanks to Upton for voting against the Government. 'Such a Senator,' declared the Mayor, Sheriff, and Burgesses, 'adds lustre to his station in the Legislature, and commands respect to that august body.' Dobbs no doubt felt rebuked for having voted the other way, but at the same time he opined that the Patriot Party was doing the country harm. In a letter to his son, early in 1754, he wrote: 'As to Irish affairs I wish they may end well, but if party [feeling] runs high, and they cant cool, things must turn out ill then, and many will take sanctuary in my colony where I shall prepare settlements for my friends.'[18]

Pending the completion of his commission as Governor of North Carolina and the drawing up of his instructions, Dobbs put his own personal affairs in order, and settled his estates 'in the counties of Antrim and Kildare, or elsewhere in the kingdom of Ireland,' on Conway, and made all the necessary preparations for his voyage to America to 'commence a new life.' However, the vexatious delays continued and on 31st January, 1754, he wrote to his son:

'I should be in America by this time . . . My affairs are not yet come to at the Board of Trade. I expect it this week, but something relative to Nova Scotia intervened . . . which has postponed it, but this day week I expect that it will be first for next Tuesday, and once it is begun they will proceed on it until it is over. The first thing will be my appointment. Once that is fixed the rest will soon be dispatched.'[19]

In the same letter he informed Conway that a ship 'with my French families is arrived at New Bern,' and added that his efforts to secure additional colonists were meeting with success. 'I have a gentleman,' he wrote, 'who will undertake to send over annually 1,000 Palatines and Germans, one third of which will pay their own passage, or he will engage to carry them over at 20s. a head, paid by the colony, so that we shall soon settle all our lands.'

During the next few weeks Dobbs spent much of his time with the officers of the Board of Trade helping to draw up the instructions given to all governors for the correct discharge of their office. He also submitted a memorial to the King in Council 'for ordinance and standards for a new fort erected at Cape Fear, and a memorial to the Board of Trade to get a Company of Foot to garrison the fort and for some other forts that are bound to be built in the colony.' [20] He also made provision for the future payment of his salary, and in a letter to Ward he stated that he had presented a memorial to the Treasury 'for an appointment of my salary from this side, as the quit-rents at present are just sufficient to pay the Establishment which is many thousand pounds in arrears.' [21] This request was agreed to, and Dobbs's salary was paid in Britain; unlike his predecessors, therefore, he was not dependent upon the colony for his salary, nor likely to find it many years in arrears as in the case of Johnston. [22]

During the long period of his enforced wait in London, Dobbs continued to impress upon the Government the need for a vigorous course of action against the French. The advice he now proffered could no longer be brushed aside or looked upon as the imperialistic clamour of a headstrong patriot. French action, particularly the erection of a series of fortifications on the Ohio, now threatened the British colonies, and a state of undeclared war ensued. In a letter to Conway, Dobbs remarked that, as a result of his insistent demands, his government in North Carolina had been instructed 'to repel force with force,' and he added: 'We shall erect forts, and plant beyond the mountains in an extreme fine country finely watered and with the best land in the world.' [23]

The French threat to the British colonies in America had grown more apparent during the last few years, and by 1753 it was fairly clear that the French were not going to submit to British claims in the Ohio Valley, and were in fact eager to fight for supremacy in America. The first move in this direction was to drive the English traders and settlers from the Ohio Valley, and erect a series of blockhouses on the Ohio and Allegheny rivers, and thus bar British expansion and settlement in a westward direction. The action of the French was particularly galling for the gentlemen of Virginia and the English prospectors of the Ohio Company who, keenly alive to the French threat, saw all hope of settling their newly acquired land seriously menaced by the erection of the strongly armed Fort Duquesne. Rowan, in the course of a letter to Samuel Smith which was transmitted to Dobbs, remarked pessimistically, 'I am afraid our Ohio Company goes badly.' [24]

In America, Dinwiddie, the Governor of Virginia, the province most seriously affected, did all he could to discourage the French from their warlike preparations, but as already noted, his initial efforts, under the able colonial officer George Washington, were utterly futile through no fault of his own. Efforts to bring about a union of the colonies, and present a solid front against the common enemy were defeated, either by the ineptitude of the several governors or the short-sighted policy of the colonial assemblies.[25] At home, fretting and impatient, Dobbs continued to bombard the Government with briefs and memoranda in an effort to awaken it to the serious situation developing; he was no longer a lone voice, however, for Pitt was beginning to stir the nation into action. From America, Dinwiddie penned urgent appeals for men, money, and munitions, but his appeals and the ominous rumblings of war scarcely disturbed the complacent Ministry. At length, harassed by the insistent demands of Governors Dinwiddie and Shirley, which were vigorously supported by the merchant prospectors Hanbury, Campbell, Huey, and Crymble, and forced by the rising tide of public opinion, the Government could no longer close its eyes, or ignore the warlike threat of the French.

Two years had now elapsed since Dobbs was appointed Governor of North Carolina. Some of this delay was due to the fact that in 1753 the Board of Trade was being reconstituted under the able guidance of Lord Halifax, who felt that instructions formerly issued to governors had become obsolete in many respects and that a general revision was necessary. The appointment of a new Governor to North Carolina furnished the occasion for a revision of instructions and also permitted a long and thorough examination into the affairs of the province.[26] However, the swift tide of events in America brought the delay to a speedy end, and early in June, Dobbs was instructed to proceed with all haste to Spithead and sail with an armed convoy assembled there. His plans for taking ship from Liverpool and carrying with him a number of settlers were hurriedly cancelled, and with scarcely time for farewells he joined the convoy at Spithead.

Some historians of North Carolina state that Dobbs set sail for

America with a host of needy relatives and friends earmarked for posts in the colony; in point of fact Dobbs embarked on the man-of-war *Garland*, accompanied only by his son Edward, his nephew Richard Spaight, and a few personal servants.[27] The voyage to America was dismal and tiresome in the extreme, and was dogged by foul and bitter weather. For almost twelve weeks the *Garland* and attendant ships made slow headway in heavy seas, and in a severe and unpredictable storm off the coast of Virginia the *Garland* lost a mainmast. On 6th October the ships reached Hampton in Virginia, where Governor Dinwiddie welcomed Dobbs and escorted him to Williamsburg.

Dinwiddie, an energetic, experienced, and zealous Scotsman, and Governor of Virginia for two years, had arranged a meeting of the neighbouring governors in order to draw up a co-ordinate plan to contain the French pending the arrival of a British expedition. This meeting had been timed to coincide with the arrival of Dobbs, who brought with him instructions from the Government, some £10,000 in specie, a Crown credit for a like sum, arms for North Carolina, and a commission appointing Governor Sharpe of Maryland commander of all forces 'to be raised on this part of the continent to protect his Majesty's Dominions from the encroachments and devastations of his presumptuous enemies.' [28] This move to unite the colonial forces under a single command had been voiced by Benjamin Franklin in a stirring appeal some months earlier, in pursuance of which pressure was brought to bear on the Government by Hanbury, Loudoun, and Bedford in London, who supported the claims of Sharpe for the post. Sharpe was the best choice among the governors, for he was an efficient and able administrator but, unfortunately, he was not a professional soldier.

While awaiting the arrival of Governor Sharpe, Dobbs rested from his tiring voyage, and spent a little time studying colonial life first hand, though, in this respect, Virginia did not give quite a true picture, as it was considerably in advance of its sister colonies, and boasted a higher standard of living. Williamsburg at this time contained about two hundred houses, mainly timber built, and the population exceeded a thousand people, white and black. Though the town was small, it was regularly laid out in parallel streets intersected by others at right angles, and boasted a handsome square in the centre through which ran the principal street, one of the most spacious in America, three-quarters of a mile in length and above one hundred feet wide, at the opposite ends of which were the college and the Capitol. The Governor's palace where Dobbs lodged was 'tolerably good, one of the best upon the continent,' [29] and here he was entertained with Virginian liberality.

On 19th October, Sharpe reached Williamsburg, and Dobbs presented him with the King's commission and his instructions. An interested spectator of this meeting of the governors of Maryland, Virginia, and North Carolina was George Washington, who called to see Dinwiddie following some disturbing incidents after his defeat by the French at Fort Necessity. Washington 'found the Governor busy in the entertainment of distinguished men, and in the planning of a larger war with greater means.' [30] Quite obviously the 'plan of Operations, consulted and agreed upon by Gov'r Dinwiddie of Virg'a; Gov'r Dobbs of N. Carolina, and Gov'r Sharpe of M'y'd,' [31] was little more than an expedient to meet the French challenge, for nothing practical could be attempted with the meagre resources at Sharpe's command.

Two days later, Dobbs set out from Williamsburg for New Bern, which he reached on the last day of October, having lost one day at Edenton 'by a contrary wind so fresh that the ferry boat could not pass the ferry which was above eight miles over.' [32] His friend Mathew Rowan, President of the Assembly and Acting Governor, and James Murray, the Attorney-General, met him at Bath, and accompanied him to New Bern, where he was received by two other members of the Council—John Rutherford and Samuel Swann. 'I had but four to swear me in,' Dobbs wrote, perhaps a little pettishly, but added: 'As it was chiefly a matter of form, tho' material to begin business upon, I took the several oaths required, and then administered them to the Councillors present.' [33] Thus at the age of sixty-six, Dobbs commenced the most difficult task of his life, for the Governorship of an American province was no longer a sinecure nor an office for weaklings or neophytes.[34]

North Carolina

THE APPOINTMENT of Dobbs as Governor of North Carolina was received with enthusiam by the people of the province, who, though naturally distrustful and not a little tired of royal governors, were weary of strife and years of misgovernment. The exigencies of the times were no small factors in promoting a desire for harmony in the administration, and the imminent threat of war welded the colonists together. Other factors contributing to the manifest desire for harmony and goodwill between the administration and the people was the knowledge that Dobbs was one of those most strongly opposed to Johnston's governorship, and he was known to be keenly interested in the economic and social well-being of the province; further, he had orders to repeal some of the more unpopular laws enacted by his predecessor.[1]

When Johnston died in 1752, Nathaniel Rice, President of the Council, assumed office pending the appointment of a new Governor. Rice was an old and feeble man who died six months later. Mathew Rowan being 'next in Council' took the oath of President, and exercised the duties of Governor until the arrival of Dobbs. North Carolina was fortunate in having as acting Governor a man of Rowan's calibre; he directed the affairs of the province with vigour, prudence, and ability during the difficult period that marked the beginning of the long struggle between France and Britain for supremacy in North America.

The opening stages of this struggle were marked by the pronounced efforts of the French to control the string of lakes and connecting rivers stretching almost from Quebec, the French capital in the north, to the Mississippi. In order, as we have seen, to extend and consolidate their possessions and pave the way to a linking up with Louisiana, the French had erected a line of forts from the Great Lakes to the Ohio, and thus strongly fortified they claimed possession of Virginian territory then in the process of settlement by the Ohio Company; this claim was based solely on the fact that if settlements were made in the Ohio Valley, French dreams of barring British expansion in a westward direction and linking Canada with Louisiana would come to naught. Though wholly unprepared for war, the Government in Britain issued hurried instructions to the various colonial governors to ally their provinces, and raise the necessary troops for their mutual defence, promising them immediate aid in money, men, and munitions.

Governor Dinwiddie, acting on instructions, demanded the withdrawal of French troops from Virginian territory. The demand was not acceded to. Thereupon he raised a small force for the defence of the province, and called upon President Rowan and the governors of the other colonies to come to the aid of Virginia. With commendable energy North Carolina answered Dinwiddie's appeal, and the Assembly voted £12,000 to raise and equip a force of 750 men. The newly-formed force was placed under the able command of Colonel James Innes. Incidentally, North Carolina had the distinction of being the first colony to send men outside its own frontier in defence of the American colonies.[2] Unfortunately, Rowan's prompt action was rendered nugatory by a series of events over which he had no control. Raising and equipping troops was one thing, but maintaining them in the field was quite another matter, and when Dinwiddie pointed out that he had neither money nor means to maintain or pay the North Carolina contingent, Rowan was constrained to reduce his force by a little more than half; even this force was larger than that raised by Dinwiddie in his own threatened province. The maintenance of the North Carolina troops in Virginia presented a series of problems, for the province had neither gold nor silver specie, and its paper money was not current beyond its frontier.

The unpreparedness of the colonies, lacking trained soldiers, munitions of war, and a mutually co-ordinated plan, was apparent from the outset. Dinwiddie, a capable Governor, was not a military commander, and Sharpe of Maryland lacked military training and the forceful personality to grasp leadership. The other governors showed little enterprise and were content to await events. At home in Britain an inept Government appeared almost undisturbed, and so uninformed that a dispatch sent to Dinwiddie contained enclosures for transmission to Dobbs though he had not yet left England!

Dinwiddie gave all the appearance of a panic-stricken man, and pending the arrival of Dobbs scarcely knew where to turn. It is clear from his dispatches that he placed considerable reliance upon Dobbs and anticipated his arrival with the faith of a lonely and desolate soul.

When difficulties arose regarding the maintenance of the North Carolina troops, he could only advise Colonel Innes to transmit his disbursement and charges to 'Mr. Dobbs who is hourly expected.' [3] A little later in the course of a dispatch to James Abercrombie, the Virginian agent in London, he charged that the North Carolina Assembly

> 'have conducted their forces with great improvidence, allowing every private man 3s. per day while in Carolina, in short they have exhausted the whole money before they joined the other forces. They have all mutinied for want of proper discipline. I wish Mr. Dobbs was arrived, probably he may reconcile things.' [4]

Dinwiddie's charge of mutiny is harsh and appears to have been made to conceal his own failure to provide for the men. When the Virginian troops under Washington were defeated at Great Meadows, Dinwiddie ordered Colonel Innes to fill up the ranks of Washington's troop, and march over the mountains to meet the French. He provided neither food nor money for the North Carolinians, who thereupon deserted and returned home. The depletion of Washington's force occasioned a wrathful letter from Dinwiddie to Innes in which he wrote: 'Mr. Dobbs, y'r Gov'r, I expect very soon in the *Garland* man of war into York River; he being under orders to consult with me on the present Exigen't of our Affairs. I c'd wish you was here to represent to him fully the Miscond't from the Beginning of y'r regim't.' [5]

The task of containing the French and maintaining an army in the field was quite beyond Dinwiddie's resources, and to make matters worse he was at loggerheads with the Virginian Assembly. He thereupon instructed Innes to suspend operations until the spring, but asked him to maintain his troops, build a magazine, and 'mount your guns near it for defence.' [6] Innes, with troops whom he could neither pay nor feed, and faced with the prospect of being closed up in a fortified post was compelled to disband a great part of his Carolina troop, who returned home with their arms and what horses and transport they could lay their hands upon. The understandable action of the North Carolina men was naturally misconstrued as wholesale desertion.

Throughout the year 1754 the French and colonial troops faced one another, skirmishing for position, both sides aware that a full-scale war was not far distant. When Dobbs arrived in America with Sharpe's commission, arms, and specie, he also brought the heartening news that a fully equipped army would sail from England in the spring. Pending the arrival of this army, the three governors decided to

assemble one thousand colonial troops as soon as possible and attempt
the capture of the French fort on the Monongahela, a key position in
the Ohio Valley, and hold it until the English arrived and were able to
launch an offensive. The governors also agreed to erect a fort on the
Ohio which would deny the French the use of the river in a southward
direction, and strengthen Fort Cumberland at Will's Creek on the
Potomac so that it could be used as a magazine and base for future
operations.[7] These plans were purely defensive, for there was very
little the colonists could do to drive the French from their strong
positions on the Ohio, especially as the colonists and their governors
appeared to be more concerned with their own domestic affairs than
the French threat to Virginia. In a dispatch to Lord Halifax shortly
after conferring with Dobbs and Sharpe, Dinwiddie conveyed the
sense of isolation and hopelessness he and others experienced in the
face of French threats; he wrote:

> 'The Invasion and wicked designs of the French on the Ohio has given
> me a Continual uneasiness, w'ch was increased by the supine and unac-
> countable obstinacy of the Assemblies of the different colonies on this
> Con't, y't tho' they were convinced of the progress they made, and the
> threat'g speeches they gave out they c'd not be roused to grant suitable
> supplies for conduct'g an Expedition so necessary for their safety. This, my
> Lord, is my unhappy situation, and prevented my executing his Majesty's
> Com'ds with such spirit and Resolut'n as the emergency of our Affairs
> required; however with the few men and little money I have done every-
> thing in my power.' [8]

Fully aware of the dangerous and critical situation facing the
colonies, Dobbs, on his arrival at New Bern, called a meeting of the
North Carolina Assembly. Pending the arrival of the members, he dispatched a hurried questionnaire to all the county militia commanders,
asking among other things for an immediate muster, a complete return
of the serving officers and men, and full particulars of any arms and
munitions in store. He hoped to have this information available when
the Assembly met. The returns showed a very unsatisfactory state of
affairs. Most of the officers complained that their men failed to muster,
and almost without exception they stated they were without equipment; at random we note: Captain Davis for Bladen County, 'We
have no equipment'; Captain Craven of Chowan County, 'We have
no arms'; Captain Munden, Pasquotank County, 'There is no arms,
nor ammunition belonging to His Majesty's stores in said regiment';
Captain Day, New Hanover, 'We have no arms or ammunition'; and

so it was with the rest of the counties—Tyrrell, Orange, Carteret, Anson, and Granville.[9] Having just come from a council of war, this state of affairs was profoundly disturbing to the new Governor.

The hastily convened Assembly met at New Bern on 12th December. Dobbs, at the outset of a vigorous address, reminded the members that the true basis of all good government must be really Christian.

'The first and greatest principle,' he said, 'and the foundation of all social happiness is the knowledge of true religion, and the practice of true morality and virtue, to know, love and adore the divine Being as we ought, and to obey the precepts He has revealed to us, so I think it is my duty in the first place to recommend to you the providing of a proper fund to support a sufficient number of Learned pious clergymen to reside in the Province.' [10]

This was an auspicious and pious start consonant with the religious outlook of Dobbs. He followed on this by reminding the members of their second duty—loyalty to their King, a duty that could best be proved by enacting laws to ensure the payment of quit-rents to the Crown. He then outlined briefly the new legislation he considered necessary for the proper government of the province, and asked the Assembly to pass effectual laws 'to secure your peace and properties and obtain your rights; to have justice distributed in the easiest and speediest manner without dilatory law proceedings.' He requested them, in the course of the session, to provide laws for promoting trade and industry, and 'lay our Indian traders under proper regulations, and to promote an Intimacy and Friendship and living in harmony with our Indian neighbours and allies so that we may be enabled to civilize and make them industrious, and to incorporate with them with Christian Benevolence.'

Having outlined a course of social and economic legislation, Dobbs turned to the all-important matter of defence against the French.

'I am commanded by his Majesty,' he said, 'to recommend to you in the strongest manner to provide a supply to assist the colony of Virginia whose country is invaded and his Majesty's troops slaughtered for endeavouring to repel these Invaders. The fire which has caught your neighbours' house has lately spread into your own, your religion, liberty and property are all at stake if not repelled and drove back to their inhospitable colonies. But as this subject is of the utmost importance and it will be tedious to explain the French plan calculated for the ruin of Britain and these colonies at this time; as soon as you fall upon business I shall lay it before you in a more ample manner that you may see the necessity of a speedy and effectual supply.' [11]

This address was well received by the Assembly and the members expressed their thanks to the Governor, and assured him that the legislation he proposed would be carried out with dispatch. They also acknowledged

> 'a lively sense of his Majesty's paternal care and tenderness in entrusting the Government to a Gentleman whose benevolent character and experience in Publick Affairs gives us the most sanguine hopes that under his prudent administration an end may be put to all the divisions under which this Province has already too long groaned and that peace and happiness may succeed party and rancour.' [12]

With this promising start the Assembly settled down to business, and it would seem that much of the bitterness and divided loyalties of the past were merged in a more peaceful and friendly atmosphere. True to his promise that he would deal more fully with the critical situation arising from 'the grand plan of France to ruin and distress the British colonies,' Dobbs submitted a stirring statement to the Council and Assembly.[13] In his statement he made no effort to disguise his hatred of the French and his fervid zeal for the destruction of French power which 'for nearly two centuries laid a plan for enslaving Europe by ruining the liberties of the Germanick body and Protestant interest of Europe.' In the course of his statement he traced briefly the rise and growth of Bourbon France, but pointed out that in spite of 'Gallick' intrigues

> 'which enabled the French to acquire a Dominion more extensive and rich than any empire ever known on the Globe, the Prudence, magnanimity and steady conduct of our most Gracious King, the Father of his People, who supported by the Courage, Wealth and naval power of the British Empire . . . hath defeated the Gallick future schemes in Europe.'

This defeat, Dobbs pointed out, only enraged the French, who, realising 'that British liberties and Protestant succession cant be conquered or reduced,' laid a plan 'to ruin British commerce by confining, invading and Conquering all our American colonies.' This plan to enslave and conquer the American colonies was a matter of immediate importance. Already, Dobbs reminded the members, France, 'contrary to the most solemn treaties,' had deprived Britain of the greater and best part of Nova Scotia, and formed settlements on the St. John's to ruin the trade of New England and the Northern Colonies. Now they were stirring up the Indians and erecting forts from Canada to Louisiana to 'distress and confine our colonies betwixt the mountains and the Eastern Ocean . . . and so forming a chain of above 2,000 miles to prevent our corresponding or trading with our Indian allies.' This scheme to enslave the colonies was, he claimed, 'hatched in hell and supported by the Church of Rome.'

In an appeal for unity he said that 'the French imagining (for which they have some ground) that the several colonies are like a rope of sand each guided by selfish partial views, and that each planter is more wedded to his own private gain than to defend the Rights of his Community, or of the neighbouring Colonies.' If this French view were right, which he doubted, then 'we must submit to be slaves to France, become their hewers of wood and Drawers of water, supporting them with enormous taxes.' He did not believe they would accept this state, nor were they likely to fall into it, for 'God Almighty, who by his Providence under the conduct of our Messiah hath in many remarkable instances defeated all Popish schemes when the Protestant interest and Liberties of Britain seemed to be on the brink of ruin.'

In a fervent appeal for an all-out effort to defeat the French, Dobbs continued:

> 'In this critical situation let his Majesty's faithful subjects of the Colony of North Carolina shew that we are true sons of Britain whose ancestors have been ever famous for defending their valuable Religion and Liberty, and that we are still inspired with the same spirit of liberty, and are determined to support our Religion and civil rights and hand them down to posterity.'

In defence of these rights he asked the Assembly to grant an immediate supply to 'assist in the general defence of the colonies,' and not to imagine that because the danger 'is at a distance that they will leave the brunt of it to others,' nor imagine 'that Britain loaded with debts and taxes will defend them and Indulge them in living without taxes or assisting in the general defence of the colonies.' Dobbs, like Franklin, Washington, and other leading colonists, realised that they could not expect any immediate help, and that even when help came success would depend in a great measure upon the colonists themselves. He therefore urged them to stand upon their own feet and fight in their own defence.   His closing words are worthy of the man.

> 'Let us behave like generous brave men and true Christians,' he said, 'and for a little while confine our appetites and luxuries and part with a reasonable part of our wealth to preserve the remainder and our happy constitution in Church and State; this will shew the Gallic Monarch, and his insatiable Ministry, that we are not to be intimidated or bullied out of

our rights, and that if he should insist upon his romantic scheme of surrounding, confining and enslaving us, that we shall jointly and unanimously support our valuable religion, liberties and properties, with our
lives and fortunes; and that whilst we behave like brave men and true
Christians we are sure of the Protection of God, and that we shall not only
be happy in this world but to endless ages.'

Dobbs's lengthy statement was warmly received, and printed copies of
it were distributed throughout North Carolina, and dispatched to
other colonial governors and also the Government in Britain.[14]

A harmonious session of the Assembly marked the early months of
Dobbs's governorship. A large appropriation was granted to pursue the
war against France, and for raising troops for the defence of Virginia.
Laws were passed to provide for the payment of quit-rents, and more
important perhaps was the framing of new laws for the establishment of
a proper judiciary and an improved jury system. The almost total lack
of a parish or religious organisation in the colony was something Dobbs
viewed with concern and anxiety. When, therefore, the Assembly
passed an Act for the setting up of parishes and providing for a vestry
system, it enacted a measure very dear to him. The establishment of a
strong and virile Protestant Church, not only in North Carolina but
throughout the American colonies, meant a great deal to him, and this
is abundantly clear from his subsequent letters to the Society for the
Propagation of the Gospel, and indeed from his writings generally.

Early in 1755, General Edward Braddock arrived from England to
assume command of the colonial and royal forces in America. In
North Carolina a small force was being raised for service with Braddock under the command of Edward Dobbs, the Governor's son—
a regular British officer, and the young colonial Hugh Waddell, who
had already been in service under the North Carolina Commander
Innes, and proved himself to be a brilliant soldier. As soon as the
troops were raised, Edward Dobbs was sent with his company to Fort
Cumberland, and Waddell was dispatched to superintend the building
of Fort Dobbs on the frontier and garrison the area. Despite the
meagre resources of the province, every effort was made to place it in
a proper state of defence; a number of small posts were set up and garrisoned, the militia was re-organised, drilled, and armed from the
supplies Dobbs brought with him from England, and a force was
raised for service in Virginia or elsewhere. Some months later four
companies of North Carolina troops, including Captain Dobbs's company, were dispatched to New York to assist in operations there. The

sending of troops to New York was done entirely on Dobbs's initiative, as he was not satisfied that they were being properly utilised in Virginia, and he wanted the North Carolinians to play a more active part in the offensive against the French. On arrival at New York, Governor Shirley requested that a field officer with experience be appointed to command the North Carolina contingent, and Captain Dobbs was accordingly placed in command.

Dobbs embarked upon his career as Governor with a lively zeal and a genuine desire to do what he could for the good of the colony; in fact, his efforts in this respect were not unlike those of his earlier years when he set out to provide a liberal and thoughtful solution to the economic and social problems of the Irish people. In one of his first communications to the Board of Trade in January 1755, he wrote in detail on the needs and requirements of the province, and suggested methods for the improvement of the social and economic life of the colonists.[15] He stressed the need for more clergy 'to instil good principles and morality into the inhabitants and proper schoolmasters to instruct their youth.' He drew attention to the utterly defenceless state of the province, the lack of forts, arms, and munitions, and the long undefended coastline. Trade, he pointed out, was considerably retarded by a lack of sufficient harbours from which large ships could remove lumber and other exportable products. He informed the Board of Trade of his efforts to encourage a silk industry for which he had, some time earlier, brought over a number of French families 'to carry on and instruct the inhabitants of the province in the several branches of the said industry.' To encourage the 'raising of mulberry trees, the breeding of silk worms and winding of silk,' he had expended four hundred pounds. He claimed that the raising of flax seed had been successfully undertaken, but the want of a direct trade with Ireland, where a market existed, hampered the undertaking. This brought Dobbs to a subject on which he had very strong and decided views, namely, the deleterious effects of the Navigation Acts on Irish and colonial trade.[16]

In his communication to the Board of Trade, he pointed out that the Navigation Acts deprived the

'southern colonies of sending most of the enumerated commodities direct to Ireland being obliged to enter every ship first in England, and then to land and reship their goods inhances the price so much without benefit to England that very little of the produce from hence can be sold in Ireland, and they are obliged to take all they want with ready money from Norway to the Baltic. Thus it stands as to naval stores, masts, yarns, bowsprits, tar, pitch, turpentine, rice, indigo, &c. As to rice it seems very surprising that it should be allowed to all countries south of Cape Finisterre and not be allowed to be carried to Ireland for at least their own consumption.'

As an economist and a patriot interested in the economic development of Britain and the colonies, he appealed to the Board of Trade for a relaxation or repeal of all Acts militating against the free flow of trade within the empire. 'If these difficulties were removed,' he wrote, 'then we should have an immediate trade with Ireland for our produce and take linnens in return, and be able to make remittances to England for their manufactures.' As with so many aspects of British trade and policy, Dobbs saw far ahead, and though he could not have anticipated the final effects of the Navigation Acts so far as the American colonies were concerned, he realised, as Huskisson and Wallace did more than half a century later, that the same Acts served only to engender a spirit of hostility and place a brake on international trade. 'These things,' he exclaimed, 'are so obvious when thought of, that I am surprised these confining laws should not be repealed.' In support of his appeal, he enclosed a memorial from the merchants, traders, and planters of North Carolina wherein it was pointed out that there were many products that 'might be exported to Ireland, Spain and Portugal or to the Streights to great advantage who now take these articles from Norway and the Baltick with ready money' if the restrictions imposed by the English Parliament were repealed or relaxed.[17]

Besides pleading for a repeal of the Navigation Acts and an extension of colonial trade, Dobbs, early in the year 1755, submitted a detailed proposal to the Board of Trade calling attention to the need for copper coinage in North Carolina. The lack of specie, he claimed, not only hampered trade, but nullified the colony's effort in the war against France. Needless to say, his proposals elicited no response.

When the first session of the Assembly finished on 15th January, 1755, and stood prorogued, Dobbs was in the happy position to report that it had been harmonious and co-operative in every way, and that a large number of important measures had received his assent. With the prorogation of the Assembly and the dispersal of the members to their homes and plantations, Dobbs was free to undertake a close and intimate study of the colony he administered.

Two important problems confronted him at the outset, the first being the erection of a number of forts for the protection of the province, the second was the need for establishing a new administrative capital. With regard to an administrative capital, both New Bern and

Wilmington could lay claim to the title, but Dobbs did not consider either of them satisfactory: New Bern was not centrally situated nor easy of access to the northern parts of the province; equally important, neither New Bern nor Wilmington boasted suitable buildings for administrative purposes, nor was there any suitable Governor's house; in fact, since his arrival in the province he had to be content with a small rented house at New Bern, with neither field nor paddock attached, and altogether unsuitable for the needs of the Governor.

On 9th April, Dobbs set out from New Bern 'to view the river Neuse and proceeded up it to near 100 miles to the falls to see what proper situations were upon that river for the seat of Government.' [18] A few days later he came upon a tract of land in the neighbourhood of the present town of Kinston which appeared to him suitable for the establishment of a capital; he describes the countryside as 'fine rising ground from the Ferry, dry, healthy and good springs; and extends a considerable way pretty level back from the river, where the lands are very good, altho' they are piney at some distance from the river.' Pleased with his mission, Dobbs, on his return to New Bern, promptly arranged to purchase the land on which he proposed to build the capital. In a letter to the Board of Trade he gave some details of his plans, and was of the opinion that 'the Assembly will proceed Briskly in erecting publick buildings and offices which have been so long unsettled that almost all old records are lost.' The lack of a suitable seat of government with adequate offices and public buildings contributed in no small way to the problems of the Administration. With the establishment of a centrally situated seat of government, many of the problems of administration would be overcome, and Dobbs hoped that

> 'all publick officers who ought to keep to their offices in the Capital should also reside in or near it, and members of the Council should all have houses there and half of them in rotation should reside half-yearly at the Capital, and not always be obliged upon emergencies to send expresses above 100 miles each way to summon a Council.' [19]

Dobbs rested for a few days on his return to New Bern, and then set out by sloop for the northern town of Edenton on Albemarle Sound. The purpose of this voyage of close on two hundred miles through almost landlocked Pamlico Sound was 'to fix upon a place to erect a fort or battery and Barracks to protect ships in the Harbour out of which they were taken by privateers in the last war.' [20] In the course of his voyage northwards he surveyed the entire coastline minutely, and carried out soundings where possible. From this survey and the knowledge gained of the coastline, he drew up plans for the different types of forts and batteries suitable for the sandy and marshy dunes stretching along the coast; in making these plans his experience as an engineer stood him in good stead. His journey took him to the east of New Bern to the neighbourhood of Beaufort, where a provisional site had been selected for a new fort. Dobbs did not approve of the site and suggested a place some miles southwest, where he 'found a fine sandy point well fixed, above water five or six feet, where the roots of trees in the sand make a sure foundation for a battery, where they have good water and wood for firing, and fixed with the commissioners to raise a fascine Battery.' [21] North Carolina was fortunate in having a Governor experienced in public works, but the passing years have so changed the face of North Carolina that little of consequence remains of the colonial province, and no records exist to associate his name with any extant public building.

From Beaufort, Dobbs sailed around the Shackleford Banks to Cape Lookout, which he describes as a fine harbour, and decided that it would be a suitable place to build another fort, as 'this harbour is the best altho' small, of any harbour from Boston to Georgia, and may be of utmost consequence to the Trade and navigation of England where all our cruisers can ride in safety as in a mill pond, and warp out at any time in an hour.' Dobbs thought so well of Cape Lookout as a harbour that in his report to the Board of Trade on the state of the province, he pointed out the need for erecting not only a fort but a barrack at this point, though he felt that the cost of doing so would be of

'too great Consequence to be attempted by any sum that can be raised in this Province, and if done must not only be built but maintained for some time at the expence of Britain until the Provinces on the main unite in their general defence, for this harbour is of general use to all the Provinces, and to all trading ships from Britain passing this coast.' [22]

Like so many other suggestions submitted to the Government, nothing was done to provide for the defence of Cape Lookout or to develop it as a safe harbour for trading-ships and naval vessels.

While Dobbs was engaged in his survey of the North Carolina coastline, Braddock requested him and the governors of Massachusetts, New York, Pennsylvania, Maryland, and Virginia to confer at Alexandria in Virginia in order to work out a concerted plan of action against the French. Dobbs did not receive Braddock's summons until his return to New Bern some weeks later, and by that time the meeting was over. However, Dinwiddie wrote to him and informed him that Braddock intended attacking the French immediately, and added the personal note: 'Y'r son left y's last Friday; his comps. went from Hampton to Alex's the Tuesday before; I supplied them with powder and shott and w't clothing he may want, he will be supplied at Alex's from the cloth'g I had from Engl.' He assured Dobbs that 'y'r son shall always have my advice.' [23] Captain Dobbs's transfer to Alexandria coincided with the opening of Braddock's campaign against the French, which in the initial stages was directed against the French stronghold on the Monongahela.

Though a declaration of war was hourly expected, Dobbs set out from New Bern on 17th June 'to view my lands, and at the same time the western frontier, and to fix a place to station our frontier company, and propose viewing the South Carolina line.' [24] In the course of a detailed account of this journey he wrote: 'I took my roote by the Heads of the New River,' from thence he proceeded by the northwest branch of the Cape Fear River to Duplin Courthouse, and at Gibson's store he turned northward to the hills dividing 'the streams that fall into the Peedee.' He continued in a northwesterly direction until he reached a point 'where the four counties of Anson, Rowan, Orange, and Cumberland meet,' and where 'the land rises to be mountainous or very steep hills, and continues so to the Unwarry which falls into the Yadkin.' In this hilly area, Dobbs set off on horseback to climb the highest hill from whence he could view the countryside.

> 'From a height,' he wrote, 'I could see as far as my eye could reach from westward by the north to the southeast, over the tops of all the trees these rich dry rocky hills I think very good for vineyards, for they can choose any aspect and any height to plant them on, so as to prevent their ripening too early or bursting with August or summer rains.'

He journeyed along the banks of the Yadkin, which he described as 'a beautiful river where is a ferry,' and found the land 'very rich level ground, free from rocks or gravel, but all a dark rich red, and some inclining to yellow or the richest loam, here they sow barley, wheat, rye, oats, and have yards to stack it in.'

Dobbs continued his journey northwards to Salisbury, the newly established county town of Rowan. 'The town is but just laid out,' he noted, 'the courthouse built and 7 or 8 log houses erected.' Proceeding by way of the South Yadkin River, he fixed upon a place on the third Creek which he considered suitable to build a fort to protect the back settlers. Returning from this point, he travelled in a southwesterly

direction to the limit of the Granville line 'which is as yet run no
farther upon Cold Water Creek on the Catawba path.' Here he wrote:
'I was within three miles of the North-west corner of my lands, which
lye upon Rocky river, and its several branches.' After a short ride, he
found himself among a group of settlers, men and women from Ulster
and other parts of Ireland. He had travelled many miles to visit them,
and they welcomed him for his friendly interest, and as the Royal
Governor of the colony.

'There are at present 75 families on my lands,' he wrote. 'I viewed
betwixt 30 and 40 of them, and except two there were not less than from
5 or 6 to 10 children in each family, each going barefooted in their shifts
in the warm weather, no woman wearing more than a shift and one thin
petticoat; they are a colony from Ireland removed from Pennsylvania, of
what we call Scotch Irish Presbyterians, who with others in their neighbouring tracts settled together in order to have a teacher of their own
opinion. Besides these there are 22 families of Germans or Swiss, who are
all an industrious people, they raise horses, cows and hogs with a few sheep;
they raise Indian corn, wheat, barley, rye and oats, and make good butter
and tolerable cheese, which they sell at Charlestown, having a waggon
road to it, tho' 200 miles distant.' [25]

Among the hills Dobbs found traces of iron ore and spoke with a
German miner who had 'just brought down his family to my land
upon the symptoms of its being a mineral country . . . he had but just
got his tools when I was obliged to come away, but he showed me
some samples of ore struck off from the spary rock.' The settlers also
'produced to me near the Yadkin a mineral which is either antimony
or tin.' In this journey Dobbs was accompanied by his nephew
Spaight and some servants, and was apparently joined by Captain
Waddell with a frontier company, for he ordered Waddell 'to scout
upon the edges of the mountain, and upon their return I set out to fix
upon a proper and most central place for them to winter at and erect
a Barrack, and afterwards if found proper there to build a fort.' [26]

Dobbs returned to New Bern about mid-August, having covered
many hundred miles in the course of two months of strenuous travel,
in which he had an opportunity of 'seeing a great deal of the Country
and settlements.' Dobbs did not spare himself in his efforts to learn all
that was to be learnt about the province, and in surveying it as he did
he accomplished more than any of his predecessors. In passing it might
be pointed out that only a man blessed with a strong and vigorous constitution and a mental vision beyond the average could at the age of

sixty-six undertake such long and tiresome journeys; further, Dobbs's activities give the lie to the often repeated assertion that he was old and senile when appointed Governor of North Carolina. His enthusiasm and clarity of thought are evidenced in the detailed report of his survey which he submitted to the Board of Trade. Lord Halifax and his fellow-members of the Board, in acknowledging receipt of the report, expressed their approval of his work, adding:

'The zeal and regard which you have shewn for his Majesty's service and the Welfare of the Province, in personally taking a general survey of it with a view of fixing upon a proper place for the seat of Government and providing for the Defence of the Sea Coast, are very much to be commended.' [27]

The War with France

DOBBS'S JOURNEY through the province was abruptly terminated on the receipt of a dispatch from Governor Dinwiddie containing the 'Bad news that our forces on the Ohio were defeated, and the train of artillery taken by the enemy.' Dinwiddie's dispatch continued: 'This letter was wrote in a great hurry, and I am therefore in hopes to have this news contradicted.' [1] The defeat of General Braddock's army by the French on the Monongahela was not contradicted, however, and the death of the English commander added to the confusion of defeat.

On 28th July a messenger reached Dobbs near Salisbury with another communication from Dinwiddie, who wrote:

'I am sorry I have occasion to write to you of the defeat of our forces on the Monongahela under the Com'd of Gen'l B—k. Copy of the two enclos'd let's will give you the particulars thereof. Y'r son was not in the Engagem't, but with Col. Dunbar by some stink'g Weeds in the Woods. Y'r son's sight is hurt, but he will soon recover it.' [2]

Colonel Dunbar and his troops had not taken part in the action but were kept in reserve, and only learned of Braddock's defeat and death when they encountered hurriedly retreating stragglers, who claimed that they were being pursued by the victorious French and their blood-thirsty Indian allies. Dunbar, who was next in command, precipitately withdrew, having 'destroyed every th'g at his camp, march'd into F't Cumberland, and in a great hurry in the middle of summer march'd for winter q's.' Dunbar left his sick and wounded at Fort Cumberland, among them Captain Dobbs who was temporarily blinded with sore eyes. The affliction was not very serious, for Dinwiddie was able to assure Dobbs some days later that 'Sir Jno. St. Clair came here from F't Cumb'rl'd, says Y'r son is well, and enclos'd you have a Let'r from him.' [3] In the course of his letter to Dobbs, Dinwiddie complained bitterly of the desertion of the North Carolina troops. 'Many of y'r son's Co'y have deserted,' he wrote, 'and ab't a fortnight ago some of them went thro' this Co'ty with Horses, &c., w'ch they stole from the Fort. I wish you may find them out to punish them. . . . Inclos'd is a list of deserters from Y'r son's Co'y.'

Following the defeat and death of Braddock, Governor Shirley was appointed to command the troops pending the arrival of a new commander from England with reinforcements and equipment.

In North Carolina a friendly Assembly co-operated whole-heartedly with Dobbs, and at the end of a year of office he wrote happily to his old friend, Councillor M'Aulay:

'I thank God I have settled in the colony by keeping myself detached from any party and giving no countenance to any who would prevent the union in the province which I have steadily adhered to. I thank God I keep my health, and have purchased a plantation of 900 acres about ten miles from here on a fine navigable river . . . and will be at a reasonable distance of the seat of Government. Whether I fix it here or higher up the Neuse river I shall be within an easy day's journey of it. I have taken out a warrant to have a patent for 1,000 acres more in my daughter Fanny's name of islands and land adjoining mine on the other side of the river . . . all cypress woods and swamps fit for rice meadows, &c., which with my plantation I design to give her as an addition to her portion which will be very valuable once the capital is paid. I have parted with the Assembly in perfect harmony and done everything for Britain and the colony that they could reasonably have expected in the time.' [4]

The properties Dobbs speaks of were purchased soon after his arrival in North Carolina. As there was no Governor's house at New Bern, he prepared plans for a new residence, and, as already noted, envisaged the setting up of a capital on this property, but a little farther up the river at Tower Hill, near Stringer's Ferry. A year or two later he presented his plan to the Assembly, and a Committee appointed to examine and report on it considered the site suitable for the seat of Government.

Though now deeply immersed in American affairs, Dobbs's thoughts continually turned to Ireland, a fact noticeable in his letters to the Board of Trade, wherein he sought on every occasion to effect a repeal of the Navigation Acts to permit a direct trade between North Carolina and Ireland, which he contended would be to the mutual advantage of both countries. In his letter to M'Aulay he states:

'I have been endeavouring for the good of Ireland all I can, having sent over a strong Memorial backed by strong reason to the Board of Trade to enlarge our trade with Ireland by allowing us to send from here Indigo, rice and naval stores without touching England which will enable us to send over lumber and many other commodities to Ireland, and we can take more linnens and other manufactures.'

It is to be regretted that his efforts to open up a trade between North Carolina and Ireland failed, and that his call for the repeal or mitigation of the Navigation Acts fell upon deaf ears to the detriment of North Carolina, Ireland, and eventually Britain herself.

The defeat of General Braddock on the Monongahela brought home to Dobbs the utter defencelessness of the colony. On his return to New Bern he wrote to Dinwiddie:

> 'I delay'd acknowledging the former letters having nothing material to write, and have been above four months in different parts of the Province to observe our seacoast and western frontier in order to put them in a state of Defence, as far as this poor province can contribute at this critical juncture, until I was obliged to return Express upon account of our unfortunate Defeat and Death of General Braddock.' [5]

He informed Dinwiddie that he had given instructions to erect a Battery and Barracks for the 'defence of the Harbour at Ocracoke, which is now going on,' and added: 'As we have no artillery or Military stores we shall have an immediate occasion for Artillery, Bullets and Stores,' Fort Jackson at Cape Fear, though armed with many guns, lacked military stores, and Dobbs remarked that 'if his Majesty wou'd send 20 Barrels of Gun Powder for present use, it may be of great service, as there is none at present in the Colony.' In the same letter he informed Dinwiddie that he had given directions 'to put the frontier in the best state of Defence against Indian Incursions,' and in order to help in the war he assured him that he would 'get the Assembly, who meet the twenty-fourth September, to exert themselves to the utmost to put a speedy end to the French schemes, by confining them to their own limits, and if there shu'd be a war to expel them from this continent, without which we can never be safe and easy.'

Dinwiddie's reply was doubly welcome, for it was brought to New Bern by Captain Dobbs, who was returning home to recuperate. Apparently his eye affliction was completely cured, and Dinwiddie wrote: 'I congratulate You on his recovery of the Distemper in his eye.' [6]

The Assembly met on 25th September, and Dobbs, in a vigorous address, enjoined the members to vote all the aid they could to meet the changed circumstances following Braddock's defeat.

'The flame has already reached our Border,' he reminded them, 'and God Almighty has extended his correcting arm and made a Breach upon us, upon account of our wantoness, luxury and neglect of the practice of our religious duties and moral virtue, and we are now to fight *pro aris et focis*, and it requires the united forces of all the Colonies notwithstanding our great superiority to withstand their arms supported by the whole power of France.'

He informed the members that Britain was at that moment providing money and equipping an army to the fullest extent of her resources, and he urged them to grant an appropriate aid,

'for a proper sum cheerfully granted at once will accomplish what a great sum may not do hereafter.' He continued: 'I therefore earnestly recommend it to you to grant as large a supply as this province can bear not only to defend your own frontier and sea coast but also to act in conjunction with our neighbouring colonies.'

He realised fully the immense difficulties facing the province, the lack of coin and bullion, and a paper currency unacceptable across the frontier, but despite these difficulties he requested them to

'support the credit of your bills by giving what may be hereafter issued a security on your lands and laying a penalty upon those who reside in this province who shall give any preference to Gold or Silver at a discount upon our bills, or who shall for the future contract for gold or silver and refuse to take our paper currency in payment for goods sold in our neighbouring colonies. This will effectually support our credit when our neighbours can pay the balance due to this province in our own bills.' 7

Though the exigencies of war constituted a prior claim on the administration and demanded all their efforts, Dobbs did not wish that the internal affairs of the province should suffer in consequence. 'The revisal of your laws is absolutely necessary,' he said, as was also the need for erecting county or parish schools 'for the education of your youth, and the knowledge of religion and moral duties.' Regarding the desertion of North Carolina troops he said:

'The desertion of your companies is becoming so excessive from the base principle of the lowest class of men for want of education that they carry off their arms and livery and steal horses to carry away, and appear publickly in this province without being secured by any Magistrate, that it would be necessary to introduce forthwith a mutiny bill.'

He also asked the Assembly to enact a law to 'oblige planters who have small properties to bring up their children to industry, or bind out their children to necessary trades as many of them breed up their children to sloth and laziness.' To encourage people to pursue useful trades, he suggested that 'Artificers' wages might be regulated by affording the necessaries of life cheaper.' In closing his address, he enjoined the Assembly to enact proper laws for the benefit of the Indians, particularly to provide for their education and upbringing, and guarantee their safety by punishing anybody who killed, wounded, or maimed an Indian or negro slave.

The members of the Council and Assembly assured Dobbs that all the matters offered for their consideration would be expeditiously attended to. They thanked him for his interest in the province, adding:

'Amidst all the calamities that threaten us we think this province singularly happy in being under the conduct of your Excellency's prudent, mild and equitable administration, your zeal, sir, for his Majesty's service so long approved hath since your arrival here prompted you to such application and fatigue in the affairs of Government as few could be able for, and fewer willing to undergo.'

On this harmonious note the Assembly settled down to work.

Though Dobbs returned from his journey through the province in very good spirits, a sultry August and September, as well as his anxiety with the turn of events in the neighbouring province, imposed a heavy strain on him, and for some weeks he was confined to his house, 'seized with a Lax and Dyarrhea.'[8] The summer had been abnormally dry and sultry, and autumn fogs made New Bern unpleasant. In the circumstances, Dobbs was constrained to prorogue the Assembly after a short session. In closing the session he said:

'Since this unseasonable hot season hath made this neighbourhood sickly I shall no longer detain you, and must thank you for the several good laws you have passed, and shall only recommend to you the putting the several laws you have passed in execution in your several districts, and to take care that the Militia be in readiness in case of any invasion, and to raise and keep up a spirit against a perfidious Enemy who are determined to deprive you of your religion, liberty and possession.'[9]

Dobbs informed the Board of Trade of the early prorogation, pointing out that 'the season having been very sickly with Agues and intermittent fevers by a long dry season . . . and one third of the members of the Council and Assembly laid up from time to time I closed it as soon as I could.'[10] Despite the short session, the Assembly granted a supply of £10,000 for His Majesty's service to raise three companies of men, and a sum of £7,500 for the purchase of glebes, and the erection of churches and public buildings. He warned the Board of Trade that should the war continue he did not think that any further aid could be granted without depreciating the currency of the province, and he was doubtful if the members 'were inclinable to keep it up.' In this communication he recommended that his son be appointed a member of the Council. While the recommendation savoured of nepotism, Dobbs had good reason for his action; he felt that if he nominated a person from either the northern or southern counties the representation jealousies which enflamed the province during Johnston's administration might break out afresh, since 'the parties are only smothered yet not quite laid aside I expect recommending one either from the Northward or Southward might raise the flame, so to prevent Solicitations I was advised to recommend my son.' Edward Dobbs was accordingly appointed a member of the Council of North Carolina, and shortly afterwards Dobbs's nephew, Richard Spaight, a young man of somewhat erratic temperament, but shrewd and able, was also appointed to the Council.

Early in December 1755, the Board of Trade requested Dobbs to supply a detailed report on the defences of North Carolina, including the attitude of the Indians in the event of a declared war with France. It would seem from this request that the home Government had fully awakened to the critical state of the colonies following Braddock's defeat, and realised 'the expediency of providing for the future defence of the frontiers of those colonies.' [11] Dobbs immediately drafted a long report of more than forty pages, in which he traced the growth and development of the British colonies of North America, and gave what he considered to be a strong legal and moral case not only for Britain's claim to the unsettled hinterland of the continent but also to Canada, Nova Scotia, and New Brunswick. On the 'presumption that we shall exert our undoubted right to these lands,' he submitted a plan to defend these possessions and hold them against all French claims and advances. In submitting proposals for the expulsion of the French from Canada, he harked back to an old phobia of his.

'I think,' he wrote, 'that no time should be lost in declaring the Hudson's Bay exclusive trade by Charter (without an act of Parliament to confirm it) an illegal monopoly to allow all British merchants to Trade, and British and Foreign Protestants to settle on all or any of the lands within their grant.' [12]

Having covered the ground of colonial development and expansion, which in effect was a reiteration of all the plans and schemes he had put forward in the course of his lifetime, he turned his attention to immediate needs, and set down in detail plans for the defence of the American continent. He estimated that a sum of £63,000 would be required to put the colonies in a sound state of defence, and envisaged this amount being raised 'from the United Colonies, proportionately to their wealth and numbers.'[13] In the course of his proposals, Dobbs computed that the 'number of souls of the Whites in the several British Colonies of North America' was in excess of one million people, and on this basis he assessed what each province should contribute to the common defence. The problem of finding labour to help in the building of forts and barracks also engaged his attention. To provide sufficient labour he suggested that a law be passed in England and Ireland that 'all persons guilty of larceny or small theft & pickpockets should all be transported instead of being burnt in the hand.' Vagrants could be usefully employed in the colonies 'in the Fortifications and Repairs and making Publick roads, Bridges &c; and those who were flagrant offenders upon settling the Countries about Hudson's Bay.'

With the knowledge of an experienced engineer, Dobbs described in some detail the types of forts and redoubts that should be built, advising on their construction and the armaments required for them. He had some pertinent remarks to make regarding the treatment of Indians and their exploitation by settlers and colonial administrators such as Glen in South Carolina. 'The friendship of the Indians,' Dobbs pointed out, 'can never be effectually secured without protecting them, and preventing them being imposed upon by frauds of the traders.' To prevent defrauding, exploitation, and ill-treatment, he suggested the appointment of a number of Commissioners or trustees who would look after the Indians' interests in the colonies, and provide for their settlement, education, and social well-being. The exploited Indians provided the French with a disgruntled and vengeful ally whom they used with considerable success.

Whether the Lords of the Board of Trade were in the slightest way interested in Dobbs's plans for the defence and eventual enlargement of the American colonies or not, they none the less thanked him for his communication.[14] At the same time, noting his previous comments on the outbreak of sickness in the province, the Board remarked:

'It gives us great concern to find by your letter that the Province of North Carolina has been so sickly, and that you in particular had so large a share in the public calamity, it is however a great satisfaction to us to find, that the zeal upon which his Majesty's subjects in North Carolina have shewn in so cheerfully and so liberally granting money to assist their neighbours in Virginia has not been damped by their distress and they still continue to act with so becoming a regard for the common concern. The zeal and regard which you have shewn for his Majesty's service upon this great occasion and the fatigue you have undergone cannot fail of meeting with his Majesty's approbation, and his Majesty has been pleased upon our recommendation to appoint your son to be of the Council of North Carolina in room of Mr. Craven.' [15]

Though the affairs of North Carolina throughout the year 1756 gave Dobbs little cause for concern, the deterioration of the political and military position both at home and on the American continent gave rise to anxiety. The four new companies of North Carolina troops were dispatched to New York to serve 'on Ontario Lake the most necessary operation to cut off the French from Ohio,' Dobbs reported, adding, 'my son's Company from Fort Cumberland I have ordered to join them.' These troops were destined to support the garrison at Fort Oswego, fifty miles from the French fort of Frontenac on Lake Ontario. It was in this area that the campaign against the French could boast of any success, for shortly after Braddock's defeat the amateur soldier William Johnson, with raw militia, defeated the French commander Dieskau and made him prisoner.

To add to the difficulties of the colonial governors, reports from Europe showed that the continent was bracing itself for a new war, so their hopes of obtaining trained soldiers, money, munitions, and officers appeared distinctly gloomy. A new French, Austrian, and Russian alliance had taken shape against Prussia and her English ally. The Government in Britain continued in the inept hands of the ridiculous and 'hoary Jobber' Newcastle, while the energetic and forceful Pitt, who had been pushed aside, could do no more than 'lay bare with withering satire the Premier's contemptible littleness.' [16] The state of undeclared war between France and Britain which had lasted for some years gradually broke under the stress and strain of numerous incidents. In May, France formally declared war against a Britain virtually undefended, and with a miserable army of twenty thousand men under generals as inept and incompetent as the Government itself. The Government continued to dither and was 'shivering for six months in fear of a comprehensive invasion and crying out for protection by any German or Swiss whom money could buy.' [17] A month after the declaration of war Britain lost the strategic base of Minorca, and the hapless Admiral Byng returned home to face trial and execution.

On the American continent, the colonists were more or less left to their own devices, and though the blockade of the coast by a fleet under Boscawen was relatively successful, and resulted in the capture of Nova Scotia, the French General Montcalm with a trained and well-equipped army had been able to reach Quebec, and was, at the moment of the British defeat at Minorca, pushing towards the British fort of Oswego, and reinforcing his own garrisons at Crown Point and Ticonderoga. Both sides were now poised for a full-scale war on the American continent, and in the critically developing situation the colonists lacked a general of Montcalm's calibre.

The North Carolina Council and Assembly met briefly in March, a month or two before the declaration of war, and adjourned until September. In the meantime Dobbs undertook a tour of inspection of the newly erected forts, and those in the course of erection, and was immediately faced with the problem of manning them and obtaining munitions for their defence; officers and artificers presented a still greater problem. In a letter to Lord Loudoun, the new Commander-in-Chief, Dobbs complained that he had been asked to draw up plans of forts and make the necessary estimates, but, he wrote, 'I have no Engineers here, nor know how to get one, I was obliged to act as Engineer myself & rub up my former knowledge in fortifications when I was in the army.' The lack of trained soldiers, money, and munitions was a problem confronting all the governors, and many of the Assemblies were growing impatient at the continuous demands for aid, feeling that they were bearing a disproportionate part of the war expense. Dinwiddie, in a letter to Dobbs, stated that Virginia was in much the same position as North Carolina. 'We are in great want of good officers,' he said, 'engineers and artillery, that I think we are in a bad situation . . . and our people are so dastardly that I cannot raise in them a martial spirit or raise men sufficient to augment our regiment to 1,500 men.' [18]

Early in February 1756, the Board of Trade informed Dobbs that the Earl of Loudoun had been appointed Commander-in-Chief in succession to Braddock, and would sail for America with a large body of troops and munitions. Pending Loudoun's arrival, General Shirley was acting commander, and he assembled a considerable army at Albany in preparation for a concerted attack on the French. Loudoun did not appear to be in any hurry to take over his command, and did not reach New York until August, though his two subordinate commanders, General Abercrombie and Colonel Webb, reached America some little time before him. 'These two officers landed in June,'

Bradley writes, 'and with their tardy chief, constituted, perhaps, the most indifferent trio that were ever inflicted at one blow upon a British army.'[19] Loudoun was a careerist pure and simple, and certainly no soldier; from the outset he made no attempt to conceal his dislike of colonial and provincial officers, and his treatment of Governor Shirley was contemptible.

Dobbs, in accordance with instructions from Fox, submitted a long report to Loudoun on the military situation in North Carolina; the fresh demand for a report clearly shows that little attention had been paid to the numerous reports already submitted, but as a loyal and painstaking servant of the Crown Dobbs carried out his instructions with alacrity. From this new report we gather that prior to his arrival in the province only one small fort had been erected, and it was ill-devised for defence; there was no public magazine, and only eight barrels of gunpowder; the Assembly had appropriated divers sums of money for the erection or repair of forts, 'but no steps had been taken to erect any of them when I arrived.' He was now pleased to report that Fort Johnston on the Cape Fear River had been repaired, that a new fort was in the course of erection at Ocracoke, a fort or battery had been erected at Beaufort to protect the port, and a small frontier fort had been erected in the west. Though substantial headway had been made in the matter of defences, Dobbs felt that the province was by no means properly protected, and that the long sea coast was particularly vulnerable. To safeguard the coast, he had submitted plans for a fort at Cape Lookout to the Board of Trade; this fort, planned on a large scale, was to provide accommodation for three hundred men in time of peace, and almost twice as many in war. Dobbs made it clear to Loudoun that the building and maintenance of this proposed fort could not be met by the province, but should be a charge upon the mother country. He also pointed out that owing to the relative poverty of the people, and the lack of gold and silver specie, it was not possible to maintain troops outside the province. Already four companies of North Carolina troops were fighting in the common defence of the American colonies, and it was only just that they should be maintained and paid by Britain.

By August some 7,000 Provincials and six regiments of Regulars had assembled at Albany for a conjoint effort against the strongly held French positions on the Hudson. Here the troops impatiently awaited Loudoun's arrival, growing morose and rebellious; they were in fact little more than a mob of amateur soldiers, chafing to get back as quickly as possible to their homes, and on the whole little interested in war. They were a rough, hardy lot of men, peaceful and freedom-loving, and the galling inaction and petty army regulations proved exceedingly irksome. In a deeply wooded countryside that afforded protection to their enemy they were continually subject to the snipers' bullet and the Indian tomahawk; they spent weary months clearing the forest around them, and improving the miserable roads over which their supplies moved; they spent time, too, building whale-boats and bateaux to convey the army down the lake to the French stronghold of Ticonderoga. Fighting consisted of skirmishes, raids on outposts, some scouting, and a considerable amount of scalping by the Indian allies of both sides. Living under the most primitive of conditions, the troops sickened by the thousand, and many hundred died of disease.

The months slipped by and with passing time discipline grew more lax. To make matters worse, the British perpetrated one of their usual blunders in dealing with colonial troops by insisting that British regular army officers should rank higher than Colonial officers, so that the rawest and most inexperienced British officer, a mere youth perhaps, took precedence over the experienced Colonial commander. This gaffe was perpetrated in the case of Washington, an experienced young officer, but trouble was averted by Dinwiddie and Shirley in his case. In the Albany camp there was no Dinwiddie or Shirley to smooth out these difficulties, though the sensible and experienced Winsloe did use his influence in the case of Waddell and other Colonials, but the harm had been done, and the sore became a festering wound. Winter approached and no move was made in this important seat of war. Westward, however, on Lake Ontario, the British fort of Oswego was attacked by Montcalm, who slipped away from Ticonderoga completely unobserved. After a brief but brave resistance, Oswego fell, and with it sixteen hundred prisoners, besides six heavily laden ships, two hundred barges, supplies of all kinds, and £18,000 in cash. The fall of Oswego was a bitter blow to British pride and influence.

Dobbs was informed of the fall of Oswego by Dinwiddie, who pointed out the unpalatable fact that British influence was swept from the shores of Ontario, and the Mississippi Valley was wide open to the French. 'There is reason to think,' Dinwiddie wrote, 'that the enemy 'l come down the Ohio and invade the southern Colonies, and I think we are in a very poor condition to repell their force.' [20] While a French invasion of the southern colonies was not beyond the bounds of possibility, the effect of the French victory upon the Indian tribes was a matter of grave concern. Dobbs fully realised this, and when, a month or two later, the Assembly met at New Bern, he stressed the need for cultivating friendly relations with the Indians, reminding the members that if they did not do so the French undoubtedly would, and thus make them 'our enemies and by their assistance too expel all British colonists from their Possession on this continent.' With the fall of Oswego, the Mississippi Valley was thrown open to the French, and Dobbs again exhorted the Assembly to grant an immediate aid for the defence of the province, adding that 'at this time a less sum will do more service, than a very large sum hereafter, which if delayed must necessarily be given to procure your future peace.'

Despite the critical conditions prevailing, and the many cares of office already telling on his somewhat younger friend Dinwiddie, Dobbs bubbled over with energy and enthusiasm, submitting one report after another to the Board of Trade, and keeping up a vigorous and heartening correspondence with some of his brother governors. He found time for reading and writing a long thesis of a religious and metaphysical nature, based upon biblical prophecies and portending a coming millennium following the world-wide supremacy of Protestantism and English arms. This long and peculiar work, antedating the British Israelites, bore the sombre title *An Account of the Three States of Human Nature, first in their pristine state of Innocence, second in their Present less Degraded State, third in the State they are to be restored to in the Paradisical Earth or Kingdom of God at the First Resurrection.* In one of his letters he refers simply to the work as 'my Essay upon the Grand Plan of Providence, and Dissertations annexed thereto,' and he expresses the hope of publishing it 'if please God I live to get to Ireland or England.' Dobbs, of course, never returned home, and the long manuscript in his neat, firm hand is preserved amongst his papers in the Northern Ireland Record Office.

The year 1756 came to a close. So far as Dobbs's Governorship of North Carolina was concerned, there was no cause for complaint; a spirit of harmony and goodwill prevailed throughout the province. The continuous grants for pursuing the war and maintaining four companies in the north were undoubtedly heavy burdens, but conditions might have been worse. Fortunately, the defeat at Oswego did not result in the threatened French invasion of the province. The year, on the other hand, had not been propitious to British arms, but a ray of hope ran high that the loss of Oswego in America, Calcutta in India, and Majorca in Europe would be speedily repaired. The lack of cohesion and concerted action by the American colonies, however, gravely perturbed Dobbs, Dinwiddie, and Sharpe, and all their efforts to co-ordinate the colonial forces proved disappointing. For this state of affairs the colonial governments were charged with being dilatory, lacking in public spirit, and jealously tenacious of their privileges. A recent writer remarks that their troops were undisciplined, were enlisted for short periods, and came to rendezvous ill-equipped, when they came equipped at all. In the case of Maryland and Pennsylvania, quarrels between the governors and the Assembly stopped all supplies of men and money.[21] While in the main these charges and comments are true, the fact that the colonists were ill-equipped was not the fault of the governors or the Assemblies, and as we have seen, so far as North Carolina was concerned, the utmost harmony existed, and the Assembly consistently granted aid in the common defence. The Board of Trade readily recognised this, and in acknowledging Dobbs's report on the province wrote:

'A full and satisfactory account of the State of the Province and your Government, and of your proceedings in the administration from the date of your last letter down to that period, and although this state is not in every particular so good an one as we could have wished, yet it is altogether better than we expected considering the confusion in which you found things on your arrival, and the little regard which has been shewn by your predecessor to establish that order in government and promote those measures which can alone give stability to it.' The communication from the Board of Trade concluded: 'The particular attention which you appear to have given to these matters which you have pursued for providing in a proper manner for the defence and security of the Province on one hand and the aiding and assisting the efforts which have been made by the mother country for the defence and security of America in General on the other cannot fail of meeting with his Majesty's approbation.'

In passing, the Board of Trade noted, 'We are sensible that the circumstances of the People of North Carolina will not admit of their contributing so largely to the Common cause as may be reasonably expected from the other colonies.' This sentence does admit that the Governor and Assembly of North Carolina played their part in the war against the French.

We get a more personal picture of Dobbs and his work in North Carolina about this time from a letter he wrote towards the end of October to his cousin, Judge Ward. In the course of this lengthy letter, in which he makes some pertinent remarks regarding Irish political affairs, he says: 'I thank God my health is perfectly restored by following a milk diet all the hot weather without taking wine or spirits and, now all the sickly season is over and we have abundance of tempor-

ate [?] fruits, and I have gained a great deal of flesh and am plump
altho not fat.' His leisure, he tells Ward, consists in

'reading, thinking and writing, which thank God have agreed with me very
well using exercise some times, when not making general progresses between
my plantation or villa that is to be, and this town is about ten English miles
distant, and in winter I can go in my chair and dine there, and see the
improvements making by my negroes about 14 or 15 in number, and return
in the evening, and in summer retire thither for 2 or 3 months during the
hot weather, nor do I quite forget the natural history of this province but
keep Journalls in my excursions, and make observations which may afterwards lead to writing something upon it when materials are collected to
build upon.'

With regard to the administration of the province, he writes:

'Our Assembly is once again over and we have parted good friends,
altho they have not granted so large a supply as I desired and hoped for
they having only raised £3,400 and £1,000 which they had unassigned
which they can appropriate to build a fort to protect and secure the
Catawbas Indians upon the apprehensions they are under of being attacked
by the French Indians since the loss of Oswego, as the French have now
a ready passage across the lakes to the Ohio and the wavering state of the
Cherokees who scurvily entertain French emissaries among them and to
maintain 2 companies to garrison that and another fort we have built on
our frontier this summer.'

A greater part of the letter is filled with details regarding the defence
of the province and the disposition of the North Carolina troops
'hurried over to reinforce Lord Loudoun's American Regimt., so that
my son the Major takes his command with the rest.' He writes of
erecting 'a strong Fort at Cape Lookout on the coast where there is
lately made known one of the best and safest harbours in America . . .
landlocked from all winds of which I have sent over a draught, and my
project has been so far approved as to order me to send a plan and
estimate.' He remarks that this harbour was known to Spanish Privateers, and New England Whale Fishers

'have known it for many years, but it was never made Publick nor a plan
taken of it until the year I came over, this I have advised to be built so
strong as to stand a siege, for if the French should take it they would make
another Louisburg or Gibraltar of it, so as to have three hundred men in
time of peace and 500 in time of war.'

Dobbs concludes the letter:

'As to private news I have reason to hope from England that Lord Halifax will recommend my nephew Dick Spaight to be Secretary worth about £500 p.an., and also to be of the Council as my son is already made one, and he is on the brink of wedlock with a pretty girl of 14 who has the best fortune and her mother of the best alliance in the Colony. She has a great many plantations and above one hundred negroes, the articles are synged, and nothing wanted but the wedding Cloaths from Virginia, where my man has gone to buy them and is every day expected, so that his coming with me will turn out well, as he will have the best rank and fortune in this Province.' [22]

Richard Spaight was married a few months later to Mary Moore, the daughter of John Moore of Craven County.

12

Opposition

IN FEBRUARY, 1757, Lord Loudoun called a meeting of the governors
of Virginia, Maryland, Pennsylvania, and North Carolina at Philadelphia. When Dobbs arrived at the town, he was received in a manner
befitting a Royal Governor, and greeted with a salute of guns from the
Association Battery; he was accorded a civic welcome by Governor
Denny and the dignitaries of what was then the largest town in
America. As the guest of Governor Denny at Shippen House, he had
the opportunity for the next few weeks of enjoying the amenities of
a relatively large colonial capital. In North Carolina there were no
towns as such, for the more important places—Edenton, Bath, and
New Bern—were little more than villages. Brunswick, where Dobbs
built his own house a year or two later, was but a hamlet with a few
scattered houses on the edge of a wood; Wilmington, however, was
slowly developing and growing in importance by reason of its safe and
secure harbour, and was outstripping New Bern. The traveller Peter
Du Bois remarked that 'the regularity of its streets is equal to that of
Philadelphia, and the buildings are generally good. Many of brick,
two or three stories high with double piazzas which make a good
appearance.'[1] Generally speaking, there were no public buildings of any
significance in North Carolina, not even a suitable residence for the
Governor. Philadelphia, on the other hand, was a thriving town with
three thousand brick houses, and many fine buildings; the streets were
paved, with footwalks on each side, and were lighted with street lamps.[2]

Dinwiddie and Governor Sharpe of Maryland reached the city
before Dobbs. The meeting of the three governors who had so much
in common and who had not seen each other for more than two years
was something in the nature of a pleasant reunion. The close and warm
friendship between Dinwiddie and Dobbs has already been commented
upon; both men were hard-working, honest administrators, deeply
attached to the Crown, and inflexible in their defence of Royal prerogatives. This inflexible loyalty, while tardily recognised by the

Government in England, was not conducive to harmony in provincial government, as Dinwiddie well knew, and Dobbs was later to know. In the few years that elapsed since their previous meeting, time had wrought a change. Dobbs was close on sixty-eight years of age, but he still retained a good deal of youthful vigour and enthusiasm. Dinwiddie, on the other hand, though some years younger, was a sick man, worn out by work and illness; his body was stiff and crippled with rheumatism, and he anxiously awaited the day of his recall to England.

The meeting with Loudoun had been arranged for 17th February, but for some reason or other he did not put in an appearance in the city until 14th March, much to the chagrin of the naturally impatient Dobbs, who, because of the delay, was constrained to postpone the meeting of the North Carolina Assembly and Council. With the arrival of Loudoun, the Conference got down to the business of drawing up a concerted plan of action against the French. Besides the governors, some of the military leaders were later called upon to assist in planning the campaign. Among the military leaders was Colonel Washington, one of the few colonial soldiers whom Loudoun considered worthy of trust, due no doubt to the fact that both Dinwiddie and Sharpe thought so highly of him. Though the governors remained in Conference from 15th to 27th March, their deliberations were marked by a number of social events, including a dinner given by the Corporation of Philadelphia at the State House on a scale of sumptuous grandeur worthy of more propitious times.[3]

From the deliberations of the governors it was evident that no major offensive against the French was contemplated until the following year, and plans were, in consequence, devised for a purely defensive campaign, particularly the defence of South Carolina, as it appeared to those present at the Conference that 'there is a danger of the Enemy making an attack on the Province of South Carolina, either by sea from St. Domingo or from Alabama fort in the Creek Indian on the head of the Mobile.' To provide against such an attack, the governors agreed to raise new levies of troops not only for the effective defence of their own provinces but also for the defence of South Carolina. Dobbs agreed to raise two hundred men for the defence of North Carolina, and another two hundred men to be sent to South Carolina.[4]

On the conclusion of the Conference and before leaving Philadelphia, Dobbs dispatched a report of the proceedings to the Board of Trade, in the course of which he remarked, perhaps by way of complaint:

'I have been here a month awaiting his [Loudoun's] arrival and during our consultations here, and am now ready to return in two days to my Province where I must immediately call our Assembly to enable me to send two hundred men to assist South Carolina, and raise two hundred more to secure our forts to the Sea Coasts and Western Frontiers.'

Though he had promised to secure additional troops, he was not at all certain that the Assembly would implement his promise even though the urgency of the situation demanded it. However, on his return to New Bern he called a meeting of the Assembly for 16th May, and proclaimed a day of 'solemn Fasting and Humiliation.'

When the Assembly met, Dobbs, in the course of a short address, spoke of the catastrophe of a French victory. 'Our all is at stake,' he said, 'our Holy Protestant Religion, our Liberties and Possessions are all now to be fought for.' He reminded the members that Britain was fighting desperately to secure

'their Liberties, Rights and Possessions,' and was in consequence heavily burdened, and 'without our joining to our utmost in our own defence for our own safety and in order for the future to get rid of the neighbourhood of a cruel and Perfidious enemy we must submit to Popish superstitions and Idolatory, and become slaves to the arbitrary power of France.'

He felt certain, however, in view of the dangerous situation and the zeal which the members 'have hitherto shewn in support of his Majesty's Rights and our Holy Religion . . . that you will concurr in your proportion of the Expense and Forces to be raised.' [5]

The members of the Council and Assembly in their replies to the Governor's speech assured him of their earnest desire to assist in the common defence of the colonies, and at the same time they took the opportunity of congratulating him on his 'safe return to your Government from Philadelphia, and hope that the gracious Providence that has protected you in so tedious a journey will still continue to enable you to long pursue those endeavours, which your zeal animates you for the Public.'

The Assembly agreed to raise two hundred men for immediate service in South Carolina, and provided a sum of £5,300 to maintain them for six months or longer if necessary. It was also agreed that new companies of Provincials should be raised for the defence of the North Carolina frontier which was subject to depredations by hostile Indians.

For the next few months there was little or no change in the war situation. Loudoun's ability as a commander-in-chief was marked by painful inaction, but the French and their Indian allies harried, pillaged, and destroyed isolated settlements at will. In London there was the usual scrimmage for power among the politicians, and Pitt was thrown out of office for a brief period. The sick Dinwiddie wrote despairingly to Dobbs:

> 'I am sorry there has been another thorow change in the Ministry which shews the weakness of our constitution, and of course our intestine disputes must give our enemies great advantages. This makes great confusion at home, as these changes are not in the least agreeable to the people. What will be the fate of that Nation time must tell.' [6]

Fortunately, public opinion could no longer tolerate the scheming and inept Newcastle, and Pitt was again restored to office.

Within a few weeks, Pitt set the machinery of the empire in motion. Word was dispatched to Dobbs and his brother governors, almost crushed with a feeling of isolation, that a force of more than 8,000 men supported by a strong fleet was assembling in Ireland. Most of the soldiers were drawn from Irish stations and drafted to Cork to await transport. Here for seven weeks they were royally entertained, and a public fund was raised for their women and children. Towards the end of April a fleet of warships and transports appeared off the head of Kinsale, and on the following day anchored in Cork Harbour. On 8th May a fleet of more than one hundred ships, under the command of Admiral Holbourne, sailed for America. [7]

Despite the exigencies of war, Dobbs turned his attention to the domestic affairs of the province. The rapid growth and haphazard development of North Carolina gave rise to many problems, not the least of which was the unsatisfactory collection of quit-rents and the chaotic state of land grants. The accretion of many thousands of new settlers, some mere squatters, some holding land with imperfect titles, and the fact that a considerable amount of the land granted to McCulloh, Huey, Crymble, Selwyn, and Dobbs himself had not been fully settled under the terms of the grants and was in consequence due for reversion to the Crown called for a new survey, the drawing up of complete rent rolls, and a legal registration of titles. No compact areas of land, except in the back settlements, now remained ungranted, and all lands along the navigable rivers had been taken up and settled. Though many new settlers had acquired land, there was little or no corresponding increase in the quit-rent revenue from the province; this clearly showed that the quit-rent office had failed to do its work, and that much of the land had been granted recklessly and fraudulently, and that titles were not registered with the land office. [8]

To encourage the collection of the quit-rents the sheriffs of each county were promised a proportional addition to their fees, and while this may have been necessary, it undoubtedly resulted in considerable harshness and engendered very bitter feelings between the new settlers and the law officers. With the continuous arrival of so many settlers and the consequent diminution of unsettled land, Dobbs requested the Board of Trade to limit land grants to no more than 650 acres in a single patent. He maintained that the smaller grants would be of a more convenient and economic size for the Scotch and German settlers pouring into the back country from Virginia and Pennsylvania.

In his efforts to carry out a measure of land reform and provide for the legal registration of titles and the collection of quit-rents, Dobbs embarked on a scheme of purification as it were. The Receiver-General, John Rutherford, was instructed to prepare proper accounts and compile rent rolls, while other officials, James Murray the Secretary and Mathew Rowan, were ordered to submit reports on the issues of currency in the province; John Starkey, the treasurer of the southern district, was requested to draw up a report of his office. These officials were colonial officers of long standing and of considerable influence who did not take kindly to the new and sweeping orders of the Governor, which up to a point reflected on their integrity. Murray, Rutherford, and Starkey soon headed a dissident minority in the Assembly and threatened opposition to many of the Governor's measures, which they conceived as pressing royal prerogatives over-zealously and with little regard for the Assembly and people of North Carolina. While this opposition may have had roots in an embryonic spirit of independence, it developed, in the main, from personal dissatisfaction. Dobbs, who at times could be dictatorial and ill-tempered, was not averse to removing some of these men from office and severely criticising others, thus engendering a certain amount of bitterness. In an early communication to the Board of Trade, he complained about Rutherford, remarking: 'Tho' I have no reason to doubt his being an honest man, yet I believe he is quite indolent and am told he gives himself no trouble to go about to collect the quit rents.' In preparing the ground for Rutherford's dismissal, Dobbs added: 'It certainly requires a person of activity as well as a careful and good accomptant, to be employed in that receipt, and is a place not to be given out of favour.' [9]

The first signs of disunity, and the rise of a dissentient group in opposition to Dobbs's administration, became apparent towards the close of the year 1757. Up to this time the utmost harmony and goodwill existed between the Governor and the Assembly. However, the inefficient administration of the land office, the unsatisfactory state of the quit-rent collection, and the neglect to reduce unpaid arrears—an almost impossible task under existing conditions—resulted in the Governor charging Rutherford with neglect in his office, and he coupled his name with that of James Murray, whom he charged with irregular transactions in issuing private notes; he charged both men with forming a cabal in the Assembly in opposition to him. Dobbs first raised the matter in Council, and the Council ordered that Rutherford and Murray be suspended from office.[10] The suspension of Rutherford and Murray has been the subject of much controversy, and has been adduced as evidence of Dobbs's so-called choleric and splenetic temper, but the fact remains that the issuing of private notes in payment of quit-rents—though not without precedent—was irregular, and tended to debase the already depreciated currency of the province and add to the existing chaos. In reporting the suspensions to the Board of Trade, Dobbs criticised John Starkey, and charged him with the then odious crime of being a Republican, and scheming to transfer power from the Governor and Council to the Assembly. There was, of course, some element of truth in this, but Starkey was not the only colonist to defend the sovereign authority of the colonial legislature against the overriding power of the Governor, the Board of Trade, the Privy Council, and the British Parliament. The right to legislate freely, to control the internal affairs of the colonies, to enjoy the same rights and privileges as their English brethren while maintaining a close unity and loyalty to the Crown, was the ideal and aim of the more thoughtful and progressive colonials. Their outlook in this respect was somewhat similar to that of many Irishmen of the day, and theirs was the spirit of Molyneux, Swift, and Lucas.

Though Dobbs acted correctly in suspending Rutherford and Murray, he never took any action against Starkey beyond criticising him as the leader of what he termed 'a junto,' but in no way interfering with his liberty of action. Starkey, though bitterly critical of the Governor, occupied a prominent place in the Assembly throughout the entire period of his administration. Dobbs, in spite of his intense loyalty to the Crown and the British Constitution, had a certain amount of sympathy with those who sought a greater measure of legislative and administrative independence under the Crown. To show that he was simply carrying out his duties as a loyal servant, he did what no previous governor had done, and that was to lay his instructions before the Assembly so that the members might appreciate his difficult role. With

regard to the suspension of Rutherford and Murray, the Board of Trade
approved of the Governor's action.

Undoubtedly the dismissal of these two men caused some feeling of
ill-will, but on the whole little occurred during the year to disturb the
outward calm and harmony of the administration. So far as the war was
concerned, nothing of a decisive nature took place. Holbourne's grand
fleet was scattered in a storm, and Loudoun's army simply melted
away with inaction and sickness. Montcalm, despite the attention of
the British fleet, was able to reinforce his army. On 4th August he
invested Fort William Henry, the strong British post on the south
shore of Lake George facing the French fort of Ticonderoga, and an
outer bastion of Fort Edward at the head of the Hudson. After three
days of brave but futile resistance on the part of Colonel Monroe and
his ill-equipped garrison, the fort surrendered to the French. The news
of the fall of Fort William Henry was conveyed to Dobbs by Dinwiddie, who wrote:

> 'I am sorry I have occasion to write to Yo' that our affairs to the No'w'd
> have very gloomy aspects. The Enemy invested F't W'm Henry with
> 11,000 men on the 4th this mo. They held out until the 7th., when they
> were oblig'd to capitulate, the terms not yet known. Two days after they
> besieg'd Fort Edward w'ch is supposed to be under the same fate as the
> former, and it is suppos'd they have march'd to Albany, and where they
> may stop God Knows.' He ends with the melancholy note: 'The Great
> consternation and fear N. York is in can't be described. . . . I was willing
> to give you the earliest of the News tho' bad. I have been confined with
> fever and ague for some time, wh'ch makes writing uneasy.' [11]

Fortunately for the colonies, things were not quite as bad as Dinwiddie reported. After the fall of Fort William Henry, Montcalm
turned northward again for Ticonderoga, which he reinforced, and
then disbanded his Canadian troops to permit them to return to their
homes to save the harvest. Had Montcalm advanced, the fall of Fort
Edward was only a matter of days, as well as the thriving town of
Albany, the fall of which would throw wide open the road to New
York. Dinwiddie's letter containing news of the fall of Fort William
was his last communication to Dobbs, for, broken in health, tired and
weary of the incessant toils of office, he retired to England some months
later to enjoy a well-earned rest. When Dinwiddie retired, Dobbs lost
a very good friend. Both men had much in common; they were
intensely interested in the welfare and well-being of the American
colonies, and shared a common interest in their loyalty to the Crown

and in their hatred of the French. Again, both shared a responsibility in bringing about hostilities between England and France by reason of their support of the Ohio Company, which was a direct threat to French expansionist policy in America.

The sorry plight of British arms in America aroused the people in England, who viewed Whitehall and Westminster as an ant-heap stirred to its depths with a hoard of peers, as 'plentiful as tabby cats,' who spent their time chattering, negotiating, bargaining, and intriguing while whole armies under stupid and inept generals suffered defeat after defeat. In June the Newcastle administration was mercifully swept aside, and Pitt, in a new government, set to work to clean out the dead wood left behind. News of Pitt's reappointment did not reach Dobbs until the close of the year, and he immediately wrote to him voicing his feelings.

> 'It gives me great pleasure,' he said warmly, 'to hear that you are restored to the Executive of your trust as Secretary for the Southern Department by the united Voice of the people of England, as I know you have the interest of the Commerce and safety of our American colonies so much in your power and at heart.' [12]

In the month of December, Pitt communicated with Dobbs and the Governors of Maryland, Virginia and South Carolina, informing them that

> 'his Majesty having nothing more at heart than to repair the losses & disappointments, of the last inactive & unhappy campaign, and by a most vigorous & extensive effort, to avert, by the blessing of God on his Arms, the Dangers impending on North America; and not doubting, that all his brave and faithful Subjects there will cheerfully co-operate with, and second to the utmost the large Expence and Extraordinary Succours, supplied by this Kingdom for their preservation and defence.'

He therefore asked the Governors to

> 'forthwith use your utmost Endeavours & Influence with the Council and Assembly of your Province to induce them to raise, with all possible dispatch, as large a body of men, with your Government, as the number of its Inhabitants may allow, that you do direct them to hold themselves in readiness, as early as may be, to march to rendez-vous at such Place or Places, as may be named for that purpose by Brigadier General Forbes appointed to command his Majesty's Forces in those parts.' [13]

A few days later a further circular from Pitt informed Dobbs of Loudoun's recall, and the appointment of General Abercrombie as

Commander-in-Chief, and of an immediate plan to raise at least 'twenty thousand men to join a body of the King Forces for Invading Canada by way of Crown Point . . . and if found practicable to attack either Montreal or Quebec.' [14] Pitt's plan for the ensuing year, following the dispatch of 14,000 troops under the command of able and energetic young officers, had three main objectives—the capture of Louisbourg, Ticonderoga, and Fort Duquesne. The officer commanded to lead an army against Louisbourg was one of Pitt's younger men, Jeffrey Amherst, who had the thirty-year-old James Wolfe as his second in command. The capture of the French stronghold of Ticonderoga was entrusted to the futile Abercrombie, who should have been recalled with his chief Loudoun, but fortunately he had as second in command the energetic Brigadier Forbes whose task was to reduce Fort Duquesne. A strong fleet under the command of Admiral Boscawen was also dispatched to America.

While the imperial Government under Pitt's direction set about the task of destroying the French armies in America with éclat, the hope of raising 20,000 colonial troops to assist the British regulars was most uncertain. The three provinces of Pennsylvania, Maryland, and Virginia, with a population of more than half a million white people, and the now relatively populous North Carolina, recruited no more than 2,000 half-hearted militia between them; so half-hearted and ill-assorted were the militia, and so poor was the response of these provinces, that even Washington almost despaired of his fellow-countrymen. 'Such is the example of the officers,' he exclaimed, 'such is the behaviour of the men, and upon such circumstances the safety of this country depends that nothing keeps me from resignation but the imminent danger to my country.' [15] The tardy and poor response of the colonies in providing sufficient troops for their own defence is one of the unaccountable enigmas of American history.

The failure of North Carolina to provide the quota of troops agreed upon by Dobbs at Philadelphia was a sore disappointment, and in a speech to the Assembly in 1757 he remarked bitterly: 'I wish your parsimony at this critical time may not be the occasion of a much greater expense and Trouble to you if those companies should be wanted, for then I must assemble you soon to meet again, and it will be a much greater expense to cloath and raise so many more men.' In spite of his disappointment, however, Dobbs did appreciate the fact that with its meagre resources North Carolina contributed more proportionately to the war effort than the wealthier neighbouring provinces.

With the prospect of a new and vigorous campaign against the

French about to open, and an insistent call from both Pitt and General
Forbes for still more colonial troops, Dobbs convened the Assembly
towards the end of April 1758. In opening his address he pointed out
that he was compelled to consult the Assembly 'at this most emergent
and Critical Juncture, whereon the future safety and Happiness of the
American Colonies depends,' and reminded the members that they had
now an opportunity of showing their patriotism and

> 'of getting rid forever of your perfidious, restless and Inveterate Enemies
> the French from this American Continent, and of securing, for the future,
> our most Holy Protestant Religion, Liberties and Possessions.' He went
> on: 'I have reason to hope, after the correction we have received from
> Providence for our gross neglect of His Worship and our sensualities, and
> our Treatment of the Indians, that God will now return and head our
> Armies and Councils, and the cause of British Liberties in America, but
> if we now neglect this critical time, we must give up to our cruel enemies,
> and submit to French tyranny and Popish Idolatory and Superstition,
> which God avert.'

In the course of his address he recalled his castigation of the Assembly
for what he termed its 'ill-Judged Parsimony,' but he was now confident that the members would give 'such supplies as may enable us to
exert our force with the utmost dispatch.' [16]

The members of the Assembly in their reply drew attention to the
poverty of the province, still further impoverished

> 'by the frequent Aids granted to his Majesty during the present war to
> protect this Province and assist in the defence of Virginia, New York and
> South Carolina . . . are much more than the currency at present circulating
> amongst us; that it is impossible for us to give such demonstrative Proofs
> of our zeal and ardour as we could wish ! However, notwithstanding the
> Indigency of the Country, we shall with dispatch and alacrity prepare a bill
> for augmenting the number of Forces now in the pay of this province, and
> transporting and paying them when joined to his Majesty's other forces
> under the command of Brigadier General Forbes.'

A few days later the Assembly brought in a Bill to augment the provincial forces to three hundred effective men, and an Aid of £7,000 for
'the augmentation of the said forces, and subsisting and paying them
when augmented, and for placing garrisons in the Forts on the sea-
coasts.' Dobbs wasted no time in implementing the Bill, and forthwith
issued a Proclamation that was a stirring call to arms, a fierce denuncia-
tion of popish superstitition, and a zealous laudation of Protestantism. [17]

The war against the French experienced a new momentum under

the ægis of Pitt and his young generals and resulted in the capture of Louisbourg in August. Unfortunately, this victory was preceded by the defeat of Abercrombie's troops at Ticonderoga, and the death in action of the gallant Lord Howe. The capture of Louisbourg, the Dunkirk of the north, in a combined operation of naval forces under Boscawen, and an army of 12,000 men under Amherst, with his Brigadiers Lawrence and Wolfe, was a victory marking the beginning of the end of the French empire in America. Some 6,000 French prisoners were taken and shipped to England, and all Cape Breton and the adjacent island of St. Jean fell to the English, thus opening, as it were, the front door to Quebec. Wolfe, who led the first landing party against Louisbourg, which from now on was to be the rendezvous for the ever-increasing British fleet, was recalled to England by Pitt to command an expedition planned against Quebec.

Another heartening sign of the growing determination to rid the American continent of the French was the response of the northern provinces to supply the 20,000 men Pitt asked for; in contrast to Pennsylvania, Maryland, Virginia, and North Carolina, New England responded with vigour; Massachusetts pledged her credit to the extent of half a million sterling, Connecticut was only a little behind, while New Hampshire placed one-third of her male adults in the field; altogether, these provinces raised 17,000 men. In September, the French stronghold, Fort Frontenac, the key to the west and the guardian of Lake Ontario, fell to an army of Provincials under the command of the impetuous Bradsheet. The troops of the southern provinces, under the command of General Forbes, were assembled at Fort Cumberland, Reastown, and Philadelphia, and continued but a small ill-assorted army despite the appeals of the southern governors. Pennsylvania provided but 2,500 men out of a population of more than a quarter of a million, Maryland contributed 270 very indifferent soldiers, Virginia raised two regiments of 1,400 men and such first-rate colonial officers as Washington, Byrd, and Lewis, and North Carolina sent 300 men. The four thousand southern Provincials were on the whole a motley lot, and Forbes, generally admitted an impartial judge, says of their officers that 'except a few in the higher ranks they are an extremely bad collection of broken inn-keepers, horse-jockeys and Indian traders.' Washington, as already noted, had an equally poor opinion of them, and asked to be 'distinguished from the common run of Provincial officers,' whom he characterised as a 'motley herd.' [18]

The campaign against Duquesne lacked the verve and dash of the assault on Louisbourg, due in the main to the slow assembly of Am-

herst's army in the first instance, and the difficulty of deciding on an
approach to the Ohio. Braddock's road from Fort Cumberland was
still available, but it was long and circuitous, and was thought incapable
of taking the heavy traffic of the advancing army; in consequence, a
new road was cut through the wilderness, but the work was slow
despite the energy of General Forbes and his engineer Bouquet. An
advance camp was established at Loyal Hannon, about fifty miles short
of Fort Duquesne. Early in September, 750 men under Major Grant
attempted to take this fort by surprise, but were themselves surprised
and driven back with considerable loss. As the weeks slipped by, the
outlook grew more and more discouraging. The North Carolina troops
who reached Fort Cumberland some months earlier under the command of Waddell were now placed under Washington's command with
the Maryland and Delaware contingents. On 12th November word
reached the outpost at Loyal Hannon that the French and their Indian
allies were advancing from Fort Duquesne. Washington, with 500 Virginians and 500 other Provincials including his North Carolinians, was
ordered to meet the enemy, and if possible bring back prisoners so that
some information might be obtained regarding conditions in Fort
Duquesne. On the approach of Washington and his men, the French
retreated, and in the ensuing skirmish the North Carolina troops captured two Indians, and the information they gave induced Forbes to
continue hacking a road through the forests. On 24th November the
advance patrols reached Duquesne, or more correctly what had been
Fort Duquesne, for the French had abandoned their stronghold on the
Ohio and fired it. With the abandonment of Duquesne the threat to
the southern colonies through the Ohio Valley disappeared, and the
tide of war turned northward.

The year, with its measure of success for British arms, was not un-
eventful for Dobbs and his administration. Rutherford and Murray,
still smarting under the stigma of their removal from office, continued
to raise opposition to the Governor, and going over his head, Rutherford wrote to the Earl of Granville requesting a hearing of his case by
the Privy Council. In his letter to Granville, Rutherford was careful
not to mention his dismissal from the office of Receiver-General, but
complained that his removal from the Council was unjust. He claimed
that his seat on the Council was 'an office of great Honour and no
profit' and that his suspension therefrom 'gives me the utmost concern
that I should be condemned without permission to be heard in my
defence.' Without the slightest evidence to support it, Rutherford
charged that

'it is well known that the understanding & Judgement of the Governor is wasted & greatly impaired, and also how much he is guided by his country-men residing in the province and determined to elbow out anybody in Place of Trust to make room for them. I am persuaded that the whole cause of my suspension has proceeded only from these motives.' [19]

Rutherford's charges marked the initial steps taken by a disgruntled faction to impugn the integrity and honesty of the Governor. Unfortunately the charges of nepotism, choleric temperament, and doddering senility have since clouded the name of Governor Dobbs. At this time Dobbs was sixty-nine years old and not seventy-four as many would have us believe.[20] His mind, for a man of his years, was very clear, as may be seen from reading the many letters he wrote to both the Government in England and his numerous friends; his vigour and health are amply demonstrated by the ease and facility with which he travelled through the province. As to the charge of nepotism, the only relatives Dobbs gathered around him were his son and nephew, and to provide for them in an age when the spoils of office were recognised perquisites scarcely sustains the charge. With regard to the appointments given to his son, none was of sufficient importance to warrant a charge of favouritism; the appointment of his son to command a body of North Carolina troops was justified on the ground that he was a regular army officer. It is a little more difficult to justify the appointment of his son to the Council, but this appointment had little effect, since Captain Dobbs was mainly absent on active service. Dobbs's nephew, Spaight, fared better, for from the outset he was secretary to the Governor, later secretary of the province, paymaster of the troops, and a member of the Council. With the exception, therefore, of his son and nephew, his administration was singularly free of nepotism.[21]

Rutherford's charges did not help his case, nor was Granville the right person to present it, for as the sole proprietor of a large part of North Carolina territory he was by no means friendly with a Governor who was convinced that Granville territory was an outmoded anachronism, and militated against the successful government of the province. Granville requested the Board of Trade to reconsider Rutherford's and Murray's case; at the same time he submitted a copy of Rutherford's complaints. The Board of Trade was not disposed to re-open the case, and having considered Rutherford's communication, informed Granville that

'the character and conduct of the Governor of North Carolina which has ever been as far as comes within our knowledge such as deserves countenance and Protection.' The Board concluded: 'We are humbly of the opinion that the case does not admit of the indulgence which he desires. And we must further beg leave to say that his taking upon to arraign in so extraordinary manner the Justice of the Board is in our opinion such a proceeding as deserves censure.' [22]

Though the Murray and Rutherford episode ended in a victory for the Governor, their removal from the Council strengthened the latent opposition in the Assembly. This opposition found a place in all the colonies, and was not so much directed against the person of the Royal Governor as against the superior authority of his office. In North Carolina, Dobbs heretofore experienced no difficulty with the Assembly, and though the cabals or juntas which he complained of existed, they were for the most part cliques of self-interested men with personal grievances. Dobbs, though a very liberal man, had very strong and decided views; he was stubborn and brooked neither opposition nor criticism, and being impatient and at times hot-tempered, he made enemies. Towards the close of the year he had a serious brush with the Assembly over a trivial and relatively unimportant matter. The Committee of Accounts under the chairmanship of Starkey, with whom Dobbs was not on good terms, disallowed a claim by Secretary Spaight for an account he paid by order of the Governor. While the Committee was technically correct, Dobbs in a hasty message to the Assembly complained that the disallowance of the claim of his secretary was

'an affront against me, and in it I have been treated with the greatest indignity.' He continued: 'I do not lay it to the charge of this Committee, but to the Chairman who by aiming at a false popularity pretends not only to lead the Committee but to Govern the House; Had I pretended to order it to be paid out of any improper fund otherwise appropriated, I think he, as his Majesty's Servant and Treasurer, ought in duty to have applied to me to have cleared up the point before he had the Committee to brand me with acting illegally with opprobrious words.'

Dobbs was, of course, correct in suggesting that the Committee might have consulted him, but he was wrong in suggesting that he had been branded by the Chairman, a man of considerable popularity, or the Committee, and his threat that if the Assembly continued to support the Chairman he would be at 'liberty to disapprove of the Claims of Accounts, and then no payments can be made without my Order' was riding in the teeth of the Assembly, which, though divested by

Dobbs's instructions of much of its power and liberty of action, held tightly to the public purse.

The Assembly considered the Governor's complaint, and in a measured reply stated that the members were concerned that a transaction in which the Governor's name did not appear should be construed 'a design to caste a slur' on his conduct, adding 'nothing could be further from the intention of the Committee, and are certain that nothing could be more remote from the Design of the House.' The Assembly pointed out that Spaight's claim was disallowed because of his failure to produce a vouched statement, and hoped that the Governor would be 'satisfied that nothing happened either in the House or the Committee, that might reasonably be construed as an intended Indignity to you.' The Assembly, quite naturally, defended the Chairman of the Committee, remarking: 'As to any undue influence of the Chairman of the Committee we are Strangers to it, and apprehend your ear must have been abused in this particular, as he never attempted anything of the kind in the House.' The Assembly ordered the payment of Spaight's claim, and though the matter ended amicably, it left a very bad taste behind and a certain amount of ill-feeling.[23]

Despite the exigencies of war, the question of the establishment of a new seat of Government engaged Dobbs's attention; he raised the matter in the Assembly and, though recommending a site on the River Neuse at Tower Hill, part of his own property, he left the choice entirely to the Assembly. The matter was fully debated, and after due consideration the Assembly agreed that the suggested 'site was the most convenient place' and requested 'that if it be agreeable to your Excellency that it should be applyed to that purpose and what sum would be adequate satisfaction for your interest in the said land and Plantation.' Dobbs replied:

> 'As you have thought it the properest place for the seat of Government from its Healthy situation and being most central for the Ease of the Inhabitants (though I should have been glad that it had been fixed on any other convenient Situation) I shall desire no more than the original sum which it cost me.'[24]

Dobbs's reply is of some interest in view of the fact that it was later charged that he purchased the Tower Hill property with the avowed intention of utilising it as a site for the seat of Government and reaping a rich return on the sale of land. Dobbs never pressed the Assembly to purchase his property, nor did he show the slightest desire to enrich himself at the expense of the province, but offered the property at the price he paid for it, even though its value had increased considerably since he purchased it. Though an Act was passed for the establishment of a new seat of Government, it was disallowed by the Privy Council. Some years later when the Assembly abandoned the idea of a new seat of Government, Dobbs claimed that he was entitled to the price he had paid for the Tower Hill property, and also the interest normally accruing thereon.

Dobbs found the damp and humid atmosphere of New Bern trying, and during his years of residence there suffered considerably from ague and rheumatism. In 1758 he purchased the 'shell of a house' in the neighbourhood of Brunswick, a town founded by the Moore brothers about 1725, and agreeably situated on the west bank of the Cape Fear River.[25] Within a few months the former shell of a house took shape: it was an oblong timbered structure of two storeys exclusive of basement, surrounded on both floors by a wide piazza with a protecting balustrade. Stables, coach-houses and other buildings were soon completed, and a neat fruit garden laid out; the property contained about sixty acres, which permitted Dobbs to engage once more in farming.[26] The nearby Brunswick, a small town of timbered houses with a population of about two hundred inhabitants, was in the heart of the well-settled Cape Fear district, which boasted many prosperous plantations equal in size and productiveness to all but the very largest in Maryland, Virginia, and South Carolina. Brunswick had a good, safe harbour and was used by ships carrying naval stores to Britain; in fact, more products were shipped from Brunswick to the mother country than from any other port in the colonies. A few years before Dobbs settled at Brunswick he encouraged the construction of St. Philip's Church, the cost of which came in part from a captured Spanish privateer, supplemented by private donations and lotteries. The church was a handsome building constructed with English bricks, and when completed was designated as His Majesty's chapel in the province, and a special pew, raised above the others, was set aside as the Governor's pew.

Dobbs grew increasingly lonely with the years, and his removal to Brunswick cut him off from some of his former friends, including his nephew Spaight who, on his marriage, no longer lived with the old man. For a few months he enjoyed the companionship of his son, who had been obliged because of ill-health to relinquish his command at New York, but towards the end of the year Edward Dobbs sailed for Europe to join his former regiment, then stationed at Gibraltar. The departure of his son was a wrench for Dobbs, who, despite some puritanical traits in his character, was fond of company and the fellowship of other men. Among his neighbours in Brunswick County were Mathew Rowan, John Davis, Colonel Moore, Dr. Green, and Captain Dry, but most of his older friends were scattered throughout the province. Among these was Major McWain, who had a fine plantation on the Neuse not far distant from Dobbs's estate at Tower Hill. Hugh M'Aden, a Presbyterian minister, wrote of meeting Dobbs at McWain's house, and described him as a 'very sociable gentleman.' [27] The passing years, however, had wrought a change, and in his loneliness and isolation Dobbs had grown a little more impatient, petulant, and, at times, irascible.

13

The Difficult Years

THE YEAR 1759, while bringing a welcome measure of success to the sorely tried armies of Britain, and heralding the end of French power in America, marked the opening of a trying and difficult period in colonial administration. Following the removal of the French threat, the colonies became less dependent upon the mother country and more critical of Royal government. A spirit of independence found expression in most Assemblies, and though the spirit of opposition to the authority of the governors and the rulings of the Privy Council had been very marked in some provinces, it was only during the last years of his administration that Dobbs had to contend with it. The long-drawn-out war and the consequent neglect of many internal problems resulted in a certain amount of unrest in North Carolina, and this led at times to unnecessary bitterness and unseemly quarrels between the Assembly and the Governor, which culminated in a series of charges against the administration which amounted almost to the impeachment of Dobbs.

Unfortunately, this period of unrest with its quarrels, its charges and counter-charges, has been exaggerated and magnified, and one might conclude, if one accepts all that has been written by historians, that the last years of Dobbs's governorship were brightened by the vigour of a patriotic opposition, and marred by the harsh autocracy of an enfeebled and tyrannical dotard. This, in fact, is far from the truth, and though there was a considerable amount of opposition, it was not a result of the uprising of a downtrodden people, nor did it arise from the so-called tyranny and harsh rule of an embittered Governor.[1]

The years of war had affected North Carolina; the country was weighed down with an accumulation of debt, the result of constant demands for men and money to pursue the war against France. Internal affairs had been neglected, and a spirit of unrest and dissatisfaction prevailed in many quarters. Though the war with France had moved far beyond the frontiers of North Carolina, the demand for more troops and more money was not at an end; in South Carolina the

Cherokee Indians had risen in rebellion and the Governor called on the Northern Province for aid. On the frontier and in the backward areas of North Carolina isolated settlements were threatened by Indian warriors which necessitated the maintenance of a force of Provincials at Fort Dobbs and the establishment of another fort on the Catawba River. Besides contending with warlike Indians, unrest existed in other parts of the province. Along the ill-defined boundary between North and South Carolina grants of land were made by the Southern Province of land lying in the northern area and vice versa, and this resulted in the creation of what Dobbs described as a 'kind of sanctuary allowed to criminals and vagabonds by their pretending, as it served their purpose, that they belonged to either Province.' [2]

Another hindrance to internal peace, and one responsible for much of the ensuing trouble, was the existence of the Granville district in North Carolina. This state within a state, a legacy from the days of proprietorship, comprised almost half the total area of North Carolina, and stretched from the Virginia border in the north to a line running through the present towns of Snow Hill and Princeton along the southern borders of Chatham, Randolph, Davidson, and Rowan to a little below the south border of Catawba County and westward to the Mississippi. Granville territory was the most thickly populated part of North Carolina and was the private property of the Earl of Granville.[3] This proprietorship was an incubus, and at times a festering sore on the body economic and politic of North Carolina. For many years settlers in the territory were subject to extortion, exaction, and oppression by Granville's agents, and this bred a spirit of rebellion. In 1755, a Committee set up by the Assembly found that Granville's agents had enriched themselves by giving unlawful grants of lands for which they exacted exorbitant fees, and that their conduct generally constituted 'a grievance detrimental to his Lordship's interest, and greatly retarded the settlement of that part of the Government of which his Lordship is proprietor.' [4] The exactions of Granville's agents steadily worsened, and by 1758 became so intolerable that an application was made to the Attorney-General seeking relief. The Attorney-General advised the appellants to petition either the Earl of Granville or the Assembly. Towards the end of the year, William Williams, the representative from Edgecombe County, presented a petition to the Assembly, and a Committee was set up to enquire into the conduct of two of Granville's agents, Francis Corbin and Joshua Bodley. The Committee later submitted a report which condemned the unjust exactions and malpractices of Granville's agents.[5]

The Assembly received the report but did nothing about it, and in consequence rioting broke out in Edgecombe County and elsewhere. Corbin was apprehended by a body of men, and taken some seventy miles from his house near Edenton and held under duress. He was compelled to sign a bond to return at the following spring court and disgorge all the fees unjustly taken from the people. On giving this undertaking he was permitted to return home. The Attorney-General, Robert Jones, swore on oath before the Governor and Council that he had heard 'it was intended by a great number of rioters to petition the court at Granville to silence him,' he thereupon requested that a proclamation be issued and a reward offered for discovering the rioters.[6] A stern proclamation was issued by Dobbs condemning traitorous conspiracies, and offering a reward for the discovery of Corbin's abductors. A number of rioters were arrested, but the jail was broken open and the prisoners set at liberty. Corbin took steps to prosecute the rioters, but 'being advised that if matters came to trial he would be the sufferer, as he had done things he could not justify, and that the fault would be laid to the charge of his office, he let matters drop.'[7]

Some months later the Assembly, no doubt at the behest of Corbin and his friends, charged the Governor with failing to put down the 'mobs, riots and insurrections that prevailed.' Dobbs, in replying to this charge, claimed that the Assembly exaggerated the position, and recalled the fact that Corbin and his subordinates had been severely censured by the Assembly for his exactions and malpractices; he also reminded the members that it was not the function of the Governor to proceed against the rioters, but the duty of Corbin's friend Robert Jones, the Attorney-General. The Assembly, 'severely virtuous and greatly shocked in every fibre of their law-abiding sensibilities at the traitorous conspiracies of the rioters, particularly at the arrest of the gentle Corbin, condemned both the Governor and the rioters.'[8] It would seem difficult to understand the 'severely virtuous' attitude of the Assembly, and its ganging up with Corbin, who suddenly became the gentle agent, the friend of law and order, while the rioters, with the connivance of the Governor, were condemned as a riotous mob. Saunders writes:

> 'It will not do to say that the Assembly was so actuated by a regard for the law and respect for the officers, that though they sympathised with the people in their grievances, they felt obliged to condemn the methods adopted for redress, even against such men as Corbin, for if ever a people were estopped by their record from pleading habitual reliance on purely

judicial methods for redress of grievances, the people of North Carolina would seem to be that people.' [9]

It would appear at this stage that a strong and voluble opposition party had arisen in the Assembly intent upon curbing the authority of the Governor and usurping his power. In fact, however, the opposition to the Governor was more voluble than powerful, and in the main derived its strength from a group of self-interested and ambitious men. Undoubtedly there was an incipient spirit of republicanism apparent among a few patriotic members like the venerable John Starkey, Samuel Swann, John Ashe, and a few others, but Francis Corbin, Thomas Barker, Robert Jones, and Thomas Child were not motivated by this ideal in their opposition to the Governor. These four men as Granville's agents or attorneys exerted considerable influence, and some of them, particularly Child and Corbin who had come under the Governor's displeasure, were ambitious, self-seeking men, who desired nothing more than their own elevation to positions of trust.[10]

The disallowance by the King in Council of a number of Bills passed by the Assembly at this time did not contribute to harmony, nor did Dobbs's refusal at this juncture to assent to the appointment of an agent in London meet with the approval of the Assembly. Among the disallowed Bills were the necessary Acts for the establishment of higher and lower courts, and an Act for the setting up of vestries and the payment of salaries to orthodox clergy.

With regard to these measures, the Bills for the establishment of a judiciary were assented to by Dobbs, though it would appear they transgressed his instructions and impinged upon the Royal prerogative, for Dobbs was severely rebuked by the Board of Trade for assenting to them in the first instance. The rebuke hurt him and made him exceedingly wary of assenting to any Bill that seemed likely to offend his Royal masters.[11] The Vestry Bill was thrown out by the King in Council, at the suggestion of the Bishop of London, on the purely technical ground that it did not provide that vestrymen should be conforming members of the Church of England, and the Bill gave them power to dismiss clergymen and charge them in common courts.

The appointment of a colonial agent in London was another matter that gave rise to considerable bitterness and disagreement. The need for an agent in London was manifest, and it had long been the practice to have such a colonial representative. It may be recalled that Governor Johnston and the Council of North Carolina were represented by an agent during the dispute between himself and the Board of Trade.

A great deal of the bitterness and disagreement about the appointment of an agent might be laid at the door of an intransigent Assembly that insisted on appointing an agent responsible solely to the Assembly. Further, the mode and manner of appointment was definitely wrong. Admittedly the Assembly had a constitutional right to make an appointment, but when the appointment was tacked on as an additional clause to an Aid Bill, Dobbs refused to give his assent to it. His stubborn if correct stand gave rise to a charge that he opposed the appointment simply and solely because his nominee, Samuel Smith, was not appointed.[12] The controversy dragged on for many months to the detriment of all concerned.

Early in April 1759 Dobbs received an urgent appeal from Pitt for further aid in men and money in order to bring the war against France to a conclusion. He immediately called a meeting of the Assembly at Wilmington, which took place the following month. In a strong and vigorous address he asked the Assembly to grant as large an Aid as possible. From the tenor of the opening addresses it would seem that any breach or ill-feeling between the Governor and Assembly had been healed, and that an atmosphere of goodwill prevailed. The members of the Assembly assured Dobbs that in spite of the heavy calls upon the province and its indigency, an Aid Bill would be passed. Their address closed with the words: 'We are sensible of your Excellency's steady regard for the service of his Majesty, the Welfare and Prosperity of the People under your Government, and the Trade and Happiness of all his Majesty's Subjects; and ardently wish that your administration may be long and happy.' [13]

An Aid Bill was drawn up and passed by the Assembly, but the Bill contained a number of clauses not entirely relevant to it, among the clauses being one appointing an agent in London, and another making provisions for the future disposal of the colony's proportion of a Parliamentary grant of £50,000. When the Bill came before the Upper House, Dobbs intimated that he could not assent to a Bill, however necessary, that contained irrelevant and unnecessary clauses, and accordingly advised the deletion of all such clauses. The Assembly refused to accede to the Governor's request, and insisted that the Bill should pass as drawn up. Before throwing out the Bill, Dobbs prorogued the Assembly for three days in order to permit, as he said, the members to reconsider it. Three days later the Assembly re-presented the Bill without effecting any change. Dobbs immediately prorogued the Assembly and had the Bill thrown out in the Upper House. Thus for the first time since the outbreak of the war with France no aid was forthcoming for the payment or raising of new troops. The Assembly could claim that aid was in fact granted, but that it had been ungraciously refused by the Governor.

The action of the Governor at this critical stage was, to say the least of it, impolitic, and though the Aid Bill may not have been constitutionally correct, or may have, as Dobbs thought, encroached upon the Royal prerogative, the need for aid was so pressing as to brook no delay, even in the interests of constitutional niceties. Already the war with France was reaching a decisive stage in Europe, and the French were reeling under the onslaught of the Hanoverian troops of Prince Ferdinand, who was 'performing prodigies of valour, amid fearful scenes of carnage.' The French fleet had been swept from the seas, and men, munitions, and money were pouring into America as part of a decisive plan to destroy for all time French power and influence in Canada. Wolfe, aided by a powerful fleet, had been instructed to attack and conquer Quebec, while Amherst at the head of a large army was marching to his aid by the Lake Champlain route.

The Assembly in the meantime appointed an agent in London with whom it could transact business over the heads of the Governor and Council; its first act in this connection was to present a loyal address to the King. In the course of a letter to the Board of Trade, Dobbs complained that this action was highly irregular and that the Assembly refused to join in a loyal address with the Council, or send their address through him as the proper channel for communicating with His Majesty. He also complained that a colonial agent was appointed with a salary without the approbation or approval of the Council and Governor, and was made 'entirely under a junto of the Assembly.' The action of the Assembly in appointing an agent of its own choice was not *ultra vires*, though in the interests of peace and harmony it would have been better, and undoubtedly more correct, to appoint an agent jointly responsible to the Assembly, Council, and Governor.

Having prorogued the Assembly and refused his assent to the Aid Bill because of its irrelevant clauses, and because in his opinion it impinged upon the Royal prerogative, Dobbs immediately wrote to Pitt, giving the reasons for his actions.

'They met here and are now prorogued, without passing an Aid Bill, unless the Governor and Council should give up his Majesty's prerogatives and the Rights of the Upper House to a Junto of the Assembly ... If you approve of what I have done for preserving his Majesty's prerogatives and the rights of the Council you will find it absolutely neces-

sary that I should dissolve the Assembly, since the Speaker is irritated at his
not being appointed Chief Justice, and therefore wants to make a breach
in the Province betwixt the Council and the Lower House and I am assured
he will never again be chosen Speaker.' [14]

Dobbs was not correct in his assurance, for when the new Assembly
met some months later, Samuel Swann was elected Speaker.

In the course of a letter to the Board of Trade setting out his
reasons for rejecting the Aid Bill, Dobbs requested that the Treasurers
of the province should be nominated by him and thus the power of the
Assembly might be curbed. The Board of Trade, however, did not
see eye to eye with the Governor, and in the course of a long reply to
his communication remarked: 'We have carefully read and considered
this Bill, and though we cannot but approve of your having rejected
it, yet it does not appear to us to affect his Majesty's prerogatives to
such an extent as you seem to apprehend.' [15] On the question of the
Assembly's right to appoint an agent, and appropriate by legislation
the money granted by Parliament, the Board of Trade found the
methods of the Assembly 'very regular and proper.' [16] Though ruling
against Dobbs and in favour of the Assembly, the Board was very
careful not to impinge upon the authority of the Governor, and while
the Board admitted the right of the Assembly to appoint an agent and
public Treasurers, and to devise legislation for the appropriation of
the Parliamentary grant, the Board was sensible that in these matters

'it is the Governor's duty as one branch of the legislature to see that in the
Province of these laws and the mode of framing them a proper regard is
had to the form of the Constitution and his Majesty's just rights, and
although upon this way of reasoning we see no grounds to disapprove the
Aid bill in its abstract principle, yet we think the particular Provisions of
it and the mode of framing it to be in some cases exceptionable.' [17]

On the question of the appointment of an agent, the Board admitted
the undoubted right of the Assembly to appoint one, but supported
Dobbs's contention that the appointment should have been provided
by a distinct and separate Bill, and that the Committee of Correspondence set up exclusively by the Assembly should consist of members of
the Council as well.

Of more particular importance so far as the internal government of
the province was concerned was the disallowance by the Privy Council
of the judiciary Bills on the grounds that they restricted the power of
the King, and encroached upon his prerogative, especially in the manner of the appointment of judges. Unfortunately, the disallowance of

these Bills meant that North Carolina was deprived of courts of justice for more than eight months. When Dobbs was informed by the Board of Trade of the disallowance of the Court Bills he decided to withhold the information until such time as new laws could be introduced and passed by the Assembly. This was a wise decision, and in a subsequent communication to the Board of Trade he remarked that 'the hasty repeal of these laws, which certainly wanted to be amended or repealed, was inadvertently advised by the Attorney General and Chief Justice, who did not consider that there would be a stagnation of justice.' [18] He hoped, therefore, that their Lordships 'wont blame me for delaying publishing the Repeal for two months until new laws be passed.'

During the period that the province was more or less bereft of a judicature, Dobbs was faced with a number of serious problems: in the western parts of the colony the Cherokees and the Creeks, perhaps inspired by the French, were creating disturbances by attacking isolated settlements, butchering the settlers, and destroying their homes. There was also considerable trouble in the Granville Territory, and in the south the disputed borderland between North and South Carolina was the cause of much anxiety. To add to this, Dobbs's own state of health was none too good, and his son who had been very helpful for more than twelve months left to join his regiment of regulars now stationed at Gibraltar. All told, the year 1759 was an anxious and exacting one for Dobbs, illumined only by the cheering news of the now certain and inexorable defeat of France. From the north came the news of Amherst's advance to Lake Champlain, and the French withdrawal from Ticonderoga and Crown Point, followed by the capture of Fort Niagara by Prideaux and Johnson, and the capture of Quebec in mid-September by Wolfe. Early in October Dobbs was informed of the fall of Quebec and of the signal success of British arms. He immediately issued a proclamation appointing a day of solemn thanksgiving; to mark the occasion he composed a hymn, or more correctly a pæan, which he ordered to be sung 'to the 100 Psalm tune.' The hymn, consisting of twelve verses, can scarcely claim that appellation, much less be classed as poetry; it is rather repetitious in its praise of God, adulation of British prowess, and detestation of 'papal thraldom.'

In an enthusiastic letter to Pitt, Dobbs offered his congratulations

'upon the Glorious victory over the French,' adding: 'The glorious and remarkable Interposition of divine Providence against such superior num-

bers will I hope induce his Majesty, by your active and intrepid Administration . . . to pursue his conquests until the French be expelled from this
Continent and Mississippi and Mobile.'

He informed Pitt that

> 'Upon account of such glorious success I have appointed a day of solemn
> thanksgiving, and upon this happy event and important Crisis have com-
> posed a Hymn to be sung that day through this Province, which I beg leave
> to send you, as being at present conformable to all the Prophecies according
> to my interpretation of them at this happy era 1760—for during the whole
> war I have been a little enthusiastic in my expectations; as the object of
> my Wishes for near these thirty years in regard to the British Dominion
> over North America is now so near accomplishment.' [19]

The imminent defeat of France, the destruction of a great Catholic
power, the embodiment of the scarlet woman, fitted precisely to
Dobbs's interpretation of the Scriptures, and England—the new
Messianic kingdom—was about to rule the world under a great king,
the son of David.

While we may dismiss Dobbs's flights into the field of Biblical
interpretation and his lofty conception of a Messianic kingdom, we
must not lose sight of the fact that for close on thirty years he hammered on the doors of Government offices, and penned a stream of
letters and memoranda to ministers calling for a vigorous colonial
policy, and the expulsion of the French from the American continent.
One might speculate that some of his letters and memoranda, dust-
laden and unread in the office of the Secretary of State, may have
engaged the attention of the more forceful and public-spirited Pitt,
whose plan for the destruction of the French Empire in America
differed little from the plans suggested by Dobbs many years earlier.
That he saw in Pitt some of his own enthusiasm and love of Britain
might be inferred from the closing sentence of the letter quoted above:

> 'I beg pardon, Sir, for thus transgressing upon your patience and Time,
> but my heart is so full of joy that I must give it vent and wish that you
> may long enjoy the Effects which your Zeal and intrepid active Administra-
> tion has procured to the true Protestant Church and Liberties of Britain
> to the endless glory of his Majesty and his Illustrious Family.'

The Assembly met towards the end of November at Wilmington,
a town rapidly assuming a place of importance because of its secure
harbour, easy communication with the back country, and accessibility.
By 1760 Wilmington had a population of about eight hundred people,

and a considerable number of Highlanders who settled at Cross Creek at the head of the navigation above Wilmington had, by their energy and enterprise, helped to develop its trade by shipping the products of the back country down the river, and taking in return the manufactured goods of England and the products of the West Indies.[20] In his opening address to the Assembly, Dobbs recalled with pride the 'glorious success of His Majesty's arms,' and for the first time for some years did not feel constrained to demand aid; he did, however, make a request for money to pay the troops defending the 'forts on the sea-coast and back settlements, and to provide for the necessary expense already incurred for raising and marching the frontier militia to join the forces of South Carolina' against the Indians. He then informed the members that

'His Majesty in Council having repealed seven acts . . . particularly the Acts for Establishing the Supreme and County Courts and for Appointing parishes and Vestries, it will be necessary for you to enact new laws without the clauses objected to in such a manner as may be for the General benefit of this Province and the Establishment of our Holy Religion against prevailing Sectaries.'

His address was for the most part conciliatory and showed an earnest desire to heal old wounds and foster a better spirit in the Administration. In closing his address he said:

'As the future peace and welfare of this Province will depend upon the Union and Harmony of the several parts of this Province and Branches of the Legislature I therefore recommend to you that in these Bills now necessary to be re-enacted and amended that you will consider the future general good of this increasing colony that a perfect Harmony may be preserved which I shall to the utmost of my power and capacity promote by uniting his Majesty's just prerogatives with the rights and liberties of the People.'

The Assembly, still smarting under its conceived grievances, in a reply to the Governor's speech pointedly remarked that it was 'with very sensible concern' it found that so many laws 'well calculated for the advancement of religion and the distribution of justice' met with His Majesty's disallowance. The members were persuaded that had an agent 'duly authorised at home' been in London to represent to His Majesty and his Ministers 'the importance and utility of these Laws' they might not have been disallowed. However, they promised to bring in new laws and 'shall endeavour to avoid Incerting clauses which may

by lyable to any Just Exception.' [21] The Governor's plea for co-operation and harmony was accepted in the spirit in which it was given, and
the members pointed out: 'we are sensible nothing conduces to the
prosperity of any Community more than mutual agreement among the
several Members of it. We assure your Excellency that as we hitherto
have so we constantly shall use our best endeavours to cultivate the
same.'

The hope of a better understanding and harmony between the
Assembly and the Governor was unfortunately short-lived. A Bill was
passed early in the session to enable the Treasurers to issue paper bills
of credit to pay the troops and militia and meet the contingencies of
government. Dobbs, in accordance with his Instructions which forbade the issue of paper money, refused to give his assent to the Bill.
The Assembly thereupon suggested that provision for the payment of
troops might be made by withdrawing money set aside for building
schools and purchasing glebes. As this sum amounted to only £4,000,
Dobbs pointed out that it would be insufficient to meet commitments.
The Assembly then informed him that if it was not sufficient to pay
the troops and militia 'they must remain unprovided for.' Once again
Dobbs and the Assembly were at loggerheads; the re-enacted Bills for
establishing Supreme and County Courts proved unacceptable to the
Governor, and though strongly urged by the Assembly to give his
assent, he refused to do so, claiming that they differed little from the
previously disallowed Bills. The fate of the Court Bills and the appro-
priations for the defence of the province were now inextricably bound
together, and while the Assembly had no desire to leave the troops
unprovided for, it felt that money for defence should be raised by other
means than a poll tax, which, in view of the impoverishment of the
colony, might be difficult to raise, and if levied might take some time
to collect. In consequence, the Assembly insisted that the issuing of
proper bills of credit was the more appropriate and speedier means of
providing aid. Dobbs could not agree to this, however, as the terms of
his Instructions forbade him to assent to such issues as might be considered legal tender.

There seemed no way out of the impasse, for neither side would give
ground, and early in January 1760 Dobbs dissolved the Assembly
and ordered new elections. On the dissolution he read a speech to the
members in which he roundly upbraided them for presenting Bills that
encroached on the Royal prerogative, and which in consequence he
could not assent to. Then, announcing the dissolution of the Assembly,
he hurried from the chamber, refusing to leave a copy of his speech

for engrossing in the Journals. Though the Governor had refused to assent to the Aid and Judiciary Bills, we gather from his correspondence with Pitt that he more or less approved of the Assembly's action in pressing for the issue of paper bills of credit, pointing out that as the province lacked bullion there was no other way of providing aid or meeting the commitments of the Government. He wrote:

> 'As this instruction which I will and must adhere to until released from it has put an effectual stop to the issuing any further Notes for the publick service the Assembly had no better method to raise supplies for the current service . . . but by borrowing so much again from the bills repaid to the schools as much as answered the present emergency.'

By adhering strictly to his Instructions, Dobbs was constrained, therefore, to oppose a measure which he approved of in principle.[22]

Shortly before the new Assembly was elected, the Governor received a fresh appeal from Pitt for aid. Though Quebec was in British hands, the harsh winter had decimated the garrison, and there was still a large and well-equipped French army in Canada. Part of this army, under the command of Lévis, having inflicted a severe defeat on the English at St. Foy, was marching against Quebec. Fortunately, efforts to recapture the town failed, and the French were forced back to Montreal, the capture of which would complete the destruction of the French-Canadian Empire. To achieve this, Pitt issued an urgent appeal to the colonies for both men and money. While Dobbs could not guarantee any aid until the Assembly met, he informed Pitt that he could depend upon his 'most zealous endeavours to promote the raising of as many men as we can in the short time we have to do it in upon this crisis.'

The Assembly met at New Bern on 24th April, 1760, and Dobbs in his address showed that he bore no grudge or ill-feeling against any of the members, and only desired peace and harmony. He laid the request of Pitt and an appeal from General Amherst before the Assembly, and exhorted the members to raise 'with the utmost dispatch what men can be spared in the colony, that we may exert our whole force in conjunction with his Majesty's forces from Britain to dispossess and drive the French from this continent.' He assured the members of his confidence in them and of his certainty that they would grant aid with 'that zeal which you have hitherto shown in defence of his Majesty's Right.' Turning to internal affairs, he asked the members to amend and re-enact the disallowed Court and Vestry Bills, and in a friendly manner suggested that they should unite 'in appointing an agent . . . by a particular Bill framed for that purpose which I shall heartily concur in.' [23] In a reply to the Governor's address, the members, while offering their co-operation, were not quite ready to forget the differences of the past, and they reminded the Governor that the failure to pass an Aid Bill in the previous Assembly could not be laid against them, and that the Bill had been rejected by the Council on the advice of the Governor; furthermore, the Bills for establishing courts of justice had also been rejected. This was, of course, true, but the fact remains that the Governor rejected the Bills because they did not conform with his Instructions, and he therefore asked the Assembly to omit the objectionable clauses in the Bills, which it refused to do. In regard to the rejected Bills, the members of the Assembly assured Dobbs that

> 'these matters are only mentioned in consequence of the duty we owe our constituents with whose liberties we are intrusted—And not to raise disputes with your Excellency. On the contrary it will give us the highest pleasure so far as is consistent with the rights and liberties of a free and loyal people who never refused a single Aid you have required gladly to co-operate with you in everything that may contribute to his Majesty's service and the interest of the Province.' [24]

Despite these manifestations, it was soon clear that the opposition to the Governor was by no means dead. Early in the session the Assembly resolved itself into a committee of the whole House and agreed to a number of resolutions most of which, particularly those pertaining to the raising of troops, granting aid to His Majesty, the establishment of a vestry, the setting up of superior and inferior courts, and the appointment of an agent in London, were in accord with Dobbs's suggestions, but at least two of the resolutions were directly aimed at the Governor's authority. The seventh resolution claimed

> 'that it is the Indubitable right of the Assembly to frame and model every bill whereby an Aid is granted to his Majesty in such a manner as may render the same most effectually conducive to his Majesty's Service and the Honour and Interest of the Crown, and that every attempt to deprive them of the Enjoyment thereof is an infringment of the rights and privileges of the Assembly.' [25]

The eighth resolution was a definite refusal to accede to Dobbs's request that the audited accounts of the province should be inspected by him, laid before the Assembly, and then transmitted by him to England. This was in accordance with his Instructions, and Dobbs informed the Assembly that 'if his Majesty withdraws that Instruction I shall gladly acquiesce in it.' The Assembly refused to accept the Governor's interpretation of his Instructions, and claimed

> 'That the method observed by the Treasurers was agreeable to the directions of the several laws of this Province by virtue whereof the money by them accounted for was levied and consonant to constant and uninterrupted usage—And that the methods proposed by His Excellency is unprecedented and repugnant to law.'

There was little Dobbs could do to enforce his Instructions so far as the finances of the province were concerned, and this was the experience of most colonial governors, for over the years the Assemblies had won and exercised the same control over finance that the House of Commons exercised in Great Britain, and they successfully resisted all efforts to oust them from their hard-won position of financial supremacy.[26]

Despite Dobbs's impressive call for a fresh Aid Bill, the Assembly directed its energies to framing and re-enacting Superior and Inferior Court Bills. The new Bills differed little from those disallowed by the Privy Council, and in passing them the Assembly took the unusual course of sending a message to the Governor requesting his immediate assent to the Bills. Dobbs, recalling his recent censure by the Board of Trade for passing the previous Court Bills, pointed out that he was requested to do 'what was of unusual and unprecedented Nature and that he would consult with Gentlemen who were more conversant with these affairs, and when he had done so he would send an answer in writing which may be entered on the Journals.'[27] He thereupon referred the Bills to Chief Justice Charles Berry and Attorney-General Thomas Child with a copy abstract of his Instructions.

While awaiting the advice of Berry and Child, Dobbs sent a message to the Assembly pointing out that an Aid Bill was of paramount importance. 'I must,' he said, 'in common decency and respect to the Crown give the precedency in passing an Aid Bill to every other act that is offered.' This, he pointed out, was the uninterrupted usage of the Commons of Great Britain and Ireland. The Assembly did not agree with the Governor, and claimed that new Court Bills were a prime necessity, and as there was no immediate threat to the security of the colony, an Aid Bill could wait.

The Chief Justice and the Attorney-General, having examined the Court Bills, advised Dobbs to give his assent even though the Bills deviated 'from the letter of your instructions.' This was hardly the

advice Dobbs expected in view of the fact that the previous Court Bills
were disallowed by the Privy Council on the actual advice of these
gentlemen. He accordingly refused his assent, and in a strongly worded
message to the Assembly he informed the members

> 'that the self-interested Gentlemen who have procured the repeal of the
> former laws and have taken upon them to conduct those Bills and mislead
> the Assembly have been the cause that those Salutary Laws, as well as the
> Aid bill have not been already passed by clogging those bills with unneces-
> sary clauses to diminish his Majesty's prerogatives, and lay me under a
> dilemma, to serve their own secret ends of betraying my trust and disobeying
> his Majesty's orders and instructions if I should comply with your request,
> or raise a flame against my administration in case I should refuse to pass
> those bills.'

Though fully aware of the consequence of his action, he concluded: 'I
must with great concern inform you that I cant betray my trust to the
Crown, nor shall I disobey his Majesty's orders or Instructions so
that nothing will induce me to pass the Superior Court Bill.' [28]

Dobbs had no alternative but to take the stand he did. The Superior
Court Bill not only violated his Instructions but placed the associate
justices on a more independent footing than the Chief Justice, who
was appointed from England and held office during pleasure.[29] In order
to placate the members of the Assembly, however, and provide for
some form of judiciary, Dobbs offered a compromise, and suggested
that if the Assembly made the Bill temporary for a year or until 'his
Majesty's pleasure be known' or, alternatively, expunged the objectionable clauses, and at the same time passed an Aid Bill, he would
give his assent, otherwise he claimed the Bill would be disallowed.

The compromise was reasonable, but the Assembly thought otherwise and forthwith resolved itself into a secret committee of the whole
house. This 'grand inquisition' sat for five hours and drew up a list of
grievances and charges against the Governor and Secretary Spaight
which it proposed to lay before the King. The charges, in brief, were
that large sums of money amounting to £74,000 granted over the
years and entrusted to the Governor had been injudiciously applied;
that military commissions had been granted to persons of little experience; that the Governor, without any colour of law, appointed his
nephew paymaster to the forces, and that he drew commission on the
aids, thus rendering them insufficient for their purpose; further, the
Governor out of money granted by Parliament had procured payment
of £1,000 which had never been accounted for. The Governor was

also charged with disposing of Royal Charters at exorbitant prices, and granting licences to persons to practise law who were ignorant of even the rudiments of law, and exacting fees for these licences, which was illegal and contrary to an Act of the Assembly. Dobbs was also charged with condoning lawlessness, and failing to suppress the disorders that had taken place 'in open violation of all law.' There were other charges such as the removal of all books and records from the Secretary's office 'which rendered it expensive for the generality of the People to have the necessary recourse to that office,' and election illegalities which 'infringed the rights of the subjects and tended to endanger the constitution.' The complete charges brought against the Governor and his administration were formidable and give the impression of widespread maladministration, sordid peculation, and crude nepotism, together with an autocratic and oppressive rule marked by a complete disregard of the legal rights of the people. Unfortunately, many of the charges brought against the Governor, though couched in extremely vague and general terms and unsupported by any concrete facts or evidence, have been accepted as proven despite the fact that they were easily rebutted by Dobbs, and were completely ignored by the authorities in England.[30]

Having completed its task behind closed doors and in sworn secrecy, the Assembly sitting in open session refused to accept the compromise on the Court Bill or introduce an Aid Bill as suggested by Dobbs. He thereupon prorogued the session for three days in the hope that the members would change their minds. On the following Monday he asked to see the minute book of the Assembly so that he might acquaint himself with what had happened during the secret session, but his request was refused. The Assembly, however, drew up a temporary Court Bill as suggested by Dobbs, and he immediately assented to it; an Aid Bill was also passed, but this was rejected, as it still contained irrelevant clauses concerning the appointment of an agent. Dobbs accordingly prorogued the Assembly to 9th September.

Angered by the attitude of the Assembly and smarting under the unjust charges brought against his administration, Dobbs wrote a long memorandum to the Board of Trade in which he answered each of the charges *seriatim* and in great detail, showing up his traducers in a not too pleasant light. He charged that some members of the Assembly were plotting against the Crown and executive under the leadership of the Attorney-General Child, who had been discarded by Granville and removed from the Council of North Carolina, but had been elected to the Assembly by the voters of Chowan County. Child

undoubtedly had a definite bias against the Governor and an over-
weening personal ambition; he was utterly unscrupulous and wooed
popularity by deliberately leading the opposition for purely selfish
reasons, his aspirations being no less than the Governorship. It would
seem that in his opposition to the Governor, Child had the support of
the more disinterested men such as Starkey, Swann, Moore, and Ashe,
who quite obviously bore no personal animus against Dobbs but
defended the authority of the Assembly as a legal Parliament co-ordinate in status with the Parliament of Britain, and rightly considered any
interference with this status as unlawful and intolerable.

In the final paragraph of the memorandum of grievances and
charges against Dobbs, which more than probably was drawn up by
Child, it is stated that the members

'defer mentioning many abuses of power and acts of oppression other than
those which constrained by the necessity of the times and the desponding
situation of the Province, we have already related, nothing less than the
prospect of impending ruin and desolation would induce us at this time to
remonstrate against the conduct of a Governor to the ease and happiness
of whose administration we vainly endeavour to contribute; for some time
we have remained passive under the yoke of oppression, unwilling to
interrupt the important avocations which necessarily engage your Majesty's
attention but perceiving ourselves on the brink of anarchy and ruin—We
therefore with all humility and duty most humbly supplicate your Majesty's
justice and speedy relief.'

It is clear from this declamation that some members of the Assembly
were actually pressing for the recall of the Governor, and imputing to
him acts of oppression and injustice for which there was little justification.

Considerable lawlessness undoubtedly existed, and the lack of a
judiciary very possibly encouraged the rioters, but the members of the
Assembly did absolutely nothing to palliate them, and were in consequence as much responsible for the prevailing conditions as the unfortunate Governor whom they traduced. With regard to the depredations
of the Indians, which contributed to the unsettled state of the province, there was little Dobbs could do unless he was strongly supported
by vigorous action on the part of the Assembly. While it is not easy to
dismiss the Assembly's memorandum as a mere rhetorical outburst,
the picture of impending ruin and desolation is palpably false and does
not conform to the facts. In spite of the depressed state of the finances
of the province, the depredations of the Indians, the riots and disturb-

ances, the wealth and population of North Carolina had increased considerably, and even the restrictions imposed by the Navigation Acts did not prevent a growing and increasing export trade.

In the bitter quarrels and squabbles between the Governor and the Assembly, neither side was entirely blameless, nor was the Assembly overwhelmingly anti-Governor; in fact, within the House bitterness and division prevailed, and there was little agreement between the members from the northern counties and those from the south. Many if not most of those who sat in secret session and supported the memorandum of grievances bore no ill-will against the person of the Governor, but were opposed to rule by royal prerogative and the claims of the Privy Council to overrule the measures passed by the freely elected representatives of the people. Saunders sums up the position fairly when he writes:

'To this quarrel the Governor seems not to have been a party at the outset; indeed he seems to have sympathised with the Assembly. At a later period, however, having received a different inspiration from home and a fresh batch of instructions by which he learned that the Court Bill was inimical to the royal prerogatives he went into the fight hotly, and doubtless made it warm for those who opposed him. It would seem, too, from the fact that the members of the Council who supported the Governor were denounced as his "pimps and hangers-on" that the gentlemen on the other side were, perhaps, no more cool in their temper than careful in the choice of their words.' [31]

The temporary Court Bill passed by the Assembly and assented to by Dobbs unfortunately suffered the same fate at the hands of the Privy Council as the previous Bill, and Dobbs was again severely censured, not only for giving his assent but for seeking the advice of the Chief Justice and the Attorney-General, which the Board of Trade considered 'far from alleviating the Governor's improper conduct, that it is a heavy aggravation of it.' The Board further observed that

'Upon the whole, if the Governors of your Majesty's Colonies are suffered to go on in such repeated acts of Disobedience to your Majesty's Instructions, upon points so essential to the Constitution, the Dependence of those Colonies upon the authority of the Crown and the just Government of the Mother country already too much relaxed will stand upon a very precarious footing.'

In a message from the King in Council, Dobbs was warned:

'It is our express will and Pleasure that you do not upon any pretence whatever upon pain of being removed from your Government give assent to any act, by which the Tenure of the Commissions to be granted to the Chief Justice, or other Justices of the Several Courts of Judicature shall be regulated, or ascertained in any manner whatsoever.' [32]

Thus the second judiciary Bill was annulled, a Bill which more than any other measure gave rise to much of the bitterness and was, in the main, responsible for the arraignment of Dobbs by the Assembly. Dobbs, in his efforts to rule fairly and justly and maintain a balance between the conflicting interests of the Assembly and Crown, wrote: 'Republican principles are prejudicial to the just rights of the Crown so is the prerogative when raised beyond its due limits destructive and hurtful to the just liberties of the people. I therefore made it my sole aim to preserve a due medium so that neither should predominate.'

14

Last Years

WHEN THE Assembly was prorogued, Dobbs looked forward to a few months' rest after a stormy and not too happy session. Courts were once more functioning throughout the province, there was relative peace and calm in Granville territory, and the final stages of the war with France were being fought out many miles from the North Carolina border. The peace and rest Dobbs sought and looked forward to with eagerness did not last very long, for a few weeks later he received an urgent dispatch from Governor Bull informing him that the Cherokees and Upper Creeks had declared war on South Carolina and Georgia, and that a number of traders had already been scalped and killed. Dobbs immediately summoned the Council, and on its advice called a meeting of the Assembly at Wilmington to rush through an Aid Bill to meet the impending threat to the province and for the dispatch of troops to South Carolina. The Assembly met and passed an Aid and Militia Bill of 'an unexceptional nature,' due, Dobbs claimed, to the non-attendance of Attorney-General Child and 'his northern Junto.'[1]

A few months later news reached Dobbs that the war with France, so far as the American continent was concerned, was drawing to a close. On 8th September, 1760, Montreal fell to the British, and the following day the French Governor Vaudreuil signed articles of capitulation, and the French dominion of Canada passed to British control.

When the Assembly met in November 1760, Dobbs began his address with the following words:

'It is with great pleasure that I acquaint you of the Glorious Conquest and Acquisition of all Canada by the remarkable interposition and Assistance of Divine Providence with very inconsiderable loss. The French have submitted to the terms offered without the effusion of blood, to the Immortal honour of his Majesty's forces.'[2]

With the conquest of Canada, Dobbs envisaged a speedy end to the Indian war, and informed the members of the Assembly that an offer of peace and pardon had been made to the Cherokees. He hoped, therefore, that it would not be necessary to demand any further aid as 'I shall always be unwilling to load this Province with taxes but for their safety.' He hoped that it would be possible now to devote all his energy to developing the province, economically and socially, and he asked the members of the Council and the Assembly to assist him to their utmost.

> 'I recommend,' he said, 'that you think of giving premiums to encourage the raising and export of hemp to Great Britain to be on an equal footing with your neighbouring colonies, as also upon Flax seed, and that the inspection laws might take place upon tobacco and Flour . . . as they are likely to become articles of export.'

He enjoined the members to give every encouragement for the establishment of schools. He ended his address:

> 'As it has always been my principal view and care to promote the happiness, peace and safety of this Province, and to preserve his Majesty's Just prerogative and the Just Right of the Assembly so I shall join in every measure agreeable to my Instructions from his Majesty to procure unity and Harmony, and the Peace, safety and improvement of this Province.'

The Assembly agreed to give all possible aid to South Carolina as 'the treaty with those savages may prove abortive, and we are convinced that the most effectual method of treating with Indians is, when they are under the dread of a Superior force,' and though the province 'has already emulated the most opulent in zeal for his Majesty's service . . . and contracted a large debt' the Assembly was willing at this crisis 'to join the forces of Virginia and South Carolina, with such of ours, as the Indigent and almost exhausted circumstances our Constituents will admit of.' The Assembly acknowledged its appreciation of the Governor's assurance to promote a spirit of harmony and goodwill, stating:

> 'We return to your Excellency our sincere thanks for your obliging assurance, in joining every salutary measure, for the good of the Province, agreeable to your Instructions, and that you will preserve the just rights of the Assembly, as well as his Majesty's Royal Prerogative; We are fully persuaded that both can well and ought to subsist inseparably together, and that whoever would divide them ought justly to be esteemed an enemy of both.' [3]

A further call for aid to bring the war against the Indians to a speedy end reopened an old sore. The Assembly passed an Aid Bill but reverted to the practice of adding a clause appointing an agent in London. Dobbs automatically refused to give his assent to the Bill, and immediately reported his action to the Board of Trade, pointing out that he had refused to give his assent as the Bill contained irrelevant clauses. The Board of Trade in a reply strongly censured the Governor for his action, stating that he had 'no right or propriety to interfere in the nomination of an agent so far as regards the choice of the person,' and that the representatives of the people are 'and ought to be free to chuse whom they think proper to act.' The Board was careful to admit, however, that the Governor could interfere in the mode of the appointment, adding:

> 'Though we think that the attempt of the House of Representatives to name the Agent in the Aid Bill was irregular and inconsistent with what the Crown has approved of in other colonies, yet when we consider the necessity there was for some supply to answer the exigency of the Service in the present calamitous state of His Majesty's Southern Province, we cannot but think that it was too trivial an objection to have been admitted as a reason for rejecting that supply and at the same time obstructing that mutual benefit which both the Crown and the Subject in North Carolina would derive from the Province having an Agent here.' [4]

Though the Board saw fit to censure Dobbs for refusing his assent to the Aid Bill, there was another important matter involving conflict between the Governor and the Assembly in which the Board supported him. For some years past a section of the Assembly endeavoured to hold up legislation by insisting that no Bill could be passed without the consent of an absolute majority of the whole House. This democratic ruling was embodied in the old constitution established under the original Charter, but had since been superseded by the Governor's Instructions which laid down that a quorum of fifteen members was sufficient to transact the business of the Assembly and give legality to all Bills passed. This Instruction was necessary in order to prevent the undue restriction of the work of the Assembly in the event of a boycott by any considerable number of Assemblymen. This, in fact, had been done and the House was kept in session only by continual adjournments, much to the discomfiture of the members who later claimed that these adjournments constituted a new form of tyranny on the part of the Governor, and they again insisted that no Bill should be passed without the approval of the majority of the members. This new cause of friction was in the main instigated by the northern representatives led by Child and his associates, who asserted that the business of the Assembly could only be conducted by a majority of the members, and that a quorum of fifteen members could not legally frame laws. The Board of Trade declared this to be 'a most unreasonable and Indecent Opposition to the Will of the Crown declared in his late Majesty's Instructions' and 'inconsistent with the practise and Constitution of the Mother Country and could not be defended either in Justice or Reason.' Dobbs was instructed to lay the sentiments of the Board before the Assembly so 'they will no longer persevere in so ill-founded and inconsistent a claim.' [5]

George II died on 25th October, 1760, but word did not reach Dobbs until the following February. He immediately summoned the Council and had the accession of George III proclaimed at Brunswick 'with the militia drawn out and a triple discharge from Fort Johnston of 21 guns, and from all the ships in the River.' Two days later the Council assembled at Wilmington, and in the presence of the Corporation and gentlemen of the neighbourhood the King was again proclaimed. The celebrations at Wilmington concluded with bonfires and illuminations, a ball and supper, and were marked with 'demonstrations of joy.' [6]

Some weeks later Dobbs received the King's Commission confirming him as Captain-General and Governor of North Carolina, and also additional Instructions. The new Instructions ordered that the Governor 'enjoy a negative voice in the making and passing of all laws, statutes and ordinances passed to the Prejudice of Us, Our Heirs and Successors.' By his new Instructions, which tended to curb the authority of the Assembly, the Governor was empowered to adjourn, prorogue, and dissolve all Assemblies as he judged necessary, and choose such persons as he wished as members of the Council. Further, he was authorised and empowered to appoint Judges 'and in cases requisite Commissioners of Oyer and Terminer, justices of the Peace and other necessary officers and Ministers in our said Colony.' The additional power and authority vested in the Governor was very considerable, but to Dobbs's credit it must be said that at no time did he abuse this power or authority.

A newly elected Assembly met towards the end of March 1761, and though not specifically asked, passed a Bill granting an Aid of £20,000, but containing a clause appointing an agent in London. For a time it seemed as though the old dispute between the Assembly and the Governor was about to break out afresh, but when the Bill came before the Council the members concurred with the Assembly because of 'the absolute necessity there is at this time of an immediate Grant of Aid for his Majesty's service' and 'being urged thereto in the warmest and most pressing manner by his Majesty.' With regard to the agent clause so strenuously objected to by Dobbs, the Council pointed out that though

'it would give us the greatest pleasure and satisfaction to have had the Bill passed without any tack whatever to it; Yet considering as we observed before the absolute necessity of the present Aid the many Aids which have been lost from Bills being rejected on that account only, the utter impossibility of obtaining an Aid from the people on any other terms than that of Appointing an Agent in the same bill, And also that in case the bill should receive your Excellency's assent the unhappy divisions which have for a long time subsisted in the Legislature will thereby be reconciled. For these reasons therefore we would recommend it to your Excellency to give your assent to the said Bill.' [7]

Dobbs was present at the meeting of the Council, and, due no doubt to his previous censure by the Board of Trade together with the earnest appeal of the Council, and a desire on his own part for a better understanding with the Assembly, he assented to the Aid Bill. Thus a bitter and acrimonious dispute came to a satisfactory end with a certain amount of face-saving on both sides, the Governor agreeing to assent to an Aid Bill with its extraneous clauses while the Assembly agreed to accept three members of the Council on the Committee of Correspondence, and also agreed to the appointment of an agent other than their own nominee, Mr. Anthony Bacon; the agent agreed upon being Mr. Cuchet Jouvencel. Though Dobbs had been censured by the Board of Trade for not assenting to a previous Aid Bill containing a clause not germane to it, when at length he gave his assent he was warned by the Board of 'the irregularity of this Practice and the many evils and Inconveniences which must necessarily arise from it,' and the Board suggested 'that when the time of Mr. Jouvencel's appointment shall expire you will recommend it to both houses of the Assembly to pass a separate law for the appointment of an Agent, and that you will not upon any pretence whatever consent to an appointment made in any other manner.' [8]

The remainder of the session was comparatively calm and peaceful, and when the Assembly was prorogued in the late spring of 1761, Dobbs was able to turn his attention to his own personal affairs. He had now reached the venerable age of seventy-two, and although his mind was clear and his body active, his powers of concentration were growing feeble, and it was noticeable that the numerous problems which had engaged his attention over the years were becoming tele-scoped into one another; memoranda and reports previously sub-mitted to the authorities in England and decided upon, were re-opened and re-submitted by him. This common fault of age was impatiently noticed by the officers of the Board of Trade, who on more than one occasion reprimanded Dobbs for his reiteration, and in the course of one letter of complaint remarked upon

'the great difficulty and embarrassment which have attended the considera-tion of every point to which all your letters to us have reference from the very incorrect vague and incoherent way in which they are expressed, in so much that in many cases it is almost impossible for us to discover your meaning or apply any consistent construction to what you propose.'

The Commissioners of the Board continued: 'Your letters to us con-tain little more than repetition of propositions made to them upon which you have received their sentiments and Opinions very fully and clearly expressed in their letters to you.' [9] Though the Board thought fit to censure Dobbs for his repetition and the vagueness of mind occa-sioned by years, the Board's own uncertainty, and the ease with which regulations and instructions changed almost from week to week were not above reproach. To censure the Governor one month for not assenting to a Bill, and months later to censure him for assenting to a similar Bill is but an example of what he had to contend with. Despite a certain amount of vagueness and repetition, allied with a slight difficulty in following his line of reasoning, due in the main to care-less punctuation, his mind was clear, and for a man of his years his grasp of affairs was extraordinarily keen. This is perhaps best evidenced in a long report of considerable value on the Government, population, climate, soil, and economic conditions of North Carolina submitted about this time to the Board of Trade. The criticism of the Board hurt Dobbs very much, and in a letter a year or two later he recalled this unjust criticism, saying, 'I shall not at present trouble your Lord-ships with a longer letter, lest you should blame me as Lord Sandys did for writing long letters to the Board.' A recent commentator who studied Dobbs's reports and letters notes that the insertion of marks of punctuation renders his writing clear and correct, and remarks that as a close observer of events he wrote very hurriedly and without re-vision, yet if he is read with care there is little difficulty in following his meaning and line of thought.[10]

From a private letter to his old friend and adviser, Alexander M'Auley of Dublin, we get a slight picture of a busy and conscientious Governor about this time. In the course of this letter Dobbs wrote:

'I have had so large an intercourse and correspondence by letter and dispatches, publick and private, and so great an undertaking in finishing and revising my essay upon the Grand Plan of Providence and the dissertations annexed to it which I thank God I have now ready for press, and which has taken up all the time I had to spare from the Publick business that I have little time to write to my other good friends, and particularly to you, and I am now very busy answering the dispatches and orders which I have just received from England to proclaim his present Majesty whom God long preserve that I have scarce time to write to my friends.'

In the course of this letter he adverts to the economic state of Ireland, and also asked M'Auley to draw up deeds conveying his Kildare estates to his son Edward, whom he also proposed to leave 'all I have a title to in this Province except what I design to my daughter Fanny.'

He speaks of himself and gives a picture of a man growing old in exile.

'I find,' he says, 'many of my good friends are gone to their everlasting habitations, and have reason to thank God for sparing me so long among so many contemporaries. As to me with health and memory sufficient as to finish what I engaged in and lived to see my long projected plan of driving the French out of the continent and I hope out of America I may say accomplished, nothing being now wanting to my wishes but Mississippi and their islands, and the opening to the Hudson Bay Trade which I think must immediately follow, and converting these colonies will soon be in our power.'

He recalls in this letter the part he played in the formation of the Ohio Company of Virginia, which he claimed contributed to the eventual destruction of French power in America. In closing the letter, he again thanked God for sparing him so long, adding, 'my health continues good in my time of life and this has been the most sickly season ever known in this Province.' Indeed, conditions during the preceding autumn and winter were extremely bad, and to add to the difficulties facing the province great herds of cattle were carried off by a 'fatal distemper brought into South Carolina by a raw hide.' Writing of this affliction, Dobbs remarked that many people with hundreds of cattle 'have not ten left. I can scarce get milk in my tea, but I hope it is now over.' [11]

The prorogued Assembly did not meet in the autumn as arranged, but, following new elections, met at Wilmington early in March 1762. In the meantime a new European alliance threatened Britain's existence. Negotiations at Paris in 1761 to mark the end of the Seven Years War were abruptly broken off by Pitt on learning of the Family Compact between France and Spain. With his usual energy Pitt declared war on Spain, and again turned to the American colonies for aid. Amherst, the Commander-in-Chief in America, immediately dispatched a letter to each of the colonial governors setting down the number of troops required from each province. In his letter to Dobbs, Amherst requested 'that the quota to be raised by your Province agreeable to the Proportions from the other colonies is one hundred and thirty-four.' When the Assembly met, Dobbs placed Amherst's request before the members, and in the course of an address said:

> 'I must therefore recommend to you, in the warmest manner as you shall answer it to your constituents and Posterity, that you will with unanimity and dispatch testify the same zeal you have hitherto shewn by raising as large a Quota of troops as this Province can bear upon the beneficial terms laid before you . . . upon account of this unexpected Spanish War.' [12]

A few days later the Assembly presented an address to Dobbs and, transposing the Governor's words to 'we shall answer to our Constituents and Posterity,' refused to raise the troops requested, adding, 'we are sorry to observe, that at this time, we cannot without reducing the Province to the utmost distress, add to the Intolerable and Accumulated load of Taxes we are already groaning under.' The Address continued: 'If we form a Judgement of the future from the Past we are but little encouraged to hope any supply that may be granted would much contribute to the service of his Majesty or the interest or advantage of the Province.' [13] North Carolina was no longer threatened nor in danger, and the new war with Spain was England's affair. The conquest of Canada had freed the colonies from the menace of France and in consequence tended to weaken their dependence upon the mother country. The need for further burdens and sacrifices no longer existed, and the colonists not only in North Carolina but in the other provinces were keenly aware of this. Dobbs, a loyal and uncompromising servant of the Crown, could not approve of this attitude; to his way of thinking the colonists were Britons, the sons and grandsons of Englishmen and Irishmen whose first, indeed whose only loyalty should be to Britain and the Crown; any deviation from this was a violation of allegiance.

When Dobbs received the address from the Assembly, he issued an angry reply, in the course of which he pointed out that North Carolina was the least taxed of all the American colonies. He adjourned the Assembly for a day so that the members might reconsider their decision and informed them of their duty to the Crown.

'I find,' he said, 'that all the other Provinces willingly submit to his Majesty's demands, and it grieves me and every loyal breast in this Province, to find that you only should prove refractory to and not comply with his Majesty's just demands, which are so necessary to procure the future peace and safety of this and all other colonies.' . . . 'When you therefore seriously consider the situation of affairs in Europe and America, and that a powerful enemy is raised against us, the King of Spain, who not only endeavours to prevent our having a safe and honourable peace, but also with a view of ravishing from his Majesty all the conquests we have made, and the Laurels and trophies he has gained by his victorious arms, conducted by Divine Providence, after Britain expending eighty million pounds to secure and perfect her American colonies; Your noncompliance at this time, would lessen you in the eyes of all his Subjects, and you will lose the honour you have already obtained in so zealously assisting his Majesty to the utmost of your Ability.'

In a final appeal he remarked: 'I must therefore warmly request you, that you preserve the esteem and good opinion his Majesty has of you, that you will forthwith repair to your House, and reconsider the several letters and papers laid before you and come to an immediate resolution without loss of time.' [14]

The members of the Assembly were adamant in their resolve, and claimed again that the province was unable to bear the expense and charge of raising the supplies demanded by Amherst and supported by the Governor. Again Dobbs prorogued the Assembly in order to 'give you an opportunity to reconsider my last speech to you to know if you will consent to his Majesty's demands for an Aid.' He warned the members that 'his Majesty can and will confer Favours or withhold them from you, according as you support his government and prerogative, and comply with his instructions to me.' This threat had no effect, and the members of the Assembly in reply to the Governor reaffirmed their previous resolve, stating that the Governor's speech

'was most maturely considered, and the Resolution then taken, with the Greatest deliberation; that this Province being already burthened with a heavy debt, occasioned by several large Grants for his Majesty's Service in the support of the Common Cause since the commencement of the present war with France and the present impoverished circumstances of the Inhabitants by reason of the said grants, render them unable to bear the expense and charge of raising the supplies required by your Excellency in that speech; The same Motives, Sir, which Induced us to enter into that Resolution, permit us to acquaint you, still prevail with us to adhere thereto. . . .' [15]

The fact that the North Carolina Assembly refused to grant an Aid to His Majesty on this occasion does not mean that the province was tottering on the brink of ruin, and that its financial and economic state was at a low ebb.[16] All the colonies suffered somewhat from the burden imposed by war, but it cannot be doubted that if North Carolina had been immediately threatened a substantial Aid Bill would have been passed, but in view of the small repayment made by the English Parliament for the efforts already made, plus the fact that there was no apparent threat to North Carolina, and perhaps to discomfit the Governor and win a measure of popularity among the people, the Assembly held tightly to the colony's purse-strings, the only powerful weapon in its control. Though the Assembly refused an Aid Bill, it did empower Dobbs to raise a body of men to garrison Fort Johnston and Fort Granville, and as proof of its loyalty presented an address to the King assuring him 'of their firm and loyal attachment to your Majesty's Royal Person.' In this address the Assembly reversed its previous decision to set up a capital at Tower Hill on the Neuse, and requested that His Majesty would signify his assent to move the seat of government to New Bern 'whereby we may be permitted to erect a suitable house for the Residence of Your Majesty's Governor, and other Edifices as may be requisite for the safe keeping the Public Records, and for other Public uses.' This was a complete *volte-face* and set at naught all the decisions of the Governor and previous Assemblies, whereby it was agreed that New Bern was unsuitable for many reasons to be the seat of government, and that the site offered by Dobbs at Tower Hill was more suitable.[17]

The final refusal of the Assembly to raise the quota of troops requested by Amherst infuriated Dobbs, and calling the members before him he informed them that 'it was with the greatest concern that I shall be obliged to represent to his Majesty, the little regard you have had to his so warm and pressing demands for a proper Aid at this so remarkable crisis.' Continuing, he reminded them with some little disregard of facts that they showed little concern to prepare laws recommended to them for the encouragement of trade and the education of the youth of the province, and that at the outset of the session the members deliberately acted in opposition to His Majesty's prerogative and instructions by refusing to meet without a majority of the whole Assembly when fifteen members was deemed a quorum.

'The great opposition you have made,' he said, 'by refusing a proper aid to his Majesty by which, as far as in your power, you have delayed and prevented our having a safe, speedy, and honourable peace, is so Flagrant and impolite that those members who have opposed it well deserve the censure instead of the thanks of their Constituents for their ill-judged Parsimony, by which they deserve to lose the favour of the best of Kings.'

Dobbs's assertion that the Assembly delayed and prevented a speedy peace is of course an oratorical exaggeration. To the members' complaint that they had been put to considerable expense by the Governor's repeated action in calling frequent meetings of the Assembly followed by adjournments, prorogations, and dissolutions, for which they themselves were responsible, Dobbs replied in a forthright and somewhat autocratic manner by immediately dissolving the Assembly and informing the members

'that I may give no cause of future Complaints against me of putting the Public to expence, by paying for your attendance, I cant with decency or propriety pass any other bills, when the business you were called upon has been neglected. I therefore put an end to this meeting without making it a Session, which will save the Publick the Expense of your attendance, so much complained of, and will prevent any future complaints against me, for the expense of the publick in calling too frequent Assemblies.' [18]

Having dissolved the Assembly, Dobbs immediately communicated with the Board of Trade, stating that he had been unable to obtain the aid requested as the members were as 'obstinate as mules,' and that he in consequence 'with some resentment dissolved the Assembly and have appealed to their constituents for their behaviour.' Dobbs's later action, while justified by events, was undoubtedly autocratic and dictatorial and unlikely to help him in his future dealings with the Assembly. With the unco-operative Assembly out of the way, Dobbs proceeded on his own initiative to raise the quota of troops requested by Amherst, and advanced his own money to raise recruits, and then charged it to the colonial agents in London, 'which I hope his Majesty will approve of and direct them to pay.' Writing some time later, Egremont, the new Secretary of State, informed Dobbs that 'the King very much approves of your resolution to raise the 134 recruits required by Sir Jeff. Amherst, notwithstanding the Assembly

had refused to concur in any measure for that purpose.' The King's
concurrence and approval were not likely to help Dobbs or render his
action acceptable to the Assembly; on the contrary, it made the
Assembly more critical, and strengthened its resolve to maintain a
firm grip on the provincial purse.

At this time Dobbs had to contend not only with a recalcitrant
Assembly but with a series of problems affecting both his official and
private affairs. In his endeavour to fix a boundary line between North
and South Carolina, straighten out the muddled McCulloh grants,
and dispose of the still unsettled portions of his own grants, he ran
into new difficulties.[19] Surveyors sent to mark the unsettled grants
found that land close to the frontier, originally granted to Dobbs or
McCulloh and his associates, had been assigned to settlers by the land
office of South Carolina, and when they attempted to lay out and
adjust the boundaries of the illegally settled land they were attacked
and lives were lost.

Despite his great age, Dobbs decided to visit the disputed area.
Because of the riotous behaviour and the arrogant and rebellious
speeches of the leaders of the illegal settlers, and in view of the re-
survey being carried out, he had notices issued in advance informing
the settlers that he intended inspecting his property 'to ascertain the
line of my grants.' On his journey southward through Anson and
Mecklenburg Counties he was accompanied by his London attorney
Samuel Smith and two servants. The party was later joined by Colonel
Robert Harris, the Lieutenant-Colonel of the Anson County Militia,
who had purchased some of Dobbs's property, a surveyor, and 'chain
Carrears and three or four more who knew the lines.'

The party soon ran into trouble when accosted by James Loosh,
who claimed to be a Justice of the Peace from South Carolina, and
appeared to be in possession of land belonging to either Dobbs or
George Selwyn. Loosh, who was attended by a body of armed horse-
men, intimated that he would oppose by force any attempt to survey
lands in his possession. To avoid bloodshed, Dobbs and his party withdrew, but Loosh, 'after being joined by the rest of his posse,' pursued
them. In the course of a letter to Governor Boone, Dobbs gives a vivid
description of what happened. He wrote:

'They appeared while we were sitting on the ground at breakfast.
Colonel Harris mounted his horse by the time they came up and expecting
to be attacked he desired the gentleman with me to lend him one of his
pistols to defend himself if attacked. Upon their coming up without more
ado one, White, who acted as a constable appointed from Charlestown

seized upon him on horseback, and Loosh who was on foot seeing the pistol in his hand, called out he has a pistol, and laid hold of it and forced it from him, upon which I went up and asked him how he came in so riotous a manner to seize a gentleman in my presence, employed in my service, and he said he took him by a power from the Governor of South Carolina, and would carry him to Charlestown as a prisoner.' [20]

Subsequent events show that Dobbs, though an old man, was physically fit; in fact, the long and tiresome journey through the southern and lawless part of the province on horseback gives the lie to those who would have us believe him to be a decrepit and senile old man incapable of even coherent speech or thought. Dobbs approached the constable who had laid hold of Colonel Harris and commanded him to desist in the King's name, then he

'seized the Bridle and pushed the constable with the end of my cane, upon which he held up a pole over my head, and said if any offered to oppose or strike him he would knock him down, or whatsoever person he should be, upon which finding such insolence to me backed by such a body of armed men assembled with a design to do mischief, and Justice Loosh ordered him to detain and carry off his prisoner, I thought it prudent to allow them carry him off to another Justice one Wyly ... who had so much sense to keep out of this riot though he attended them on foot a great part of the way.' [21]

Wyly knew Dobbs; he was in fact one of a group of North of Ireland families whom Dobbs had settled in North Carolina some ten years earlier, but who had apparently gravitated to South Carolina. The armed frontier settlers, hardy, lawless pioneers, had no more respect for a Royal Governor than they had for the local sheriff, and one of the party, McFerran, had forcibly possessed a plantation that Dobbs had promised to sell to Colonel Harris, who, when he found McFerran in possession, fired the wood, 'and the flames spreading to McFerran's house frightened his wife so that she miscarried.' [22] McFerran claimed that Harris had done this deliberately to drive him from the land, and he had therefore obtained a warrant from Loosh against Harris. The armed mob claimed the warrant was valid, and, despite expostulations from Dobbs, insisted upon carrying Harris away, and detaining him for some hours in an effort to make him relinquish all claims to the land.

While the ill-defined boundary between North and South Carolina had long been responsible for the unsettled conditions in the south, the encroachment and lawless behaviour of some South Carolinians tended to aggravate matters. As a result of his own experience, Dobbs wrote to Governor Boone of South Carolina condemning the lawlessness of the frontier settlers, the high-handed action of Justice Loosh, and the illegality of the southern province in issuing grants for land which he and his associates had possessed since 1747. Referring to the insulting behaviour of Loosh and his armed posse, he said:

> 'As to what concerns me as Governor for the insults offered to me in this Province upon the frontiers Had they been disputable I shall only say had your Excellency been so insulted in this Province had you entered it, I should upon your application immediately turn out such a Magistrate without any further enquiry, and much more so when such Justice has no lands in either Province by any title from the Crown but what he holds by force in lands patented by order from the Crown.' [23]

Boone replied expressing regret for the insulting behaviour of Loosh who was 'highly blameable for his want of compliance to you,' but he added, 'it is impossible to say he has been criminal.'

Having spent the greater part of the month of July inspecting his own grants, and endeavouring to carry out his instructions of 'quieting the Associates of Huey and Crymble in their possessions,' Dobbs returned to his home at Brunswick. There was very little he could do about the disputed frontier lands until he called the Council together in October. In the meantime, to use the words of Saunders, Dobbs committed the supreme folly of old age by marrying a very young girl. The marriage of Dobbs and Justina Davis, a girl of fifteen, took place at St. Philip's Church at Brunswick. Few actions of his long and varied life excited more ridicule and comment. Saunders, a just and honest historian, remarks that if Dobbs 'did indeed escape the drivelling imbecility of old age he committed its supreme folly by marrying a young girl.' A vicious lampoon purporting to be a letter from a Gentleman of North Carolina to a friend in Maryland describes the events leading to the marriage and states that 'our old Silenus of the Envigorating age of seventy-eight who still damns this province with his baneful influence grew steadily enamoured with Miss Davis a lovely lady of sprightly fifteen of a good family and some fortune.' The lampoonist goes on to suggest that she was 'persuaded to be a Governor's Lady although she loved and was loved' by another, but her friends, on discovering that Dobbs had conveyed his estate, even 'his Potato Lands near Carrickfergus,' to his son, brought the young couple together 'to consummate the marriage Hymen attends Venus and Apollo adds Ringlets and ten thousand charms to adorn the lovely pair.' Dobbs apprised of the misalliance 'orders his horse to the Chariot and feebly in his course would emulate a Youthful passion he enters her parents house demands the lady, and is conducted into the apartment of Youth, Love and Virtue.' [24]

The bitter lampoon may be dismissed as a mendacious flight of fancy. If there is any truth in the suggestion that Justina Davis was in love with a young man, the fact lies buried with her bones; her only other love whom she married after her husband's death was not a young man but Governor Abner Nash. Despite the gross disparity of age and the certain knowledge of the ridicule their marriage would inspire, Dobbs and his young wife were happy, and her companionship was a solace in his lonely old age.

Towards the end of the year, Dobbs suffered a stroke which paralysed one side of his body and left his lower limbs almost useless. Though seriously impaired in body and limb, he sedulously attended each meeting of the Council, and with the concurrence of the members his nephew Spaight was permitted to sign a number of blank commissions and most letters for him. In spite of his physical disability, he addressed the opening session of the Assembly in November 1762 with all his usual vigour, and informed the members, not with the triumphant air some historians would have us believe, but with disappointment, that eight Acts passed in the previous session had been disallowed by the King. In conveying this information to the Assembly, Dobbs warned the members that they could gain no benefit by 'opposing his Majesty's just prerogatives' and that he would oppose all Bills departing from his Instructions 'because of the severe reprimand I had from his Majesty.' He asked the members to amend the disallowed Bills, particularly the Court Bills, and the Bill for 'fixing an Orthodox clergy and establishing vestries.' He reminded the members that they must be 'sensible of the prejudice this colony must suffer by the Assembly encroaching upon his Majesty's just prerogatives and disobeying and not complying with his instructions that it only served to break the happy union between his Majesty and his Subjects.'

In an effort to bring about harmony between the different parts of the Legislature, he said:

'Notwithstanding the many Calumnies cast upon me for endeavouring to preserve his Majesty's prerogative and obey his Instruction I shall always endeavour to concur with you in Enacting such laws as may promote religion and Industry and promote your commerce and secure your peace and possession at home, provided the bills you desire are agreeable to his Majesty.' [25]

There was no air of gloating triumph in the Governor's speech; on the contrary, he stated facts with a sincere desire that a spirit of harmony and good will should prevail, and quite clearly the majority of the members desired the same. Unfortunately, no *via media* existed or could in fact exist between colonial assemblies firmly maintaining their freedom to enact laws consonant with the conditions and rights of the people, and the immutable prerogatives, and inflexible instructions, firmly binding the executive authority in the person of the Governor to the mother country.[26]

The Council hastened to assure Dobbs, in reply to his address, that no calumnies or charges against him emanated from that body, and informed him of their earnest desire and wish to co-operate in every way with him. The Assembly, in a reasoned and thoughtful reply, showed a conciliatory spirit, too, but the members pointed out that they failed to see in what way the rejected Bills encroached upon the Royal prerogative. The members noted that the Governor had placed before them a number of Bills which had been rejected by the Board of Trade, and they requested that they might have the reason or reasons why the Board disallowed, in particular, the Vestry Bill. Dobbs was unable to give them this information for the simple reason that he was, as he said in the course of a letter to the Board of Trade, 'at a great loss to know the true reasons given for the repeal.' Unfortunately, his refusal to give information which he did not possess has been ascribed by some historians to what they are pleased to call his petulant and choleric temperament.

The session of the Assembly continued to the end of the year 1762 with disagreements on the wording of a number of Bills, but on the whole a great deal of the former bitterness was absent.

Dobbs's health continued poor, and as he had lost the use of his legs he could be moved about only in a wheel-chair. The death early in January of his nephew and helpmate Richard Spaight added to his afflictions. Spaight, whom the anonymous gentleman of North Carolina referred to as a man of motley caste, was by no means a person of outstanding ability. On the whole, however, he appears to have been a conscientious and honest official despite charges to the contrary. He had married into a well-known North Carolina family six years earlier, and his wife, 'a pretty girl of 14,' bore him a son who many years later was to don the mantle of his grand-uncle as Governor

of a free and independent North Carolina.[27] Spaight's death affected
Dobbs and aggravated his illness. In a message to the Assembly early
in 1763, he requested that the session be brought to a speedy conclusion as 'my health requires that I should return home before the
winter sets in.' With his health impaired and the gloom occasioned by
the death of his nephew, Dobbs anticipated his return home, but
beyond mentioning the matter to the Assembly, he postponed taking
any action so far as the Board of Trade was concerned. For the next
month or two his health showed little improvement, and his chaplain
at Brunswick, the Reverend John McDowell, in a letter to the
Society for the Propagation of the Gospel, wrote:

'This has been a fatal year to us Europeans here, his Excellency Gov[r].
Dobbs has been in a very bad way all this winter, having lost the use of his
legs, occasioned by cold he caught in November at the Genl Assembly.
And his nephew Mr. Spaight one of the King's Council & your late Secretary is lately dead, he came over with his Excellency and was a very
sprightly gay young man.' [28]

With the unremitting care of his dear Jessy, Dobbs made a remarkable recovery, and by the late spring of 1763 was able to move about
again with the aid of a stout stick. Thoughts of returning home
gradually receded, and beyond pointing out in a letter to the Board of
Trade that he considered New Bern an unhealthy place for the seat
of government, because with its damp air he 'had been nigh death
thrice,' he gave little indication of the gravity of his illness. His
recovery was fairly complete for a man of his age, and we find the
Reverend James Reed of New Bern writing in June: 'It has pleased
God to restore our Govr. to a perfect state of health, his recovery
indeed is very surprising, for he had for a considerable time lost the
use of both his feet.' Mr. Reed continued: 'I am in great hopes that
it will please God to prolong his life to hold another Assembly for the
clergy are still destitute of any legal provision.' [29] This referred to the
disallowed Vestry Bill, in the absence of which all the vestries in the
province were dissolved, and the entire Church system, such as it
was, completely disorganised.

As soon as he was able, Dobbs removed to Wilmington, and
throughout the year 1763 held all meetings of the Council there. In
February he was informed by Lord Egremont that the Treaty of Paris
had been signed, thus bringing to an end the war with France. By the
terms of the Treaty, all French possessions in North America were
ceded to Britain. Some weeks later Egremont forwarded the King's

proclamation announcing the peace, and returning his thanks to the colonies for their effort in the common cause. Dobbs had the peace proclaimed throughout the province with worthy ceremony, a peace he remarked that 'has secured us so great an Empire on this continent.' In the course of a letter to Egremont, he wrote:

> 'After this glorious acquisition which has answered my most sanguine endeavours to promote I have nothing to wish for but the opening the trade to Hudson's Bay and discovery of the Passage to the Western American Ocean which I have laboured to obtain these thirty years, and then I should die in peace.' [30]

Even as an old man Dobbs never lost his interest in the Northwest Passage. For close on thirty years he entertained this great dream which first brought him into prominence and won him the support and friendship of Lord Halifax and many other political leaders. He now hoped, since Canada was a British possession, that others would take up where he left off and search for the Passage he had failed to discover.

The defeat of France and Spain and the subsequent Treaty of Paris removed all foreign threats to the southern provinces, but the omnipresent Indians—the Creeks, Choctaws, Cherokees, Chickasaws, and Catawbas—among whom the seeds of mistrust, doubt, and fear of the white man had been assiduously sown by experience had still to be contended with.[31] The accretion of new territory in the south and the now urgent need for a peaceful *rapprochement* with the Indians prompted the Board of Trade to suggest to the Governors of North and South Carolina, Virginia and Georgia that a Congress of the Indian chiefs should be held as soon as possible at Augusta in Georgia. At the same time goods of considerable value were shipped to Charlestown by the Board as gifts for the Indians and an earnest of goodwill and friendship.

Early in September, 1763, Dobbs sailed by sloop to Charlestown, where he was warmly received by Governor Boone. In the course of the next few days both men agreed upon a plan to send Commissioners and Surveyors to mark a temporary boundary line between North and South Carolina, and thus put an end to the lawlessness in the disputed areas. Dobbs and Boone travelled together to Augusta some two hundred miles away, where they were welcomed by Governor Wright of Georgia. Wright was a wise and tactful governor and a native of South Carolina who had succeeded Governor Ellis, an old friend who had been associated with Dobbs in his Northwest Passage scheme.

Governor Fauquier of Virginia joined the others at Augusta, and a day or two later the chiefs of the six Indian nations met the governors. From these deliberations there ensued 'a treaty of Perpetual Peace and Alliance with the Chickasaws, Choctaws, Upper and Lower Creeks, Cherokee, and Catawbas Indians, and a settlement of all their claims and boundaries with Virginia, North and South Carolina and Georgia to their satisfaction.' [32] The arrival of a concourse of Indian chiefs accompanied by their braves was nothing unusual in Augusta, a town that had grown out of Indian trade, and whose cobbled streets were ever noisy with the sound of the hooves of laden pack-horses from the backlands.

Dobbs returned to Charlestown with Boone, and while recuperating from the tedious journey to Augusta he enjoyed a little of the hospitality of the thriving capital of the great slave-owning state. Charleston at this time ranked fourth among the American towns, and claimed to be a replica-in-little of Augustan London; it housed some of the wealthiest citizens in America. Whether Dobbs approved of the luxurious living of its citizens, whom Governor Glen—fourteen years earlier—had feared would suffer the same ruin as the ancient Romans because of their love of luxury, we do not know, though on occasion he wrote reprovingly of the immorality and excessive gambling of the 'ill instructed inhabitants' of North Carolina.

Dobbs returned to Brunswick in December and arranged for an immediate meeting of the Assembly at Wilmington. The meeting proved abortive, as the northern members refused to attend in protest against what they considered to be arbitrary action of the Governor in raising the troops requested by Amherst, proroguing the previous session of the Assembly, and disallowing the expenses of the members. Further, they objected to all meetings of the Assembly at Wilmington, which they considered a most unsuitable place. Though the northern members refused to travel to Wilmington, a sufficient number of Assemblymen gathered there to form a quorum, but in the absence of so many others they refused to meet 'to make a House, nor would they adjourn.' Dobbs adjourned the meeting of the Assembly from day to day in an endeavour to induce the members to come together. They were adamant in their refusal to attend, whereupon he let the members 'dissolve themselves for non-attendance and immediately put out writs to choose new members.' It could be said that this action of the Governor was harsh and arbitrary, but it is difficult to see what else he could have done under the circumstances.

The Reverend James Reed, the missionary at New Bern, writing

in December to the Society for the Propagation of the Gospel, remarked:

> 'The Assembly were to have met at Wilmington . . . but there were not
> then a sufficient number of Members arrived to make a house and that it
> was current opinion that there would be no session of the Assembly this
> winter. Wilmington is not at all central, but a remote part of the Province
> where t'is quite inconvenient for the majority of the Assemblymen to attend
> and our Governor is too infirm to meet them at any other place.'

This was true in part, but only in part, and Reed continued:

> 'In short the Province is in great confusion for want of the seat for
> Government being fixed, and the approaching dissolution of the Governor
> presents us with gloomy prospects, upon his decease I expect that old
> Quarrels will be renewed, old grievances repeated, and the whole Province
> disunited and divided into the old parties of North and South.' [33]

The sharp cleavage between the old settlers of the north and the
newer settlers of the south had bedevilled the province during a great
part of Johnston's administration. Much of the opposition to Dobbs
may be traced to the at times bitter rivalry between the older and more
thickly populated northern counties and the newer southern counties
and not to any lively spirit of patriotism.

Following a new election, the Assembly met at Wilmington on
3rd February, 1764. By this time Dobbs had recovered the use of his
limbs and was more or less able to walk with the aid of a stick; he
complained, however, of considerable swelling of his legs, and found
movement very painful at times. Though his body suffered from the
ravages of age, his mind for a man of his years was singularly clear and
alert, and in spite of his infirmity the tiring and exacting journey to
Georgia did not upset him. The Upper House of the Assembly was
not unmindful of his exertions, and in a congratulatory message to
him said:

> 'It is with great pleasure we embrace this opportunity of congratulating
> your Excellency on your safe and happy return from the Congress of
> Augusta; the Zeal your Excellency has shewn in obeying his Majesty's
> Orders, and your attachment to the Publick Welfare in so fatiguing a
> Journey, at a time when your bad state of health rendered such an under-
> taking very dangerous demands our most Grateful Acknowledgement.'

The warm and gracious address of the Upper House was repeated by
the Assembly, whose members acknowledged the zeal displayed by the

Governor 'in such an advanced time of life and declining state of health to undertake so long and Hazardous a Journey.' Both Houses assured Dobbs that they would willingly concur in passing the Bills suggested by him to encourage the raising of hemp and flax, increase the trade of the province, and provide for the building of churches, schools and glebes, and re-enact such laws as had been amended or disallowed by the King in Council.[34]

The friendly and co-operative attitude of the Assembly was apparently due to the fact that a number of the northern members refused to attend, though some of those opposed to the Governor, including Starkey, whom Dobbs claimed was the leader of the Junto, took their seats and contributed to what proved to be one of the most harmonious and useful sessions of the Assembly. While a number of contentious matters gave rise to a wordy exchange between the Assembly and the Council, when the prorogation took place on 10th March, 1764, Dobbs had given his assent to a number of useful Bills. Some of the Bills were important, including a new Vestry Bill, a Bill for building a school and residence for a schoolmaster at New Bern, a Bill to encourage the cultivation of flax and hemp, as well as Bills for the suppression of excessive gambling, the pilotage of the Cape Fear River and of prime importance, a Bill empowering the public treasurers to draw the proportion of money granted by Parliament to the American colonies. In all, twenty Bills were passed during the session. The passing of a satisfactory Vestry Bill gave Dobbs great pleasure, and in the course of a letter to the Reverend Daniel Burton of the Society for the Propagation of the Gospel, he wrote:

> 'I after some struggles, since my last have got a better bill for the maintenance of the Orthodox Clergy . . . and a much better Vestry bill wherein the incumbent is to be always one of the Vestry, and they have power to raise ten shillings upon every taxable person annually in each County, to be applied to build Churches and Glebe houses and to purchase glebes and also to maintain schoolmasters in each parish.'

In this, as in other letters to the Society, he made a strong appeal for the sending out of a body of missionary clergy and schoolmasters to the colonies. He pointed out that owing to the rapidly increasing population the need for clergy and teachers was greater than ever.

> 'With few or no schools,' he wrote, 'for the education of Youth, and only a few Lay readers to serve the Several Chappels erected in the several Counties this is the reason for our Sloth, Indolence and Immoralities and occasions numerous Sectaries of all denominations, except Papists, having

many Strollers, particularly Anabaptists or dippers, there being so few
qualify'd to give regular Baptism, when this is considered, and the increasing
British Empire on this continent, I am convinced that his Lordship of
London will willingly part with a great part of his Diocese and join in
soliciting to procure Bishops, and others with Episcopal power to ordain
and Visit the Clergy in the Several provinces on this Continent, and to
erect proper schools for the education of Youth for a succession of persons
qualified to be put into orders.' [35]

The low state of the Established Church was a cause of concern to
Dobbs, a deeply religious man. On the death of the Reverend John
McDowell, in November 1763, there were only six Church of Eng-
land clergymen left in the province; four of whom, Dobbs claimed,
performed their duties diligently, while two others, John Moir and
Joseph Miller, 'by all I hear do not behave as clergymen ought.'

The Governor's impaired health continued fair throughout the
year, and though he suffered considerable pain, his interest in North
Carolina showed no signs of slackening. When the Assembly was prorogued in March, he prepared a report on North Carolina somewhat
similar to the one he had drawn up some eight years earlier. This
report was submitted to the Board of Trade as perhaps a valedictory
from his Governorship. It is an important document, and provides an
interesting commentary on the state of North Carolina in the year
1764. From the report we learn that the population of the province
exceeded 120,000 people. In the economic field considerable progress
had been made, resulting in an increasing export of pitch, tar, turpentine, lumber, animal products, cereals, and tobacco. A number of
bolting mills had been erected from which a considerable quantity of
flour was exported to the West Indies. In this, as in previous reports,
Dobbs called attention to the restrictions and burdens imposed upon
trade by the operation of the Navigation Acts; once again he made a
strong plea for the lifting of these restrictions in order to open up a trade
with other countries, particularly with Ireland; such a trade, he claimed,
would serve the economic interests of both countries.

For almost thirty years Dobbs pleaded for a relaxation of the British
restrictions on trade, conscious that these restrictions seriously affected
the economic development of the colonies. His plea in 1764 fell on deaf
ears just as Burke's did some years later; by then it was too late, for the
guns of the American colonists were more forceful in tone than the
language of a great orator or the pleading of a wise Governor.

The End

AFTER TEN strenuous years of Governorship, Dobbs felt that his health might improve if he could obtain leave of absence and return to England for a time. Long separation from his family, his home, and his friends, and the knowledge that his span of life was nearing its end no doubt contributed to his desire to return home. In April 1764, he wrote to Lord Halifax requesting leave of absence, and at the same time sent a personal note to Lord Hillsborough, President of the Board of Trade, whom he had known as a younger man. Hillsborough wrote to Halifax:

> 'As we are fully convinced how necessary and essential to his Majesty's Service it is, that all his Majesty's Servants and Officers in America should personally attend their Duty, we shall at all times be very cautious of recommending requests of this nature, but the circumstances of this Gentleman's case, who is upward of seventy years of age, who has resided in his Government near ten years without intermission and undergone great fatigue, will we hope justify the Application we have the honour to make to your Lordship.' [1]

The recommendation was acceded to by the Ministry, and on 26th April, Colonel William Tryon, a cultured young officer of the Queen's Guards, was appointed Lieutenant-Governor of North Carolina.[2]

Two months later, Dobbs received word from Lord Hillsborough that Colonel Tryon had been appointed 'to administer Government during your absence from the Province.' The dispatch continued: 'You may therefore be preparing for your departure on the arrival of Col. Tryon who proposes to embark for North Carolina the latter end of this summer.' [3]

During the succeeding months the Governor's health continued to improve, and we gather from a letter to the Society for the Propagation of the Gospel from the Reverend James Reed that Dobbs was enjoying good health. In the course of his letter Reed wrote:

> 'Tis with great pleasure I embrace the present opportunity of acquainting you that the clergy of North Carolina are at length favour'd with legal encouragement, the Assembly met at Wilmington this last spring & passed a Vestry act thro' the influence of our worthy Govr. to whom the clergy of this Province can never sufficient express their gratitude. His life is dear & precious to us & the good state of his health he appears at present to enjoy gives us no small hope that his days will be considerably prolonged, we have great reason indeed to offer up our most fervant prayers for his preservation & health for we can never expect a more sincere friend in his exalted station to the real interest of the Christian religion.' [4]

In preparation for his return home, Dobbs wrote to his son Conway in July:

> 'I have wrote to Lord Halifax for leave to go over if my health continues in order to get rid of my lameness. My feet continuing still swelled though I am strong and can walk a little without a staff. I am glad to hear that my grandson is so fine a boy and likes his books. I hope God will preserve him to you as my family is weak ... I hope in God to see you in Ireland or England. I long to hear how all my friends are.'

And then he enquired about the neighbouring families who had lived close together for almost two hundred years, such as the Edmonstons, Dalways, and Uptons. Nor did he forget his life-long interest in the economic well-being of the country he had served to the best of his ability as a younger man. 'I hope,' he wrote, 'we shall soon have a trade opened with Ireland for Hemp, Flax and their seeds. . . . We have given premiums to carry hemp and flax to Ireland, and hope to export several hundred hogsheads of flaxseed next winter.' He ended, 'My dear Jessy enjoins in love to you.' [5]

His young wife showed a keen interest in his family and sent Conway and his sister Fanny a barrel of rice, and a 'small box of New England spermaceti candles.' When Dobbs sat down to write to Conway, he had not received permission to return home, but a day or two later he received Halifax's letter, and he immediately added a postscript.

> 'Just after sealing this letter,' he said, 'I received an express from Charlestown with his Majesty's leave of Absence. I don't think I shall go away till March, and as my dear Jessy proposes going with me if it will

answer your convenience to meet us in London, and we might lodge together at half the expense to each.'

Dobbs later wrote to his friend Samuel Smith in London and asked him to make all the necessary arrangements for his voyage home. Smith, in the course of a letter to Conway, said that he had applied to Lord Egremont 'about a sloop of war to bring the Governor over next spring,' adding, 'his Lordship is well disposed to oblige him if it is practicable.'[6] The time suggested by Dobbs for his departure, the spring of 1765, has a certain interest, for when Tryon arrived at Cape Fear on 11th October, 1764, and was informed that Dobbs did not intend relinquishing his office until the following spring, he was greatly surprised. 'This I own was a thunderbolt to me,' he said. Tryon's position was delicate and somewhat difficult, as he fully expected to take office on his arrival in the province. It would seem that the Board of Trade acted with more than usual alacrity in appointing him, for Dobbs had made it clear to Smith, Egremont, and Conway that, health permitting, he intended remaining in the province until the spring.

Tryon was annoyed and disappointed; he complained in a letter to Halifax that the lack of employment over the winter would be burdensome. 'Among my lesser disappointments,' he said, 'is the want of a house, as the Governor has declined letting me his villa till his departure.' This was a disappointment, but it was one which Dobbs himself had experienced, for he had been constrained to rent a house at New Bern until he purchased his property at Russellboro'. Dobbs did at least offer hospitality to Tryon, who, despite his complaints, admitted that 'the old gentleman has been so polite in his offers to accommodate my family till I can get fixed elsewhere, I mean to behave to him with the respect that is due to his character, age, and infirmities.'[7]

The Assembly met at Wilmington and continued in session until the end of November. At the close of the session, Dobbs informed the members of his impending departure. In the course of a warm address, the Council tendered its 'unfeigned and grateful acknowledgment' of his labours in North Carolina.

'Your Excellency's wise, steady, and uniform administration has always been (judging from consequence) for promoting his Majesty's service, and at the same time productive of the best and most extensive advantages to his Majesty's loyal Subjects. . . . We are happy in being able to distinguish that administration not only unsullied but publickly tried and benevolent as yours demands our grateful acknowledgements. . . . We most ardently wish you all happiness and prosperity with an agreeable arrival in Britain, and a speedy recovery of your health, together with a most gracious reception from his Majesty & his Ministers for your unwearied endeavours to serve his interests and the Province.' [8]

The Lower House was more constrained in its address, and for the first time used the phrase 'the Commons House of the Assembly' to describe itself, thus adopting a description used by Dobbs when he compared the legislature of North Carolina to the British Houses of Parliament. In the course of this address the members acknowledged Dobbs's zeal 'in promoting the rights of the crown,' and assured him of their attachment to the King and the steady support of his government; they trusted that on the Governor's return to the Royal Presence he 'will faithfully represent our loyalty.' In closing the address, the Assembly wished Dobbs 'a pleasant voyage and a safe arrival in Britain, and that your native air may have all these salutary effects for the re-establishment of your health that you can wish.' [9]

In a reply to both Houses, Dobbs gave a gentle admonishment to the members.

> 'Before my departure,' he said, 'I think it is my duty to inform you as Governor that by some hasty and inconsiderate resolutions you have come into, by being overruled by some young Members who dont rightly understand the Constitution of Britain and the Colonies, you have taken upon you to interfere in the executive power over this Province, which is his Majesty's sole right which he has delegated to the Governor for the time being and his Council.'

The particular encroachment on the Royal prerogative he alluded to was the Assembly's claim to dispose of public monies without the concurrence of the Council and Governor, which was undoubtedly illegal, since the legislature consisted of the Assembly, Council, and Governor. In the expiring winter of his life, however, Dobbs was quietly patient like a tired and ageing father gently admonishing a wayward child.

> 'Tis as a friend,' he went on, 'I mention to you to prevent your interfering with his Majesty's undoubted Prerogative the executive power of the Government that you may not embroil yourselves with the Crown which at the end you must submit to and must be highly prejudicial to the welfare of this Province.' He concluded: 'However in what manner so ever you take this information and advice I shall think it my duty to lay the loyalty of the Inhabitants of this Province before his Majesty in the most favourable light; and to promote the peace and happiness which can only be procured by a perfect harmony between his Majesty and the

General Assembly of this Province which will be the means of procuring favour which otherwise they cannot expect.'

He thanked the members for their kind addresses and acknowledgement of his endeavours 'to promote the true Interest and Welfare of this colony by promoting a happy union between his Majesty and the Inhabitants of this Province.' [10]

With the prorogation of the Assembly, Dobbs returned to Russellboro' to rest and prepare for his voyage home in the spring. Here were the library of books he had gathered over the years, his papers and manuscripts, all in fact that made his villa a haven of rest and peace. His last Christmas in North Carolina was brightened by the tender and solicitous care of his young wife, and by the presence of his young grandnephew. For the next few months Dobbs and Jessy were busily occupied gathering together the accumulated possessions of ten years, and looking forward with eager anticipation to a return home. On 25th March—a week or two before he was due to sail—while engaged in the task of packing he had a seizure, and under Jessy's anxious and watchful eyes he was carried to his bed. From this seizure Dobbs never fully recovered consciousness, and two days later died in his wife's arms. Tryon, in a dispatch to Lord Halifax, wrote:

'Last Thursday Gov. Dobbs retired from the strife and cares of this World. Two days before his death he was busily employed in packing up his books for his passage to England, his physician had no other means to prevent his fatiguing himself than by telling him he had better prepare himself for a much longer voyage.' [11]

A month later the young widow wrote to Conway:

'The melancholy Subject that gives ociation for my writing to you effects me so much that I hardly know what I write. Alas I have loste my ever Dear Mr. Dobbs which makes me almost Inconsolable, he went to the Fort with Lord Adam Gordon on a Party of Pleasure and Caught a violent cold & after a few days illness departed this life the 28th of last March he died in his senses the violence of his disorder made him delirious at Times but when his reason beamed out his serenity of minde resigned himself up to his Heavenly Father with that nobleness of soul which few can equal. I have lost one of the best and tenderest of husbands and you a kind and most affectionate father. I condole with you on so great a loss. I should have wrote to you by a vessel that sail'd a few days after his death, but my mind was overwhelmed with grief. Mr. Powel Tooke a copy of the Will and said he would enclose it to Mr. Ned Dobbs by the Vessel I mention therefore make no doubt but you have received the Melancholy news of his death before this can reach you. Coll. Tryon is now at New Bern which prevents my sending a copy of the will under the Colony seal but as he returns and an opportunity offers for England I shall send it properly attested to Capt. Dobbs. I once flattered myself with the pleasing expectation of seeing you in company with my dear Mr. Dobbs, but the Divine power of Events otherwise determined it, and however reluctantly we must submit I cant help enclosing a Newspaper for the sake of the respect therein paid to the memory of one of the best of men by a Friend which I dare say will be agreeable to you. I am, dear sir, with all possible regard yrs affectionate Mother, Justina Dobbs.' [12]

Dobbs was interred in the incompleted Church of St. Philip, which he had designated as the King's Chapel in North Carolina.[13] With the passing years his grave has disappeared, but somewhere in the shade of the now ruined church there lie the remains of a man who, despite his faults and frailties, can lay claim to immortality, and be reckoned 'among the ablest and most intelligent Governors of his time.' [14]

16

Conclusion

AN APPRAISAL of Dobbs—of his life, his work, and achievements—presents difficulties. He was a man of many parts, and each part must be considered on its merits. In the first place, he was an Irishman with a very marked and definite interest in the land of his birth, and he was an economist with ideas much in advance of his times. He was a zealous reformer, a projector, imperialist, and colonial administrator. He was many other things—an engineer and architect, a soldier and a leader, a student of science and a practical and progressive agriculturist. He was a thoroughgoing Protestant, and a patriotic Briton who believed implicitly in the constitutional authority of the Crown; the Revolution, the Toleration Act, and the Bill of Rights were his guiding principles. In politics he was a Whig, and his Whiggery had much of the pristine character of its mentor, John Locke, from whom he absorbed many of his ideas. Politically these ideas accorded, a little crudely perhaps, with the perfect form of the Whig theory of government as enshrined in the writings of Edmund Burke.

When Dobbs entered the Irish Parliament, he did so as a reformer, fully bent on providing measures for the social and economic betterment of the country. The Irish Parliament, however, had little power or authority, and, generally speaking, its members displayed no interest in the country. Thirty years earlier William Molyneux endeavoured to assert the legislative independence of the Irish Parliament, but the case he so ably made in 1693 was largely vitiated by an Act of the English Parliament in 1717 which declared that it had 'full power and authority to make laws and statutes . . . to bind the Kingdom and people of Ireland.' [1] This Act removed all significant or practical vestige of independence from the Irish Parliament, so that it was little more than a gilded room for dispensing government largesse to the ruling minority; small wonder indeed that Swift described it as a den of thieves and a harpies' nest.

Though Dobbs entered the Irish Parliament allied to the English

ruling party, which for the most part displayed a cynical indifference
to the harsh lot of the Irish Catholics and a like indifference to the
economic state of the country, he refused to close his eyes to the
appalling conditions prevailing; he censured his indifferent country-
men, and sought, particularly by a Parliamentary Act, to encourage
tillage, and thus provide the basis of an agricultural and social policy
suitable to the needs of the Irish people. He strongly urged, both in
Parliament and in his writings, the need for increased tillage and land
reclamation, so as to provide work for the workless, and a new and just
system of land tenure to secure a frugal living for the small farmer, the
cottier, and the peasant. Though he supported the penal legislation
against Catholics on political grounds, he advocated a relaxation of
some of the penal laws so as to permit Catholics to lease land on equality
with their Protestant brethren. He found himself in opposition to the
English interest by his disapproval of the Navigation Acts and other
measures militating against the free export of Irish woollen and other
manufactures.[2]

In his *Essay on Irish Trade*, Dobbs predated Adam Smith in many
respects, particularly in his constant reiteration that the wealth of
a nation grows from the full employment and production of labour, and
that the free flow of trade throughout the world should not be retarded
by restrictive or protective measures save in exceptional circumstances.
Though Adam Smith claimed that the Navigation Acts 'were wise as
if they had been dictated by the most deliberate wisdom,' he was constrained to admit that they were injurious in many respects, and this
was also Dobbs's contention.[3] While admitting that there may have
been a need for the Navigation Acts, Dobbs maintained that free trade
within the bounds of the empire was essential in order to bind the
colonies and mother country in a single comity of nations, each
sharing in the wealth and productivity of the other. His ideas of a
colonial empire when studied side by side with those of Adam Smith
are interesting, and the student of political economy cannot fail to be
struck by the similarity of ideas and the parallelism of argument and
presentation.

Early in his career, Dobbs became convinced that the Irish Parliament was an unnecessary and useless luxury, and at best was simply an
institution for asserting and maintaining the ascendancy of the ruling
minority. It was obvious to him that an institution based on such
principles could not be maintained for all time, nor could the Catholic
majority be denied a voice therein. The preservation of the Ascendancy, therefore, and a more liberal treatment of Irish Catholics could

only be guaranteed by a close union with the Protestant Parliament of Britain. Dobbs also favoured union on the ground that it would be to the mutual advantage of both countries, and offered the only satisfactory solution for the economic and social regeneration of Ireland.[4] He was, therefore, a convinced unionist, one of a long line of Irishmen who genuinely believed that Ireland and England were bound together by many ties.

Dobbs was more than an Irish economist, however, and while there may be a tendency to dismiss his letters, memoranda, and papers on various aspects of colonial development as vague theories, we must accept them as the ideas of a man intensely interested in the social and economic development of Britain and her colonies, and very much in advance of his time. The Walpole attitude of *quieta non movere* which distinguished British colonial policy for many years was distasteful to the imperially minded Dobbs, to whom colonies represented more than great tracts of the world painted red on the map. He conceived the colonies as part and parcel of Britain, sources of wealth and power, not merely appendages to be left alone to work out their own salvation, and contribute in some indefinite way to the wealth of Britain without either direction or guidance. The colonies were assets to be used and developed for the benefit of both Britain and the colonists themselves. In this respect his interests and ideas were colonial rather than English in the narrow sense of the exploiting merchants; he was an imperialist and ideally empire-minded.[5]

His letters and memoranda sometimes give the impression that he was a theorist and an impractical visionary, but Dobbs was neither a theorist nor impractical. His belief in a closely knit empire was not a dream, nor was his belief in the existence of a Northwest Passage, nor was he quite the fanatic and beholder of visionary lands 'with the greatest talent the eighteenth century ever knew for misconstruing geography.'[6] *An Account of the Countries adjoining to Hudson Bay* is a vigorous and absorbing book. By no stretch of the imagination can we call it the work of an impractical dreamer, nor is it 'a shining example of what the imagination can do when it has a blank map to work on, and is handicapped by no empirical knowledge whatsoever,' as a recent writer asserts.[7] This harsh stricture is only true in the light of present-day knowledge. Though Dobbs failed to find a virtually non-existent Passage, his efforts cannot be written off as a total failure, for it was as a result of his efforts that the Hudson Bay area was thoroughly explored, mapped, and plotted. The two expeditions organised and planned by him were in line with traditional British exploration.[8]

Dobbs's long and bitter controversy with the Hudson's Bay Company, and his efforts to destroy its monopoly, while at times questionable, were in the main incidental to the greater issues involved. He viewed the Company, like many others, as a fat, wealthy monopoly sated with its profits, and sleeping in inglorious ease while the French increased their power and influence in northern Canada, even to the shores of Hudson Bay. Burpee has rightly pointed out that Dobbs was more alive to the French threat than were the proprietors of the Company, and it was not until he stirred the Company into action that any move was made to counter the French trader. In his efforts to find a Northwest Passage, and provide another route for British trade and expansion, Dobbs was in every sense a carrier and exponent of the expansionist and imperial energies that intended to make the Pacific a British instead of a Spanish lake.[9]

Though Dobbs's expansionist dreams in this respect failed, his other imperial schemes were not quite failures. His role in the formation of the Ohio Company of Virginia, overlooked and ignored by historians, was very important, as also were his efforts to obtain settlers for the merchant proprietors of North Carolina. The fact that there was no Halifax at the head of the Board of Trade before 1748 accounts in no small way for Dobbs's failure to provide settlements in Labrador, Newfoundland, and Nova Scotia, for Walpole's policy of inaction was perfectly congenial to Newcastle and his coterie, who were uninterested and completely indifferent to the plans and schemes submitted by Dobbs.

There is little need to enlarge on the last few years of Dobbs's life as Governor of North Carolina. In his letters seeking this appointment he set down very clearly the objects prompting his action. In the main he sought a post that would enable him to give practical effect to his ideas on colonisation. Unfortunately, he entered the colonial service at a time that was anything but propitious for his schemes; the ten years of his governorship were marked by a war which, though greatly extending the British empire, also initiated the movement towards its disruption so far as the American colonies were concerned. Walpole and his successors left colonisation largely to private enterprise, with the result that the colonies were not incorporated as an organic part of the British body politic but were largely self-governing and had developed a political life of their own.[10] When Halifax came to the Board of Trade in 1748, his more vigorous colonial policy was just too late, for more and more power had come to reside in the colonial Assemblies. The colonies depended very little on the mother country, and the only badge of bondage was the monopoly of trade safeguarded by the Navigation Acts.[11]

It is not necessary to go over the points of disagreement between Dobbs and the Assembly which became more marked as the war with France drew to a close. The causes of the disputes are more or less self-evident and were bound to arise by the nature of the incompatibility of the Governor's instructions and the aspirations of the colonists. It is unfortunate that the history of Dobbs's administration has been overshadowed by too much emphasis on these disagreements, which were bound to arise, especially in the case of governors like Dobbs, who tried to carry out their duties armed with the new instructions of a revivified Board of Trade—instructions carefully devised to curb the growing power of the colonial Assemblies. The works of writers such as Dickerson and Beer throw considerable light on the difficulties of colonial governors, and enable us to dismiss for the most part many of the harsh charges levelled against very able administrators, and in the case of Dobbs rebut the charges that his disagreements with the Assembly and his so-called autocratic behaviour were motivated by personal spite, choleric temperament, and splenetic hostility.[12]

The constructive work of Dobbs in North Carolina has been overshadowed by the false picture of an enfeebled and tyrannical dotard continually warring with the Assembly. Osgood's statement that Dobbs was one of the ablest governors of North Carolina is more in accord with facts than the verdict of earlier historians.[13] Dobbs was not without his faults; he was stubborn, individualistic, and hot-tempered. He was an old man when he assumed office, and the difficult period of the French war did not contribute to a peaceful, easy, and prosperous administration. However, we must not lose sight of the fact that the work of Dobbs as a colonial builder extended over a period of more than twenty years, during which time he played an important role in the colonisation and settlement of North Carolina. He was in the forefront of the opposition when Johnston's administration had provoked trouble in the province; and on his own appointment to the post he roused the people in their defence of the colonies, not perhaps very successfully, but the then relatively poor province did contribute something in the common defence against the French. Besides sending a quota of troops to fight outside the province, Dobbs showed commendable energy in the erection of forts and defensive outposts and in reorganising the militia.[14]

In the social and economic development of North Carolina, the work of Dobbs cannot be overlooked or lightly dismissed. In spite of opposition at home, he established a church organisation when the religious life of the province was at a low ebb. He was instrumental in starting a silk industry, and initiated a scheme of bounties for the cultivation of hemp and flaxseed. He set up a postal service and encouraged the craft of printing.[15] In an effort to increase the export trade, he sought time and again to effect a change in the commercial system by pressing for a modification of the Navigation Acts so as to permit closer commercial relations between Ireland and America, and open a trade with Spain and Portugal.

Had it not been for the war with France, much might have been achieved in the social and economic development of North Carolina, and the large sums of money spent in the defence of the colonies would have been devoted to more enduring purposes. Though war retards progress in many spheres of human activity, the rapid progress in the growth of North Carolina and a significant increase in trade and population was most marked during this period.[16] The interest shown by Dobbs in this growth and development is proven by his many journeys through the province, and his long reports to the Board of Trade. In the earlier years of his administration he carried out the most comprehensive survey of the coastline and drew up plans for new harbours; we can only regret that his plans for a seat of government at Tower Hill miscarried, otherwise he would have left behind him an enduring monument to his memory.

There are a few points meriting a moment's consideration. We can dismiss many of the charges brought against Dobbs and his administration. His love of 'filthy lucre' is an exaggeration, and though he realised the value of money like any normal man, there is no proof that he enriched himself as Governor of North Carolina. He undoubtedly made money during his lifetime, but at the same time he expended a small fortune on many of his schemes. His Northwest Passage ventures cost him many hundred pounds and gave no return; the expenditure on his North Carolina property in a final analysis showed little profit, while his investment in the Ohio Company was an absolute loss. It would seem, therefore, that what money he earned was promptly poured into other ventures and schemes that brought little or no return. His salary as Governor of North Carolina was not paid by the province, and his fees of office did not amount to more than four hundred pounds per annum.[17]

Dobbs has been charged with nepotism, but this charge is readily disproved. He certainly elevated friends and supporters to the Council of North Carolina, but this was not unusual; in fact, it would have been difficult if not impossible to carry out the functions of a Governor if he had not done so, and his action in this regard differs little from the governmental systems of our modern democracies. With the exceptions of the appointments given to his son and nephew, there appear to be no grounds for the charge of nepotism.

In a final analysis, we can say that Dobbs was an able and talented Irishman. He loved the country of his birth in a practical way, and was proud of his English heritage. He was an imperialist, and to him Britain and the Crown were the instruments designed by Providence to rule the world. He was a robust Protestant, upright and God-fearing; up to a point he was intolerant and fanatical in his hatred of the Catholic Church, which he looked upon as a tyrannical oligarchy. He was a thoughtful, if at times profuse, writer, who wrote hurriedly and carelessly but nevertheless had something profound to say. His two most important works, the *Essay on Irish Trade* and *An Account of the Countries Adjoining to Hudson Bay*, are of value and considerable merit in their limited way.

Dobbs was essentially a man of action. He was stubborn and egotistical, swayed by his own conclusions and judgements, which were often faulty. He was hasty, impatient, and did not accept either advice or criticism. Because of his impatient and volatile temperament, he made enemies, yet he had a warm and kindly streak in him, and willingly helped his needy relatives, and at all times showed a warm regard for his own poor tenantry and the impoverished peasantry of Ireland. He was a temperate man in an age of intemperance, and strongly disapproved of gambling, vice, and loose living generally. He possessed a vital and forceful personality that impressed itself on nobility and commoner alike. Allied to this were drive, initiative, and tireless energy which, though often misdirected, were never without purpose for good.

Dobbs does not rank among the greatest men of his age, and though he was the friend of Walpole, Newcastle, Pelham, and the other leaders of the Cleveland House coterie, he played no part in the political life of the country. Had he been an Englishman by birth, or even a member of the Irish aristocracy, he might well have occupied a place with the parliamentary group governing England from the rise of Walpole till the destruction of the Whig aristocracy under Chatham. But Dobbs was not an Englishman nor an Irish aristocrat, nor had he at the outset of his career the wealth or patronage to achieve a position of importance in the Whig oligarchy of his day. He lived in an age when a man of his ability and energy could satisfy his ambitions only by aligning himself with the wealthy merchants, courting the ruling class, and obtaining their patronage. This, of course, Dobbs did, otherwise he would have lived the small life of a country squire.

To label Dobbs as an ambitious man grovelling at the feet of the Whig leaders and the merchant princes does him scant justice. He was a man of ability, and this is proven by the fact that only a man of his ability could successfully have put across so many of his ideas and won the esteem of the worldly-wise merchants, and the confidence of the more able politicians who judged him a shrewd, capable, and far-seeing man. The eminent merchant-economist Gee expressed his surprise at Dobbs's grasp of business affairs, and the enterprising merchants, who were wiser than the politicians, readily accepted him. Able politicians such as Chesterfield and Wager supported his Northwest Passage project, while Newcastle, Pelham, and Halifax had sufficient faith in him to entrust him with an American governorship when that appointment was no longer a sinecure.

As Governor of North Carolina, Dobbs endeavoured to maintain what he conceived to be a just balance between the executive authority, for which he was responsible, and the aspirations of the colonists, which he never wholly condemned. In an impossible position, he tried to serve two masters with equal zeal, and in doing so drew upon himself the criticism of both. His life as a colonial governor has been overshadowed by too much emphasis on the less important events of his career, and, like many other able governors, he has suffered eclipse by the legend of the Revolution, yet he played a part in the building of a Commonwealth which, despite artificial differences, is still linked to Britain by a common heritage and a common tongue.

Notes

v. = volume

CHAPTER I Pp. 9–16

1 Spenser, *Brief note of Ireland*. Calendar of State Papers, Ireland, 1598–99, p. 414.
2 Burke, *Landed Gentry of Ireland*.
3 Fynes Moryson, *Rebellion in Ireland*, Book 2, p. 78.
4 McSkimin, *History of Carrickfergus*, p. 220.
5 Information about the Dalway Family from manuscript material in the possession of Miss Joan Gardiner.
6 The Egmont Papers, v. 1, pt. 1, p. 53.
7 McSkimin, *History of Carrickfergus*, p. 476.
8 Ibid., p. 38.
9 Rutty, *History of the Quakers in Ireland*, p. 325.
10 Dobbs, *Description of County Antrim*. Castle Dobbs Papers, D.O.D. 162. 6.
11 Ibid.
12 Ibid.
13 Ball, *Correspondence of Swift*, v. 1, p. 28. *Scepsis Scientifica, or Confest Ignorance of the Way of Science, An Essay of the Vanity of Dogmatic and Confident Opinion,* was written by Joseph Glanville, Court Chaplain to Charles II.
14 Young, *Fighters of Derry*, p. 87.
15 Family Bible.
16 McSkimin, *History of Carrickfergus*, p. 71.

CHAPTER II Pp. 17–25

1 Jackson, *The Inniskilling Dragoons*, p. 34.
2 War Office Records.
3 McSkimin, *History of Carrickfergus*, p. 485.
4 Both Dobbs and Ward had a common grandfather in Archibald Stewart of Ballintoy.
5 The Kildare estate 'contained ten castles, 100 messaiges, 100 lofts, 2 dovecots, 2 mills, 100 gardens, 20 orchards, 5,000 acres of land, 500 acres of meadow, 500 acres of pasture, 400 acres of wood, and under 200 acres of heath, and 12,000 acres of moor, bog and Marsh.'
6 Hall, *History of the Bank of Ireland*, pp. 23 et seq.
7 Lecky, *History of Ireland in the 18th Century*, v. 1, p. 197.
8 Boulter's correspondence gives perhaps the best picture of the Bishop-ruler in eighteenth-century Ireland.
9 Swift in a letter remarks that he regarded the Rev. R. Dobbs as one

of the three most worthy clergymen in Ireland. *Correspondence,* v. 3, p. 818.

10 Lecky, *History of Ireland,* v. 1, pp. 45 et seq.
11 Boulter's *Letters,* v. 1, pp. 7–10.
12 Records of Carrickfergus, 1724.
13 Castle Dobbs Papers, D.O.D. 162. 23.
14 Castle Ward Papers, Book 4.
15 *Transactions of the Royal Society,* v. 32, p. 89.
16 Ibid., v. 34, p. 128.
17 Ibid., v. 36, p. 140.
18 Conway was a brother-in-law of Catherine Walpole.
19 Letter from Dobbs to Conway. Castle Dobbs Papers, D.O.D. 162. 33.

CHAPTER III   Pp. 26–33

1 Alexander M'Aulay was the author of *A Treatise on Tillage* and a pamphlet on tithes entitled *Property Inviolable*. He was a friend of Swift, who bequeathed him 'the Gold box in which the freedom of Dublin was presented to me, as a testimony of the esteem and love I have for him.' M'Aulay was legal adviser to Dobbs.
2 Hall, *History of the Bank of Ireland,* p. 426.
3 *Journal of the House of Commons, Ireland,* v. vii, pp. 16, 21, 50.
4 O'Mahony, *Viceroys of Ireland.*
5 Lecky, *History of Ireland in the* 18*th Century,* v. i, p. 195.
6 Swift, *Short View of the State of Ireland.*
7 *Journal of the House of Commons, Ireland,* v. vii, p. 50.
8 Clarke, *Thomas Prior,* p. 16.
9 *Journal of the House of Commons, Ireland,* v. vii, p. 83.
10 McCullock, *Literature of Political Economy,* p. 147.
11 Boulter's *Letters,* v. 2, p. 15.
12 Castle Dobbs Papers, D.O.D. 162. 21.
13 Ibid.

CHAPTER IV   Pp. 34–43

1 McCullock, *Literature of Political Economy,* p. 46.
2 Castle Ward Papers, Book 4.
3 Swift, *The Modest Proposal for Preventing the Poor of Ireland from being a Burden to the Parents and Country.*
4 Nicholson's Letters, British Museum Add. MSS. 6116.
5 Boulter's *Letters,* v. 1, p. 181.
6 Mountmorris, *Impartial Reflections on the Present Crisis,* p. 6.
7 Berry, *History of the Royal Dublin Society,* p. 9.
8 Clarke, *Thomas Prior,* pp. 24 et seq.
9 Ibid.
10 Castle Dobbs Papers, D.O.D. 162. 25.
11 *Dictionary of National Biography*. See Dorset.
12 McSkimin, *History of Carrickfergus,* p. 78.
13 Castle Dobbs Papers, D.O.D. 162. 25.
14 Castle Ward Papers, Book 4.

15 Houghton Papers, Cambridge University, 1908 and 3097.
16 Castle Dobbs Papers, D.O.D. 162. 25.
17 Boulter's *Letters*, v. 1, p. 31.
18 Houghton Papers, Cambridge University, 1908.
19 Ibid.
20 Castle Dobbs Papers, D.O.D. 162. 33.
21 Ibid.
22 Ibid.
23 Houghton Papers, Cambridge University, 1908.
24 *Liber Munerum Publicorum Hiberniæ*, pt. 2, p. 106.
25 *Journal of the House of Commons*, Ireland, v. 6.

CHAPTER V Pp. 44–59

1 Mackay, *The Honourable Company*, pp. 3 et seq.
2 Castle Ward Papers, Book 6.
3 Ibid.
4 Ibid.
5 Hervey's *Memoirs*, v. 2, p. 47.
6 *A Vindication of the Conduct of Captain Middleton*, pp. 3 et seq.
7 Bryce, *The Remarkable History of the Hudson's Bay Company*, pp. 62–68.
8 Mackay, *The Honourable Company*, p. 77.
9 Bryce, *The Remarkable History of the Hudson's Bay Company*, pp. 62–68.
10 Castle Ward Papers, Book 6.
11 Ibid.
12 Castle Dobbs Papers, D.O.D. 162. 37.
13 Ibid., 162. 54.
14 Houghton Papers, Cambridge University, 3097.
15 Morton, *A History of the Canadian West to* 1870–71, p. 210.
16 *A Vindication of the Conduct of Captain Middleton*, p. 52.
17 The correspondence between Dobbs and Middleton is contained in *A Vindication of the Conduct of Captain Middleton*, London, 1743.
18 The Criticism filed with the Admiralty is printed in Middleton's *Vindication*, pp. 1 et seq.
19 *A Vindication of the Conduct of Captain Middleton*, p. 8.
20 Introduction to James Isham's *Observations on Hudson Bay*, edited by E. E. Rich, p. lxii.
21 *A Vindication of the Conduct of Captain Middleton*, p. 2.
22 Ibid., p. 3.
23 Burpee, *The Search for the Western Sea*, pp. 226 et seq.
24 Mackay, *The Honourable Company*, p. 85.
25 Morton, *A History of the Canadian West to* 1870–71, p. 212.

CHAPTER VI Pp. 60–70

1 Castle Ward Papers, Book 7.
2 Ibid.
3 Ibid.

4 Ibid.

5 *Journal of the House of Commons, Ireland*, v. 7, pp. 759 et seq.

6 Clarke, *Thomas Prior*, p. 43.

7 Castle Ward Papers, Book 7.

8 Ibid. Also *Commons Journal*, v. 24, pp. 738, 762, 791, 805, 817, 824, 845, 848, 891.

9 Ellis, *A Voyage to Hudson's Bay by the Dobbs Galley and the California in the years 1746 and 1747, for discovering a North West Passage*.

10 Castle Ward Papers, Book 7.

11 Ellis, *A Voyage to Hudson's Bay*, p. 16.

12 Ibid., p. 21.

13 Ibid., p. 22.

14 James Isham's *Observations* . . . *and Notes and Observations on a book entitled, A Voyage to Hudson's Bay in the Dobbs Galley*, 1749, pp. 266 et seq.

15 Castle Dobbs Papers, D.O.D. 162. 52.

16 *Transactions of the Royal Society*, v. 44, pp. 471–2.

17 Castle Dobbs Papers, D.O.D. 162. 52.

18 Isham's *Observations*, pp. 204–5.

19 Ellis, *A Voyage to Hudson's Bay*, p. 231.

CHAPTER VII   Pp. 71–81

1 Osgood, *The American Colonies in the* 18*th Century*, v. 4, p. 152.

2 A short account of the McCulloh grants is given by Saunders in his Introduction to the *Colonial Records of North Carolina*, v. 5, pp. xxx–l.

3 *Dictionary of National Biography*.

4 Castle Dobbs Papers, D.O.D. 162. 52.

5 Ibid.

6 Ibid.

7 Lawson, *Travels in Carolina*, p. 73.

8 *Colonial Records of North Carolina*, v. 5, p. 381.

9 Ibid., pp. 792, 797, 844.

10 Ibid.

11 Smith, *The Thirteen Colonies*, p. 383.

12 *Colonial Records of North Carolina*, v. 5, pp. 792, 797, 844.

13 Ibid.

14 Osgood, *The American Colonies in the* 18*th Century*, v. 4, pp. 172–3.

15 The following letter was sent to each subscriber from London on the 8th February, 1748:

> 'The Gentlemen of the Northwest Committee, who were chosen by a general meeting, and took upon themselves the trouble of managing the late expedition for the discovering of a Passage by Hudson's Straits to the Western ocean; have desired me to acquaint you that they have sold the two ships *Dobbs Galley* and *California*, and paid off all the people who went that voyage (except the Captains whose conduct is not as yet cleared up to the Committee) and for that purpose they have been obliged to advance near £1,500 over and above all that the ships and effects have produced, which the Committee hope will be reimbursed them, in equal proportions by every subscriber, as nothing can be more equitable.

'At the same time that I am directed to make the reasonable demand, I am also desired to inform you, that the Committee have petitioned His Majesty in Council, for a Grant for ever, of all the lands in Hudson's Bay, not immediately occupied by the Company, and an exclusive right to trade in all that country for a certain number of years, which we have great reason to believe will be granted us, our expectations being founded on the opinion of the Attorney General and others learned in law, that the Hudson's Bay Company have not by the Charter an exclusive right to the trade of those parts, and we have good grounds to think that they have forfeited any right they might have had from that charter by their not fulfilling the conditions of it.

'The prayer of our petition is founded upon the great expense the subscribers have been at in the late attempt, the probability of a Passage, and the great loss the public sustained by the not settling and enlarging the trade of that vast continent. If we succeed in our solicitations, the advantages to those who are originally concerned must be very great; therefore we think it just to make an offer to all the subscribers in proportion to their shares, but as this application is attended with expense, it is expected that each subscriber will not only pay up his deficiency on the late expedition which will be about £21 upon each of the 70 subscribers, but advance £10 more towards the charges of applying for this new Charter; and that you will by return of post allow me to draw in the name of the Committee for the £31 English to entitle you to any share in the future advantages. So far those who may be taken in upon the new plan, that were not concerned in the late expedition, they must pay up as much as each of the original subscribers have been out of pocket, which will be thrown into the stock of the new projected company who are to be incorporated.

'Sam. Smith, Sec.'

Castle Ward Papers, Book 7.
16 Draft Petition to Parliament of Merchant Adventurers, Castle Dobbs Papers, D.O.D. 162. 55.
17 Castleward Papers, Book 7.
18 Parliamentary Committee appointed in March 1748.
19 Mackay, *The Honourable Company*, pp. 86 et seq.
20 Bryce, *Remarkable History of the Hudson's Bay Company*, pp. 62–68.
21 Appendix to *Commons Journal*, 1749.
22 Castle Ward Papers, Book 7.
23 Ibid.
24 Ibid.
25 Appendix to *Commons Journal*, 1749.

CHAPTER VIII Pp. 82–94

1 *Transactions of the Royal Society*, v. 46, pp. 536–538.
2 Boulter's *Letters*, v. 1, p. 8.
3 Lecky, *History of Ireland in the 18th Century*, v. 1, p. 461.
4 Walpole, *Memoirs of George II*, p. 281.
5 Castle Dobbs Papers, D.O.D. 162. 60.
6 *Insula Sacra et libera*, London, 1753.
7 Lecky, *History of Ireland in the 18th Century*, v. 1, p. 466.
8 Dobbs, *Essay on Irish Trade*, v. 2, p. 65.

9 Lecky, *History of Ireland in the* 18*th Century*, v. 1, p. 466.
10 The two manuscripts are preserved among the Castle Dobbs Papers.
11 Castle Ward Papers, Book 8.
12 Castle Dobbs Papers, D.O.D. 162. 53.
13 Ibid., D.O.D. 162. 61.
14 Ibid., D.O.D. 162. 60.
15 Bailey, *The Ohio Company of Virginia*, pp. 17 et seq.
16 Osgood, *The American Colonies in the* 18*th Century*, v. 4, p. 267. Winsor, *Narrative and Critical History of America*, v. 5, p. 570. List of Original Members of the Ohio Company, P.R.O., C.O.S. 1423. Bailey, *The Ohio Company of Virginia and the Westward Movement*, 1748–1792.

   Though Dobbs was one of the principal figures in the Company, and claimed responsibility with Hanbury for obtaining the grant, his name does not usually appear in any of the accounts of this remarkable Company, due no doubt to the fact that the Castle Dobbs and Castleward Papers have only now been studied. Among these papers are copies of the later sale of Dobbs's interest in the Company, and particulars of the original agreement between the partners. From the information contained in these papers it is clear that Dobbs and Hanbury were the active agents in promoting the Company in England, and in obtaining the grants of land.

17 Bailey, *The Ohio Company of Virginia*, p. 25.
18 Public Record Office, C.O.5, 1327/53–57.
19 Bailey, *The Ohio Company of Virginia*, p. 58.
20 Ibid., p. 35.
21 Gist, *Journals*.
22 Castle Ward Papers, Book 8.
23 Public Record Office, C.O.5, 1328/53–57.
24 Banta, *The Ohio*, pp. 65–76.
25 Castle Dobbs Papers, D.O.D. 162. 72.
26 Bailey, *The Ohio Company of Virginia*, p. 202.

CHAPTER IX   Pp. 95–106

1 Faris later obtained an appointment as Collector of Customs in North Carolina.
2 Castle Dobbs Papers, D.O.D. 162. 48.
3 Ibid., D.O.D. 162. 52.
4 Ibid.
5 Ibid., D.O.D. 162. 57.
6 Ibid., D.O.D. 162. 61.
7 Ibid., D.O.D. 162. 63.
8 Ibid., D.O.D. 162. 65.
9 Ibid.
10 Ibid., D.O.D. 162. 64.
11 This portrait hangs in the dining-room at Castle Dobbs.
12 Castle Dobbs Papers, D.O.D. 162. 64.
13 Ibid.
14 Pococke, *Travels in Ireland*, p 112.

15 Castle Dobbs Papers, D.O.D. 162. 69.

16 *Journal of the House of Commons*, Ireland, v. 7, pp. 759 et seq.

17 Lecky, *History of Ireland in the* 18*th Century*, v. 1, p. 459.

18 McSkimin, *History of Carrickfergus*, p. 494.

19 Castle Dobbs Papers, D.O.D. 162. 69.

20 Castle Ward Papers, Book 8.

21 Ibid.

22 The salary of £1,000 per annum was paid by the Treasury from the Barbados 4½ per cent. duty. Labaree, *Royal Governments in America*, p. 333.

23 Castle Dobbs Papers, D.O.D. 162. 69.

24 Ibid., D.O.D. 162. 67.

25 Beer, *British Colonial Policy*, pp. 17–30. On 29th December, 1754, Franklin wrote:

> 'All the Assemblies in the Colonies have, I suppose, had the Union Plans laid before them, but it is not likely, in my opinion, that any of them will act upon it so as to agree to it, or to propose any Amendments to it. Every Body cries, a Union is absolutely necessary, but when they come to the manner and Form of the Union, their weak Noodles are perfectly distracted' (*Franklin's Writings*, v. 3, p. 242).

26 Osgood, *The American Colonies in the* 18*th Century*, v. 4, p. 202.

27 Wheeler, in his *Historical Sketches of North Carolina*, and other historians state that Dobbs brought many relations with him, and also a printer named Rice whom he encouraged to carry on his trade.

28 Sharpe, *Correspondence*, v. 1, pp. 139, 184.

29 Burnaby, *Travels through the Middle Settlements of North America*, pp. 33–34.

30 Freeman, *George Washington*, v. 1, p. 436.

31 *Colonial Records of North Carolina*, v. 5, p. 144.

32 Ibid.

33 Ibid.

34 Labaree, *Royal Governments in America*, p. 131.

CHAPTER X   Pp. 107–121

1 Saunders, Introduction to the *Colonial Records of North Carolina*, v. 5, p. xl.

2 *Colonial Records of North Carolina*, v. 5, p. 144.

3 *Official Papers of Robert Dinwiddie*, v. 1, p. 277.

4 Ibid., p. 297.

5 Ibid., p. 270.

6 Ibid., p. 277.

7 *Colonial Records of North Carolina*, v. 5, p. 144.

8 *Official Papers of Robert Dinwiddie*, v. 1, pp. 269, 277.

9 Dobbs Papers in the State of North Carolina Department of Archives and History, Raleigh.

10 *Colonial Records of North Carolina*, v. 5, p. 213.

11 Ibid., p. 213.

12 Ibid., p. 215.

13 Castle Dobbs Papers, D.O.D. 162. 73.

14 Ibid.

15 *Colonial Records of North Carolina*, v. 5, p. 314.

16 Crittenden, in his book *The Commerce of North Carolina*, 1763–1789, claims that the Navigation Acts and similar trade restrictions did not militate against North Carolina, and asserts that 'in spite of the fact that from time to time a little grumbling was heard there can be little doubt that, all aspects of the question being considered, North Carolina profited by being part of the British System' (pp. 43 et seq.). Crittenden's painstaking work gives a reasonable picture of the trade and commerce of the province as viewed by a twentieth-century scholar, but Dobbs wrote from experience of the deleterious effects of the navigation laws so far as Ireland was concerned, and the denial of a direct trade between North Carolina and Ireland was definitely harmful to both countries.

17 The Board of Trade freely admitted that the proposed alterations appeared advisable, in the light in which Dobbs put them, but contended there were many difficulties in making any changes, adding: 'whenever . . . the times will admit of a Consideration of this matter, the whole will be entered into together' (Board of Trade, N. Carolina, 22, pp. 194, 195).

18 *Colonial Records of North Carolina*, v. 5, pp. 341 et seq.

19 Ibid.

20 Ibid., pp. 343 et seq.

21 Ibid., p. 346.

22 Ibid., p. 347.

23 *Official Papers of Robert Dinwiddie*, v. 2, p. 24.

24 *Colonial Records of North Carolina*, v. 5, p. 353.

25 Fort Dobbs, according to Saunders, was located between Salisbury and Statesville, but Collet's map would appear to place it north-west of Turnersburg.

26 *Colonial Records of North Carolina*, v. 5, pp. 353 et seq.

27 Ibid., p. 416.

CHAPTER XI   Pp. 122–136

1 *Official Papers of Robert Dinwiddie*, v. 2, p. 123.

2 Ibid., p. 181.

3 Ibid., p. 185.

4 Castle Dobbs Papers, D.O.D. 162. 72.

5 *Colonial Records of North Carolina*, v. 5, p. 419.

6 *Official Papers of Robert Dinwiddie*, v. 2, p. 202.

7 *Colonial Records of North Carolina*, v. 5, pp. 495 et seq.

8 Ibid., p. 440.

9 Ibid., p. 520.

10 Ibid., p. 940.

11 The Board of Trade asked the governors for their opinions on three points: first, the best general system for the defence of the frontiers, types of forts that should be erected, and an estimate of the number of soldiers required; second, a scheme for managing Indian affairs; and third, 'what will be a proper fund to be established for making a

constant and permanent provision for these services, with the least
burthen and inconvenience to His Majesty's Subjects' (Beer, *British
Colonial Policy*, p. 48).

12 *Colonial Records of North Carolina*, v. 5, pp. 462 et seq.

13 Governor Shirley of Massachusetts replied on similar lines, but
estimated that 6,480 troops would be required, while Dobbs thought
2,800 would be sufficient (Board of Trade, Mass. 74, Hh. 68).

14 'The British Government did not adopt these suggestions, though they
came from men of conspicuous ability who, from long and faithful
service in the colonies, were in the best position to advise wisely' (Beer,
British Colonial Policy, p. 49).

15 *Colonial Records of North Carolina*, v. 5, p. 563.

16 Robertson, *Chatham and the British Empire*, p. 62.

17 Ibid., p. 64.

18 *Official Papers of Robert Dinwiddie*, v. 2, p. 494.

19 Bradley, *The Fight with France for North America*, p. 147.

20 *Official Papers of Robert Dinwiddie*, v. 2, p. 494.

21 Bradley, *The Fight with France for North America*, p. 147.

22 Castle Ward Papers, Book 7.

CHAPTER XII   Pp. 137–153

1 Du Bois, *Travels in North Carolina*.

2 Andrews, *Colonial Folkways*, p. 53.

3 *Pennsylvania Gazette*, 24th March, 1757.

4 *Colonial Records of North Carolina*, v. 5, p. 751.

5 Ibid., p. 753.

6 *Official Papers of Dinwiddie*, v. 2, p. 536.

7 Bradley, *The Fight with France*, pp. 169 et seq.

8 Osgood, *The American Colonies in the 18th Century*, v. 4, p. 208.

9 *Colonial Records of North Carolina*, v. 5, p. 145.

10 Ibid., pp. 945–60.

11 *Official Papers of Dinwiddie*, v. 2, p. 691.

12 *Colonial Records of North Carolina*, v. 5, p. 792.

13 Ibid., p. 743.

14 Ibid., p. 945.

15 Bradley, *The Fight with France*, p. 205.

16 *Colonial Records of North Carolina*, v. 5, p. 999.

17 Beer, in his *British Colonial Policy* (p. 62), notes:

'Nothing was expected from the Carolinas, but thanks to the efforts
of Governor Dobbs a small force was sent from North Carolina.' In the
course of a letter to Pitt, Dobbs wrote: 'We passed an Aid bill . . . to
make up three companies we had on foot here of 50 men to 100 each,
so as to send three hundred to join General Forbes . . . and have raised
50 more in two companies to defend the forts on the sea coast. I have
engaged a sloop to carry two companies immediately to the Potomac
river in Virginia, with what additional men they can raise, and to leave
three additional officers to raise and follow them as soon as possible, and
the 3rd company is to march immediately from our western frontier . . .
to Winchester in Virginia . . . but the misfortune of this province is that
we have no cash . . . and though we can raise and pay men in the

province yet we have no credit to pay them out of the Province' (*Pitt Correspondence*, v. 1, p. 341).

18 Bradley, *The Fight with France*, p. 209. Pitt, *Correspondence*, v. 1, p. 372.
19 *Colonial Records of North Carolina*, v. 5, p. 958.
20 A number of historians, including Ashe, Winsor, Wheeler, Wiley, Haywood, and Williamson, predate Dobbs's birth by five years.
21 Two other relatives, the Reverend Alec Stewart, and a nephew, Cornet McManus, were given appointments.
22 *Colonial Records of North Carolina*, v. 5, p. 959.
23 Ibid., pp. 1098 et seq.
24 Ibid., p. 1070.
25 Russellboro' was originally owned by the Moore family, and later sold to Captain John Russell, but after his death reverted to the Moore family, from whom it was purchased by Dobbs. The house appears to have been picturesquely situated overlooking the Cape Fear River (Sprunt, *Tales and Traditions of the Lower Cape Fear*, pp. 67–71).
26 Letter from Tryon to Sewallis Shirley in the possession of Mr. Bruce Cotton of Baltimore.
27 *Colonial Records of North Carolina*, v. 5, p. 1211.

CHAPTER XIII Pp. 154–172

1 Saunders, Introduction to the *Colonial Records of North Carolina*, v. 6.
2 Ibid.
3 Ashe, *History of North Carolina*, v. 1, p. 267.
4 *Colonial Records of North Carolina*, v. 5, pp. lvi et seq.
5 Ibid., v. 5, pp. 1088 et seq.
6 Ibid., v. 6, p. 79.
7 Ibid., v. 6, p. 295.
8 Saunders, Introduction to the *Colonial Records of North Carolina*, v. 5.
9 Ibid.
10 Corbin was dismissed from the Council and from the Colonelcy of the Militia.
11 *Colonial Records of North Carolina*, v. 6, pp. 56, 180.
12 Samuel Smith was nominated for the post by John Campbell of Bertie County, one time Speaker of the Assembly. The nomination was agreed to by the Council, and the Assembly recommended that Smith be appointed 'agent of the Governor and Council.' The recommendation does not appear to have been implemented, and Dobbs recalls that during the debate on the appointment of an agent 'Mr. Smith's name was not so much as once mentioned' (*Colonial Records of North Carolina*, v. 6, pp. 77, 307).
13 *Colonial Records of North Carolina*, v. 6, p. 99.
14 Ibid., v. 6, p. 32.
15 Ibid., v. 6, p. 55.
16 In 1757 Parliament granted the sum of £50,000 to Virginia and the Carolinas to compensate for service against the French; North Carolina received £8,000.
17 *Colonial Records of North Carolina*, v. 6, p. 100.
18 Thomas Child and Charles Berry.

19 *Colonial Records of North Carolina*, v. 6, pp. 62 et seq.
20 Andrews, *Colonial Folkways*, p. 39.
21 *Colonial Records of North Carolina*, v. 6, p. 219.
22 Ibid.
23 Ibid., v. 6, p. 347.
24 Ibid., v. 6, p. 371.
25 Ibid., v. 6, p. 380.
26 Labaree, *Royal Governments in America*, p. 400.
27 *Colonial Records of North Carolina*, v. 6, pp. 400 et seq.
28 Ibid., v. 6, p. 409.
29 Labaree, *Royal Governments in America*, p. 400.
30 Dobbs's reply to the charges brought against him fill more than forty printed pages and is given in full in the sixth volume of the *Colonial Records*. The reply is an interesting commentary on some aspects of the domestic and internal affairs of North Carolina. Dobbs defends all his actions with candour and vigour, and at the same time shows up his principal accusers in a most unsavoury light.
31 Saunders, Introduction to the *Colonial Records of North Carolina*, v. 6, p. lx.
32 *Colonial Records of North Carolina*, v. 6, p. 691.

CHAPTER XIV   Pp. 173–194

1 *Colonial Records of North Carolina*, v. 6, p. 266.
2 Ibid., p. 449.
3 Ibid., p. 451.
4 Ibid., p. 539.
5 Ibid., p. 540.
6 Ibid., p. 520.
7 Ibid., p. 633.
8 Ibid., pp. 642, 695, 703, 748.
9 Ibid., p. 725.
10 Morrison, 'Arthur Dobbs of Castle Dobbs and Carolina,' *South Atlantic Quarterly*, v. 16, pp. 30–8.
11 Castle Dobbs Papers, D.O.D. 162. 78.
12 *Colonial Records of North Carolina*, v. 6, p. 803.
13 Ibid., pp. 800–37.
14 Ibid., p. 836.
15 Ibid., p. 834.
16 'The tide of emigration that ten years earlier was setting so strongly to Western Carolina was, however, checked because of the Indian war. Yet at the conclusion of peace North Carolina had a population of about 100,000 whites, and more than 10,000 negroes. On the Cape Fear there were forty saw-mills producing some 30,000,000 feet of lumber annually, and there were exported from that river 36,000 barrels of naval stores' (Ashe, *History of North Carolina*, v. 1, p. 304).
17 *Colonial Records of North Carolina*, v. 6, pp. 692, 695, 703, 748.
18 Ibid., p. 836.
19 In a letter from Henry Eustace McCulloh to Richard Conway Dobbs, dated 22nd May, 1770, McCulloh states that about the year 1760

Dobbs began the sale of his land at £10 per acre, and it was computed that all good and valuable land had been conveyed to settlers and others. Two or three years before his death, the terms were reduced to £5, and a great number of small tracts were disposed of. 'From information received,' McCulloh wrote, 'and a consideration of the very nature of the terms it is apprehended that at Mr. Dobbs's death a very small quantity of valuable land was left and the value trifling' (Castle Dobbs Papers, D.O.D. 162. 88).

20 *Colonial Records of North Carolina,* v. 6, p. 782.
21 Ibid., p. 788.
22 Ibid.
23 Ibid.
24 This letter is printed in the sixth volume of the *Colonial Records of North Carolina,* but there is no identification of the writer.
25 *Colonial Records of North Carolina,* v. 6, p. 839.
26 Labaree, *Royal Governments in America,* pp. 420 et seq.
27 Governor Richard Dobbs Spaight.
28 North Carolina Letter Book, Society for the Propagation of the Gospel.
29 Ibid.
30 *Colonial Records of North Carolina,* v. 6, p. 992.
31 The inefficient regulation of the Indian trade by the separate colonies was an important factor in alienating the natives from the English, and was one of the immediate causes of their organised revolt in 1763 (Beer, *British Colonial Policy,* p. 260).
32 *Colonial Records of North Carolina,* v. 6, p. 712.
33 North Carolina Letter Book, Society for the Propagation of the Gospel.
34 *Colonial Records of North Carolina,* v. 6, pp. 1089 et seq.
35 North Carolina Letter Book, Society for the Propagation of the Gospel.

CHAPTER XV   Pp. 195–200

1 *Colonial Records of North Carolina,* v. 6, p. 1044.
2 Lieutenant-Governor as distinct from Governor-General.
3 *Colonial Records of North Carolina,* v. 6, p. 1045.
4 North Carolina Letter Book, Society for the Propagation of the Gospel.
5 Castle Dobbs Papers, D.O.D. 162. 83.
6 Castle Dobbs Papers, D.O.D. 162. 80.
7 *Colonial Records of North Carolina,* v. 6, pp. 1043, 1045, 1053.
8 Ibid., p. 1249.
9 Ibid., p. 1316.
10 Ibid., p. 1318.
11 Ibid., p. 1321.
12 Castle Dobbs Papers, D.O.D. 162. 83.
13 *South Carolina Gazette,* 27th April, 1765.
14 Osgood, *The American Colonies in the 18th Century,* v. 4, p. 202.

CHAPTER XVI   Pp. 201–208

1 6 George I, c. 5.
2 Dobbs, *Essay on Irish Trade, passim.*

3 Smith, *Wealth of Nations*, pp. 223, 254, and *passim*.

4 Dobbs, *Short Essay on Incorporating Union*.

5 DeVoto, *Westward the Course of Empire*, p. 219.

6 Ibid., p. 244.

7 Ibid.

8 Heawood, *History of Geographical Discovery*, pp. 329, 413, 414.

9 DeVoto, *Westward the Course of Empire*, p. 244.

10 Beer, *British Colonial Policy*, p. 1.

11 Smith, *Wealth of Nations*, p. 254.

12 Beer, *British Colonial Policy*, 1754–1765. Dickerson, *American Colonial Government*, 1696–1765.

13 Osgood, *The American Colonies in the 18th Century*, v. 4, p. 202.

14 Beer, *British Colonial Policy*, p. 62.

15 Dobbs is stated to have brought a printer with him to North Carolina, but the evidence for this is not clear. He did, however, insist on appointing a Royal Printer to the province.

16 The value of imports rose from £150,770 in 1752 to £194,170 in 1762, and exports increased from £130,887 to £181,695 (Crittenden, *The Commerce of North Carolina*).

17 Letter from Governor Tryon to Sewallis Shirley in the possession of Mr. Bruce Cotton of Baltimore.

APPENDIX

Writings of Arthur Dobbs

An account of a Parhelion or Mock Sun observed at Castle Dobbs on the 22nd March, 1721, and again a few days later. *Transactions of the Royal Society*. v. 32. London, 1722–3.

An Account of an *Aurora Borealis* seen September 1725 in Ireland. *Transactions of the Royal Society*. v. 34. London, 1726–7.

An Observation of the Eclipse of the Moon at Castle Dobbs near Carrickfergus in Ireland. 2nd Feb., 1728–9. *Transactions of the Royal Society*. v. 36. London, 1729–30.

An Essay on the Trade and Improvement of Ireland. By Arthur Dobbs, Esq., Dublin: Rhames, 1729.

An Essay on the Trade of Ireland. Part 2. By Arthur Dobbs, Esq., Dublin: Rhames, 1731.

Scheme to Enlarge the Colonies and Increase Commerce and Trade. Manuscript. 60 pages.

Notes on Currency in Great Britain and Ireland. Manuscript. 6 pages.

An Account of the Countries adjoining to Hudson's Bay in the Northwest part of America. London, 1744.

Remarks upon Captain Middleton's Defence. London, 1744.

A Reply to Captain Middleton's Answer. London, 1745.

On the Distance Between Asia and America. *Transactions of the Royal Society*. v. 44. London, 1746–7.

Reasons for settling the Coast of Labrador. Manuscript. 5 pages.

Reasons for the Great Price and Scarcity of Beaver and other furs in England. Manuscript. 8 pages.

Observations on Bees, and their Method of Gathering Wax and Honey. *Transactions of the Royal Society.* v. 46. London, 1749–50.

Some thoughts in Relation to a Union of Britain with Ireland. Manuscript. 25 pages.

A Short Essay to Shew the Expediency, if not political Necessity of an Incorporating Union betwixt Britain and Ireland. Manuscript. 31 pages.

A Proposal for extending trade with Labrador . . . via Ireland. Manuscript. 9 pages.

An Account of North Carolina. Printed in the *Colonial Records of North Carolina.* v. 5.

Essay upon the Grand Plan of Providence and Dissertations Annexed thereto. Manuscript. 250 pages.

Bibliography

MANUSCRIPTS

Castle Dobbs Papers. 1568–1845. Public Record Office, Belfast, D.O.D. 162.

Castle Ward Papers. 1691–1835. 11 vols. The Property of the Right Honourable Edward Ward, Earl of Bangor, Castle Ward, Co. Down.

Dublin Society Minute Books. 1731–1765. Royal Dublin Society, Ball's Bridge, Dublin.

Governor Dobbs Documents. North Carolina Department of History and Archives, Raleigh.

PRINTED MATERIAL

Andrews, C. M., *Colonial Folkways: A Chronicle of American Life in the Reign of the Georges.* 1919.

Andrews, C. M., *Guide to Materials for American History to 1783 in the Public Record Office of Great Britain.* 2 vols. 1912.

Arthur, J. P., *Western North Carolina,* 1730–1913. 1914.

Ashe, S. A., *Biographical History of North Carolina from Colonial Times to the Present.* 8 vols. 1905–9.

do., *History of North Carolina.* 2 vols. 1908.

Bailey, K. P., *The Ohio Company of Virginia and the Westward Movement,* 1748–92. 1925.

Ball, F. E., *The Correspondence of Jonathan Swift.* 6 vols. 1910–14.

Banta, R. E., *The Ohio.* 1951.

Beer, G. L., *British Colonial Policy,* 1754–65. New York, 1907.

Bernheim, *History of the German Settlement and Lutheran Church in North Carolina.* 1872.

Berry, H. E., *History of the Royal Dublin Society.* 1915.

Boulter, H., *Letters written to Several Ministers of State in England and some others, containing an account of the most Interesting Transactions in Ireland from 1724 to 1728.* 2 vols. 1740.

Boyd, W. K. ed., *Some 18th-Century Tracts Concerning North Carolina.* 1872.

Brickall, J., *The Natural History of North Carolina.* 1737.

Brock, R. A., *The Official Papers of Robert Dinwiddie.* 1883.

Bryce, G., *The Remarkable History of the Hudson Bay Company.* 1910.

Burnaby, A., *Travels through the Middle Settlements of North America*, 1759–60. 1775.

Burpee, L. J., *The Search for the Western Sea*. 1908.

Chalmers, G., *Political Annals of the Province of Carolina*. 1836.

Champlain Society, The, *James Isham's Observations on Hudson's Bay, 1743, and notes and observations on a book entitled A Voyage to Hudson's Bay in the Dobbs Galley*, 1749. Edited by E. E. Rich. 1949.

Clarke, D., *Thomas Prior*, 1680–1751. 1951.

Coleman, R. V., *Liberty and Property*. 1951.

Connor, R. D. W., *North Carolina*. 4 vols. 1919.

Crittenden, C. C., *The Commerce of North Carolina*, 1763–89. 1936.

Dickerson, O. M., *American Colonial Government*, 1696–1765. 1912.

Dobbs, Arthur, Works of (see Appendix).

Edgar, Lady M., *A Colonial Governor of Maryland: Horatio Sharpe and his Times*. 1912.

Ellis, H., *A Voyage to Hudson's Bay by the Dobbs Galley and the California in the years 1746 and 1747 for discovering a North-West Passage*. 1748.

Freeman, D. S., *George Washington*. 4 vols. 1948.

Froude, J. A., *The English in Ireland in the 18th Century*. 3 vols. 1881.

Gilbert, J., *History of Dublin*. 3 vols. 1874.

Grimes, J. B., *North Carolina Wills*. 1910.

Johnston, F. J., *The Early Architecture of North Carolina*. 1941.

Kelsey, H., *The Kelsey Papers*. Introduction by A. C. Doughty and Professor C. Martin. 1929.

Kimbal, G. S., *The Correspondence of William Pitt with the Colonial Governors*. 1912.

Labaree, L. W., *Royal Governments in America*. 1930.

Lecky, W. H., *History of Ireland in the 18th Century*. 4 vols. 1897.

Lefer, H. T. ed., *North Carolina History told by Contemporaries*. 1934.

Mackay, D., *The Honourable Company: a history of the Hudson's Bay Company*. 1937.

McSkimin, J., *History of Carrickfergus*. 1909.

Martin, F., *History of North Carolina from the Earliest Period*. 1829.

Middleton, C., *Forgery Detected*. 1745.

do., *A reply to Mr. Dobbs' Answer to a paper Entitled Forgery Detected*. 1745.

do., *A Reply to the Remarks of Arthur Dobbs*. 1745.

do., *A Vindication of the Conduct of Captain Middleton*. 1745.

Morton, A. S., *A History of the Canadian West to 1870–71*. n.d.

North Carolina, *Colonial Records of North Carolina*. Vols. 5, 6, and 7. 1886–90.

do., *Historical Records of North Carolina*. 3 vols. 1938–9.

do., *Index to the Documents relating to North Carolina during the Colonial Existence of the said State*. 1843.

O'Brien, G., *Economic History of Ireland in the 18th Century*. 1924.

O'Mahony, C., *The Viceroys of Ireland.* 1918.

Osgood, H. S., *The American Colonies in the 18th Century.* 4 vols. 1892.

Parkman, F., *Half-Century of Conflict.* 2 vols. 1892.

do., *Montcalm and Wolfe.* 2 vols. 1892.

Rapier, C. L., *North Carolina; a study in English Colonial Government,* 1729–75. 1904.

Rivers, W. J., *The Carolinas.* 1886.

Robson, J., *An Account of Six Years' Residence in Hudson's Bay from* 1733 *to* 1736 *and* 1744 to 1747. 1752.

Salley, A. S., *The Lord Proprietors of Carolina.* 1944.

Sharpe, H., *The Correspondence of Governor Sharpe.* 2 vols. 1907.

Smith, H. A., *The Thirteen Colonies.* 2 vols. 1901.

Spencer, C., *First Steps in North Carolina History.* 1889.

Sprunt, J., *Tales and Traditions of Cape Fear.* n.d.

Stevenson, J., *Two Centuries of Life in County Down,* 1600–1800. 1920.

Weeks, S. B., *Church and State in North Carolina.* 1895.

Wheeler, J. H., *Historical Sketches of North Carolina,* 1584–1851.

Williamson, H., *History of North Carolina.* 1812.

Winsor, J. ed., *Narrative and Critical History of America,* 1689–1763. 1887.

Wrong, G. M., *The Conquest of New France.* 1918.

Index